K

This book is due for return on or before the last date shown below.

3/10/09

Discard

DL 8119445 5

On the uses of history in recent Irish writing

Manchester University Press

ON THE USES OF HISTORY
IN RECENT IRISH WRITING

Bernhard Klein

Manchester University Press
Manchester and New York
distributed exclusively in the USA by Palgrave

Copyright © Bernhard Klein 2007

The right of Bernhard Klein to be identified as the author of this work has been asserted by him in accordance with the Copyright, Designs and Patents Act 1988.

Published by Manchester University Press
Oxford Road, Manchester M13 9NR, UK
and Room 400, 175 Fifth Avenue, New York, NY 10010, USA
www.manchesteruniversitypress.co.uk

Distributed exclusively in the USA by
Palgrave, 175 Fifth Avenue, New York,
NY 10010, USA

Distributed exclusively in Canada by
UBC Press, University of British Columbia, 2029 West Mall,
Vancouver, BC, Canada V6T 1Z2

British Library Cataloguing-in-Publication Data
A catalogue record for this book is available from the British Library

Library of Congress Cataloging-in-Publication Data applied for

ISBN   0719075858 *hardback*
EAN   978 0 7190 7585 8

First published 2007

16 15 14 13 12 11 10 09 08 07   10 9 8 7 6 5 4 3 2 1

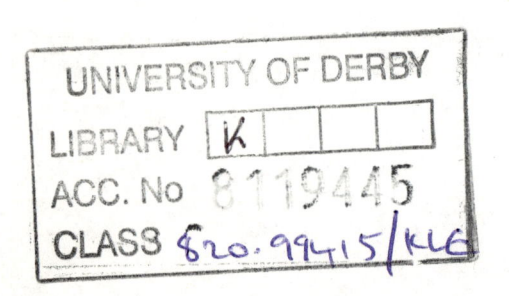

Typeset
by Frances Hackeson Freelance Publishing Services, Brinscall, Lancs
Printed in Great Britain
by Bell & Bain Ltd, Glasgow

For my mother

CONTENTS

Acknowledgements	*page* viii
Introduction	1
1 Reclaiming the early modern	12
2 Fact into fiction: novels of the Irish Famine	40
3 Staging history in contemporary Irish drama	84
4 Historicising the Troubles in Northern Irish poetry	125
Conclusion	164
Select bibliography	168
Index	175

ACKNOWLEDGEMENTS

I am grateful to the following copyright holders: to Anvil Press Poetry for permission to quote from *The Non-Aligned Storyteller* (1984) by Thomas McCarthy; to Blackstaff Press for permission to quote from *Eden to Edenderry* (1989) by Robert Johnstone, and from *Collected Poems* (1991) by John Hewitt; to Faber & Faber Inc, and Farrar, Straus and Giroux, for permission to quote from *Death of a Naturalist* (1966), *Door into the Dark* (1969), *Wintering Out* (1972), *North* (1975), *Station Island* (1984) and *The Spirit Level* (1996) by Seamus Heaney, from *Meeting the British* (1987) by Paul Muldoon, and from *A State of Justice* (1977), *The Strange Museum* (1980) and *Liberty Tree* (1983) by Tom Paulin; to the authors and The Gallery Press for kind permission to quote from *The Irish for No* (1987) and *Belfast Confetti* (1989) by Ciaran Carson, from *Selected Poems* (1988) by Seamus Deane, from *Collected Poems* (1999) by Derek Mahon, from *The Rough Field* (1976; 1989) by John Montague, from *Collected Poems* (2000) by Richard Murphy, and from *Poems 1956 to 1986* (1986) by James Simmons; to David Higham Associates for permission to quote from *Collected Poems* (1966) by Louis MacNeice; and to Martin Secker and Warburg, and Wake Forest University Press, for permission to quote from *Poems 1963–1983* (1991) by Michael Longley.

INTRODUCTION

This is a study of the uses of history in recent Irish writing.[1] I start from the – relatively uncontroversial – premise that what is often referred to as the 'unfinished business'[2] of Ireland's history has been among the most important and most evocative sources of inspiration in contemporary Irish literature. 'In this Irish past I dwell', writes Seamus Deane, 'Like sound implicit in a bell'.[3] Much contemporary Irish writing, it could be said, has been an attempt to make that bell ring, to set its 'darkness echoing',[4] to release the 'implicit' sound trapped in its cast-iron shell.

That the link between past and present is one of the foremost concerns of contemporary Irish writing is not much in dispute in current criticism. 'It would be difficult to imagine a literature', one critic has argued, 'that is so positively obsessed with the national past as the one Ireland has produced in [the twentieth] century.'[5] Another claims that 'Irish writing is steeped in history',[6] while yet another thinks that 'even a casual acquaintance with Irish literature and history discovers a pervasive tendency to use the past to explain or excuse the present'.[7] My principal reason for returning to the well-ploughed field of literature and history in Ireland is twofold. First, while many critics (like the three scholars just cited) have commented on the frequent reference to historical material in Irish writing, few have enquired into the precise nature of the conceptual link between literature and the historical imagination. Second, I want to take issue with the narrow but still dominant critical view that sees Irish writers engage with the past only as a troublesome 'burden', and that subsumes history rather prematurely under the exclusive rubric of a 'traumatic' memory. Tellingly, one of the most frequent intertextual quotes in recent criticism has been Stephen Dedalus's equation of history with a nightmare from which he is trying to awake. Elevating this statement into an a priori assumption about Irish literature's engagement with the national past means seriously to underestimate the varied, creative and often critically challenging conceptual uses of history by many contemporary Irish writers.

In this book I approach history not as a metaphorical nightmare but as a dynamic and fluid dialogue between a multilayered, future-oriented present and a polymorphous, polyglot past – a past that cannot be reduced to a single shape, form or narrative mode, that is not confined within the totality of finite time. In doing so, I join an already lively camp of critics. '[I]n contemporary Irish scholarship', Joe Cleary notes, 'evolutionist and stadial conceptions of history contend with more recent models that start with the assumption that there can be no clear-cut dividing line between past and present; in these models, every present is non-synchronous, a coeval mix of radically disjunct temporalities.'[8] Such radical models of time and history are, of course, not the exclusive privilege of literary and cultural critics; much imaginative writing in Ireland has equally subscribed to the view – whether explicitly or not – that 'our "nows" ... represent a continuous process of anticipated futures and reconstructed pasts',[9] thus effectively disputing the validity of reductive readings of Irish history as a 'burden', 'nightmare' or even 'trauma'.

Nietzsche saw the 'burden' of history as an enslavement of the spirit, an inability to forget, a desolation of the soul caused by an excessive fixation on the past. Too much history, 'oversaturation ... with history', he wrote, terrorises rather than assists humanity, throws contemporaries into a state of mental paralysis, fatally weakens their resolve.[10] To experience history as a 'burden' in this sense means both to immobilise the here and now (to disadvantage 'life', in Nietzsche's terms) and to assume a one-way traffic between past and present in which the former rules and restricts the latter. Nietzsche recommended 'the art and power of forgetting'[11] – the fleeting joys of the 'unhistorical' – as an escape route from this predicament, but a perhaps more timely cure (and deterrent against amnesia) would consist in the break-up of linear time implicit in the notion of history as 'burden'. Irish literary analysis, in my view, requires just such an approach. For the critical perspective from which all historically inspired Irish literature appears continuously to recycle the past as a nightmare runs the danger of reducing such writing to little more than a form of light release (simply 'explaining' or 'excusing' the present), a kind of therapy perhaps, while imposing upon the individual text a chronology that presses the amorphous, disordered matter of history retrospectively into a streamlined, flattened temporality. It implies a static present preceded, and then impeded, by a monolithic past.

To see the past in those terms also means to accord history an independently verifiable factuality outside its verbal representation – or its public evocation as a shared memory – and thus to assume a sense of the past largely unaffected by the textual and visual forms of recording, interpretation and transmission which enable and administer that historical sense in the first place. On the material level, there is of course a kind of self-evident plausibility about a temporal sequence in which an actual event precedes its later verbalisation. No less a radical critic of the monologic world view than Bakhtin has affirmed the essential intransigence of history in this respect, claiming that '[i]t is impossible to change the factual, thing-like aspect of the past'.[12] But, importantly, Bakhtin emphasises that the notion of 'factual' history describes only the thin outer layer of a complex set of images, symbols, perceptions, responses, meanings, etc., that together make up what he has called 'the *semantic* depths that lie embedded in the cultures of past epochs'.[13] And in *this* aspect of history, in its 'meaningful, expressive, speaking aspect', he discovers an unlimited potential for change, for it 'is unfinalisable and does not coincide with itself (it is free)'.[14] It is this 'freedom' of a polymorphous, protean past, stretching across many times and many spaces, which much historically inspired Irish literature claims as its very own domain.

If nothing else, Bakhtin's statement invites us to devote at least as much – if not more – critical attention to the present articulation of the past as to its material, 'thing-like' core. In the sense that history – whether it rewrites the past as 'trauma', 'burden' or indeed a kind of unfinalisable 'freedom' – never describes how the world might have appeared to our ancestors but rather how it appears to us, the discursive practices which make the past accessible to present ways of mental and material retrieval should be at the forefront of any critical enquiry into the formation of memory and historical consciousness. In modernity, despite the continued importance of visual and oral forms of knowledge transmission, no discursive practice has shaped our sense of the past more profoundly than literature (in the widest sense of the term). Writing, of course – whether fictional or not – comes with its own set of rules, conventions and epistemological twists. The case for a sustained attention to literary modes of narration in historiographical practice has perhaps most influentially been made by Hayden White, who borrows from Aristotle the notion of *muthos* or 'emplotment' to posit that all modern forms of history-writing, by virtue of presenting the past as narrative, follow the rules of literary plot construction.[15]

White's ideas, though not central to the argument as such, have found their occasional Irish echoes in the debates over historical revisionism in the 1980s and 1990s, when 'nationalist' historians were seen by some 'revisionists' to tamper with the historical record in the interest of 'emplotting' the Irish past as a tragedy or 'morality tale'.[16] When one of the most outspoken exponents of the 'nationalist' side in the debate defined the task of the historian as the need to exert a formative influence on national consciousness, recommending 'empathy' and 'imagination'[17] as the key techniques to achieve this, he may indeed be seen to be putting 'literary' values at the centre of his version of a fully integrative modern historiographical practice in Ireland. Yet despite such seeming convergences, even now, after the dust of the revisionist debate has largely settled, fictional and factual approaches to the past are still broadly seen to exist side by side, with little by way of contact or interaction between them, rather than as mutually reinforcing strategies of historical representation. Seamus Deane noted more than twenty years ago the detrimental effect which this artificial separation between literature and history has on historical consciousness in Ireland, where 'the two discourses [literature and history] have been kept apart, even though they have, between them, created the interpretations of past and present by which we live'.[18]

The most common argument against literature as a serious form of historical enquiry points to the 'caprice of pure fiction'[19] evident in its playful dismissal of what are sometimes taken to be non-negotiable imperatives of the historiographical enterprise, such as the chronological sequentiality of presentation, the narrative deployment of a neutral observer, the description of 'real' rather than 'invented' events, and the careful distinction between the sequential ordering of facts in time and the retrospectively constructed causalities intended to explain these facts. The point I want to make in this book is not that such arguments are unfounded (they are not) but that they are based on a narrow understanding of the function of literature, and especially its interrelation – what Ricoeur calls its 'interweaving'[20] – with history. Historical fictions, such as I am concerned with in this study, are not simply ornamental elaborations on otherwise stable contents of the cultural archive. Rather, they have the power to address the past on psychic, emotive, even spiritual levels that may effect, from within, a change of contemporary cultural sensibilities, even though they are still often (but luckily no longer unanimously) considered to be outside the bounds of serious historiography.

Luke Gibbons has noted this effect more broadly in his important work on modern Irish culture. He rightly 'insist[s] on the transformative capacity of culture in society, its power to give rise to what was not there before. Cultural representations do not simply come after the event, "reflecting" experience or embellishing it with aesthetic form, but significantly alter and shape the ways we make sense of our lives.'[21] I rank many of the poems, plays and novels discussed in the present study among such 'cultural representations' with high transformative power. To be sure, these texts are less interested than many historiographical works in a Rankean reconstruction of a 'real' past ('*wie es wirklich gewesen*'), preferring instead to speculate about less tangible realities: on what people might have done, or wished they had done, or were dreaming about doing. This is one function of literary fictions: to give expression to 'shared ideals, fantasies and values'[22] which may, in the multiplicity of their cultural meanings, open up for us the affective horizon of past (and present) societies. And while '[w]e live our lives in relation to these dreams, in self-congratulation, disappointment or resignation',[23] such fictions may tell us also about those untapped sources of our imaginative existence that lie buried in 'history'.

To read literature in this fashion requires a generous, expansive notion of 'history' as a continuous tension between diachronic expansion and synchronic contraction. I rely on a working definition of the *material* of history as the white noise of past thought and action – virtual Akasic records of a kind – only ever accessible to us in the diluted form of selective narratives and isolated snapshots, but always capable of rearranging itself and re-forming into new, unknown and unfamiliar constellations and temporalities. In this sense, what most interests me about the texts I discuss in this book is the structure of historical consciousness that they promote, whether explicitly or not. As a description for this dimension of the literary text I prefer the term 'historical imagination' – partly in the sense of the 'representative function' that Ricoeur attributed to it (meaning that through it, 'we learn to see a given series of events *as* tragic, *as* comic, and so on'),[24] but more importantly in the sense that it makes accessible an alternative past – or several such alternative, fictive 'pasts' – that are no less humanly true for being expressed in the conditional.

As a mode of collective memory, literature can hardly rival the one-directional instances of most 'official' acts of history and commemoration – whether in the form of monuments, public speeches, street names or national holidays – which rarely tolerate ambiguity as a defining aspect of their version of the past. They most commonly operate on the principle of a triadic teleology derived from centuries of biblical exegesis: 'this is who we were', 'this is who we are', 'this is who we will be'. By contrast, literature enriches the 'real' of our experience (which I take to include the historical) with deliberate fictions to evoke what Iser has called the social or cultural 'imaginary', a world beyond the real, known always only through its literary traces.[25] It is in this realm of consciousness that I want to locate the historical work of much recent Irish literature. The historical imagination opens up in these literary texts vicarious fields of possibility or resistance which allow us to experience history not as an empirical or epistemological given but as a flexible, always shifting relationship between our lived present and a multidimensional past.

It is probably clear from these opening remarks that my critical allegiance is with neither side in the debate over historical revisionism briefly referred to above – if the complexity of the debate can actually be reduced (and I doubt it can) to such a simple binary. Like other critics, I fail to see how history can ever be neutral, 'value-free' or purely factual, in the sense that there is no realm beyond speech and representation in which the *story* of the past could ever free itself from striving towards some form of argumentative and textual coherence. Language shapes and designs what it finds inhabiting the 'real', in historiography no less than in other discourses. At the same time, history in the name of a specific ideology – be it nationalism or any other – can plead spiritual liberation only at the expense of new dependencies, of submitting to a predetermined (and usually deeply moralised) hierarchy of social and political values. In any case, what seems obvious now is that the debate was as much concerned with new ways of reading the past in the light of changing circumstances (in

Ireland north and south) as with the control over the meaning of that past in the present – which is perhaps no more than saying that all serious historical work is concerned with the formation of social or cultural memory.

The centrality of memory to contemporary views of self and nation in Ireland has been noted by many critics. 'In Ireland', a student of the Irish cult of memory has written, 'the interpretation of the past has always been at the heart of national conflict.'[26] This is both true and hardly surprising. Theorists of memory from Halbwachs to Pierre Nora or the Assmanns have insisted on the extent to which 'cultural memory' (as opposed to 'personal memory', most influentially discussed by Freud) is shaped not diachronically in relation to the events of the past but synchronically in relation to the social contexts of the present.[27] Public acts of memory define *us*, not *them* (our ancestors). The interpretation of the past is at the heart of national conflict because to engage in public acts of memory means, in the first instance, to engage in a struggle *in the present* about the meaning of our own lives, rather than about the concerns of those who came before us.

To argue thus is not to blur the difference between history and memory, or between fact and myth. In Ireland, one widely held view defines 'historians and remembrancers' as 'uneasy companions, if not outright enemies'[28] by maintaining that memory is opposed to history as mythology is to science, or populism to rationality. Historical revisionism of the Irish variety derived its persuasive force from just this opposition. No less a towering figure among Irish historians than T. W. Moody argued, in a now famous essay, that '[h]istory is a matter of facing the facts of the Irish past, however painful some of them may be; mythology is a way of refusing to face the historical facts',[29] a notion shared in essence by F. S. L. Lyons who asked whether 'we [the Irish] [have] in our entanglement with history locked ourselves into a hall of distorting mirrors so grotesque that we can no longer distinguish the realities of what happened in this island from the myths we have chosen to weave about certain symbolic events'.[30] Both historians write as if such a clear separation between the brute materiality of history and the cultural meanings we retrospectively bestow upon it were actually possible, and appear temporarily to suspend the premise of their own disciplinary vocation, that all historical understanding is based on interpretation, on re-forming and reshaping the acts and 'facts' of the past into an intelligible mental pattern.

I do not believe that history operates without myths – if only the myth of its own rejection of myth – nor do I think that the only serious intellectual response to memory is its radical demystification. Rather, the production and dissemination of cultural memory deserve our serious critical attention since it is through commonly shared beliefs about the national or ethnic past – whether they stand up to historical scrutiny or not – that social communities develop an understanding of who they are and where they come from. At the same time, while much imaginative literature is directly or indirectly in the business of actively shaping memories of the past for present audiences, the term at the centre of my own investigation is not memory but history, and though this obviously does not imply a completely separate field of enquiry it does suggest a different set of key concerns.

Important for my project is first of all a concept of history as cultural reconstruction that would differ from a definition of memory, to quote a formula of Pierre Nora's, as a form of 'life'.[31] Memory, though nurtured by history, is concerned with living society to such an extent that it never quite manages to acknowledge the distance, the irretrievable *pastness* of the past, that history – cultural history – attempts to encompass.[32] Memory is aimed at a presence – the presence of the now – while history is focused on an absence – the absence 'of what is no longer'.[33] Memory always slides along a dialectical path of forgetting and remembrance, recall and oblivion, use value and impertinence, that makes it change shape with every new social alliance, all along appropriating past experience for present purposes, while the cultural history I endorse is careful never to blur or even obliterate the gap that separates us from our ancestors. If memory radically translates past language into current grammar, cultural history rejects translation as the guiding figure of historical thought. I aim throughout not to reduce literature to a form of commemorative ritual but to pay particular attention to the considerable variety of historical imaginings and historiographical theories that have been taken up by Irish writers, as well as to the noticeable concern with the future that the literary link between past and present has been made to serve.

The book is not a comprehensive survey. In each of the four chapters below I discuss a choice of texts with reference to particular historical events in Ireland's past. Since my aim was to encompass as convincingly as possible the conceptual spectrum of the historical imagination as it is articulated in recent Irish writing, I decided largely to ignore the imperatives of linear history and turn instead to material that promised to offer the most challenging and innovative approaches to the fictional rewriting of the past. The central question throughout is not just how (and why) a specific event is represented in fiction but how the relationship between past and present is re-imagined – and thus redefined – in each particular literary instance; in short, how history is conceptualised in literature. My own sense is that this kind of analysis is best achieved by way of case studies rather than sweeping surveys. I am focusing on what I see as a recognisable development within Irish writing but not a generally shared tendency, hence the prominence of the individual text. In each instance I aim to situate this text in what might be broadly identified as its 'field', or proper contextual framework, but it is only when adequate attention is paid to the specific example that the deep structure of its historical syntax comes genuinely into view.

The main organising principle of this study is generic (I use the term genre in the broad tripartite sense derived from Goethe's division of literary styles – what he called the 'natural forms of poetry' – into epic, dramatic, and lyric).[34] While Chapter 1 foregrounds a particular historical period – the Tudor reconquest of Ireland – and looks at works by Robert Welch, Brian Friel, Frank McGuinness, John Montague and Seamus Heaney, the three chapters that follow all emphasise genre by considering how the internal dynamics of certain key events in Irish history are negotiated in the novel, in drama and in poetry. Chapters 2 (novel) and 4 (poetry) focus on the reimaginings of specific historical periods – respectively the Great Famine of 1845–49, and the most recent phase of the 'Troubles' in Northern Ireland, while Chapter 3 (drama) looks principally at three plays dealing with the 1798 United Irishmen Rising (Stewart Parker's *Northern Star*), the 1830s Ordnance Survey (Brian Friel's *Translations*), and the Battle of the Somme in 1916 (Frank McGuinness's *Observe the Sons of Ulster Marching Towards the Somme*). Chapter 2 is the widest in scope and coverage; it discusses novels by a range of postwar and contemporary authors – including Walter Macken, Elizabeth Byrd, Nuala O'Faolain and Joseph O'Connor – against the background of Famine historiography and almost a century of Famine fiction by nineteenth- and early twentieth-century writers such as William Carleton, Anthony Trollope, Margaret Brew, Louisa Field and Liam O'Flaherty. The final chapter (on poetry) foregrounds the work of Seamus Heaney, Derek Mahon and Tom Paulin within the more general context of poetry on the Northern Irish 'Troubles'.

The tripartite division into genres underlying these chapters, while it may seem like a conservative choice, was suggested by the material itself. A high consciousness of genre still pervades Irish literary production, and the creative energy behind this output is best served, I think, by following the material rather than by pressing it into critical confines alien to its own pace and rhythm. Special attention to generic choices is also warranted by the unique forms of historical thought which the discursive mode of a particular genre enables. In simplified terms, while the novel is most frequently concerned with continuity and a sense of coherence over time, the basic figure of drama is the conflict between two opposing propositions, translated into an *agon* – a 'wrestling match', contest or struggle – between two characters or sets of characters (significantly, the three principal plays I discuss in the drama chapter all involve a military confrontation). Poetry, finally, gathers its force through image and metaphor, and is rarely bound to strict verisimilitude in its historical reference. Genre, in other words, is no mere accidental form; it circumscribes the literary shaping of the past in ways that enable certain modes of creative expression while limiting others. To start with prose before moving on to drama and finally to poetry is no random choice but reflects my view of the imaginative possibilities of each genre. As we shall see, in terms of their historical reference, the triadic sequence prose–drama–poetry describes a move from fact to fiction to transcendence; from recovery to play to idea; or – in terms more directly historical – from account to method to vision.

The downside of connecting genre with specific events in Irish history is that the relative eclecticism of this approach leads to the exclusion of a certain number of texts that could easily have fallen within the remit of this study – for instance, recent works dealing with the Easter Rising (by Roddy Doyle and others). I make up for such gaps by offering the study as a series of critical layers. On the surface, it is a sequence of close readings of selected texts (many of which are by now canonical) that share as a common feature a sustained engagement with the Irish past. On another level, the study is an enquiry into the cultural meanings produced by the nexus between a particular historical event and its representation in literature. Finally, on the most general level perhaps, the study considers the conceptual possibilities (and limitations) of specific literary genres to address the matter of history at all. I cannot think of a better way to explain why I think such a project is relevant than to quote the wisdom of Johan Huizinga who defined history – in the triple sense of 'that which happened', of a narrative of what happened, and of a discipline that constructs these narratives – in a deceptively simple but actually highly poignant formula as 'the mental form [*geestelijke vorm*] in which a culture accounts for its past'.[35] The imaginative power lodged in this 'mental form' makes the study of its literary expression relevant not only to an understanding of the past, but also of the present and the future.

Notes

1. Throughout this study, when referring to 'Ireland', I take the whole island into view, both north and south, while my reference to 'Irish' literature is limited to writing in English.
2. Gerald Fitzgibbon, 'Historical obsession in recent Irish drama', in Geert Lernout (ed.), *The Crows Behind the Plough: History and Violence in Anglo-Irish Poetry and Drama* (Amsterdam: Rodopi, 1991), 41–60: 41.
3. Seamus Deane, 'Return', in Frank Ormsby (ed.), *A Rage for Order: Poetry of the Northern Ireland Troubles* (Belfast: Blackstaff Press, 1992), 44.
4. Seamus Heaney, 'Personal Helicon', *Death of a Naturalist* (London: Faber, 1966), 46.
5. Geert Lernout, 'Banville and being: *The Newton Letter* and history', in Joris Duytschaever and Geert Lernout (eds), *History and Violence in Anglo-Irish Literature* (Amsterdam: Rodopi, 1988), 67–77: 67.
6. Rüdiger Imhof, 'The past in contemporary Irish drama', in Jürgen Kamm (ed.), *Twentieth-Century Theatre and Drama in English* (Trier: Wissenschaftlicher Verlag, 1999), 589–610: 589.
7. Helen Lojek, 'Myth and bonding in Frank McGuinness's *Observe the Sons of Ulster Marching Towards the Somme*', *Canadian Journal of Irish Studies* 14, no. 1 (1988), 45–53: 46.

8   Joe Cleary, 'Introduction: Ireland and modernity', in Cleary and Claire Connolly (eds), *The Cambridge Companion to Modern Irish Culture* (Cambridge: Cambridge University Press, 2005), 1–21: 19.
9   Ibid.
10 See Friedrich Nietzsche, 'On the uses and disadvantages of history for life' [1874], in Nietzsche, *Untimely Meditations*, trans. R. J. Hollingdale (Cambridge: Cambridge University Press, 1983), 57–123: 83. On history as 'burden', see also Hayden White, 'The burden of history', in White, *Tropics of Discourse: Essays in Cultural Criticism* (Baltimore, MD: Johns Hopkins University Press, 1978), 27–50.
11 Nietzsche, 'On the uses and disadvantages of history for life', 120.
12 M. M. Bakhtin, 'K filosofskim osnovam gumanitarnykh nauk' [Toward the philosophical bases of the human sciences], in Bakhtin, *Sobranie sochinenii v semi tomakh*, vol. 5, ed. S. G. Bocharov and L. A. Gogotishvili (Moscow: Russkie slovari, 1996), 7–10: 9. Thanks to David Sheperd for locating the source of this quotation, and to him and Olga Belova for confirming the translation.
13 M. M. Bakhtin, 'Response to a question from the *Novy Mir* editorial staff', in Bakhtin, *Speech Genres and Other Late Essays*, trans. Vern W. McGee, ed. Caryl Emerson and Michael Holquist (Austin, TX: University of Texas Press, 1986), 1–9: 6 (italics in the original).
14 Bakhtin, 'K filosofskim osnovam gumanitarnykh nauk', 9.
15 See Hayden White, 'Explanation by emplotment', in White, *Metahistory: The Historical Imagination in Nineteenth-Century Europe* (Baltimore, MD and London: Johns Hopkins University Press, 1973), 7–11.
16 Roy Foster, 'History and the Irish question' [1988], in Ciaran Brady (ed.), *Interpreting Irish History: The Debate on Historical Revisionism, 1938–1994* (Dublin: Irish Academic Press, 1994), 122–45: 140. Brady's volume is a very useful anthology of relevant contributions to the revisionist debate, starting in the late 1930s and ending in the early 1990s. For an assessment of the impact of revisionism on various key topics in Irish history, see D. George Boyce and Alan O'Day (eds), *The Making of Modern Irish History: Revisionism and the Revisionist Controversy* (London: Routledge, 1996).
17 Brendan Bradshaw, 'Nationalism and historical scholarship in modern Ireland' [1988], in Brady (ed.), *Interpreting Irish History*, 191–216: 215.
18 Seamus Deane, 'Heroic styles: the tradition of an idea' [1984], in Claire Connolly (ed.), *Theorizing Ireland* (Basingstoke: Palgrave, 2003), 14–26: 14.
19 Brady, '"Constructive and instrumental": the dilemma of Ireland's first "new historians"', in Brady (ed.), *Interpreting Irish History*, 3–31: 28.
20 See Paul Ricoeur, 'The interweaving of history and fiction', in Ricoeur, *Time and Narrative* [1983–5], trans. Kathleen McLaughlin and David Pellauer, 3 vols (Chicago and London: Chicago University Press, 1984–8), vol. 3 (1988), 180–92.
21 Luke Gibbons, *Transformations in Irish Culture*, Field Day Essays 2 (Cork: Cork University Press, 1996), 8.
22 Catherine Belsey, 'Reading cultural history', in Tamsin Spargo (ed.), *Reading the Past* (Basingstoke: Palgrave, 2000), 103–17: 108.
23 Ibid.
24 Ricoeur, 'The interweaving of history and fiction', 185.
25 Wolfgang Iser, *Fictive and Imaginary: Charting Literary Anthropology* (Baltimore,

MD: Johns Hopkins University Press, 1993).
26 Ian McBride, 'Memory and national identity in modern Ireland', in McBride (ed.), *History and Memory in Modern Ireland* (Cambridge: Cambridge University Press, 2001), 1–42: 1.
27 See Maurice Halbwachs, *Les cadres sociaux de la mémoire* (Paris: Librarie Félix Alcan, 1925) (or for a recent English translation: *On Collective Memory*, ed. and trans. Lewis A. Coser (Chicago and London: The University of Chicago Press, 1992)); Pierre Nora (ed.), *Realms of Memory*, trans. Arthur Goldhammer, English language ed. Lawrence D. Kritzmann, 3 vols (New York: Columbia University Press, 1996–8); and the work of the Assmanns (Jan and Aleida) who have been elaborating their concept of cultural memory [*kulturelles Gedächtnis*] over many years and in a range of different publications, for instance in Aleida Assmann, *Erinnerungsräume. Formen und Wandlungen des kulturellen Gedächtnisses* (Munich: Beck, 1999) or Jan Assmann, *Religion and Cultural Memory. Ten Studies* [2000], trans. Rodney Livingstone (Stanford, CA: Stanford University Press, 2006).
28 McBride, 'Memory and national identity in modern Ireland', 37.
29 T. W. Moody, 'Irish history and Irish mythology' [1977], in Brady (ed.), *Interpreting Irish History*, 71–86: 86.
30 F. S. L. Lyons, *The Burden of Our History*, W. B. Rankin Memorial Lecture (Belfast: Queen's University, 1978), 8.
31 Pierre Nora, 'General introduction: between memory and history', in Nora, *Realms of Memory*, vol. 1, 1–20: 3.
32 See Belsey, 'Reading cultural history', 108.
33 Nora, 'General introduction', vol. 1, 3.
34 See Johann Wolfgang Goethe, *West-östlicher Divan* [1829], *Gedenkausgabe der Werke, Briefe und Gespräche*, ed. Ernst Beutler (Zurich: Artemis, 1948), 480.
35 'Geschiedenis is de geestelijke vorm, waarin een cultuur zich rekenschap geeft van haar verleden.' Johan Huizinga, 'Over een definitie van het begrip geschiedenis' ['On a definition of the term history'], *Cultuurhistorische Verkenningen* (Haarlem: H. D. Tjeenk Willink & Zoon, 1929), 158–68: 166. Translation mine.

1

RECLAIMING THE EARLY MODERN

This opening chapter cuts across the generic division that forms the basis of the rest of this study by presenting an extended look at the way one particular historical moment – the Tudor reconquest of Ireland and attendant developments – has been represented in selected narrative, dramatic and poetic rewritings of early modern Ireland. My texts are: for prose, Robert Welch's *The Kilcolman Notebook* (1993), a fictional diary by Edmund Spenser; for drama, Brian Friel's *Making History* (1989) and Frank McGuinness' *Mutabilitie* (1997); and for poetry, sections of John Montague's *The Rough Field* (1972) and a handful of poems by Seamus Heaney (1972; 1975). These works all share a common historical focus, yet differ considerably in how they choose to represent and configure the past. I shall argue that the different conceptual forms used to encompass history in these texts range from a view of the past as an epistemological fixity to its representation as a fluid temporality subject to constant transformations and reappropriations. It is in the terms of the latter notion that the imaginative repositionings of Irish cultural identities within the narratives of the past are explicitly enabled.

Contexts: studying the early modern divide

The early modern period – specifically the sixteenth and early seventeenth centuries – has not played much of a role in the classic memorial narratives of Irish culture. Protestant memory frequently starts just at the tail end of the period, and in its popular version usually selects 1690 (date of the Battle of the Boyne) as the decisive inaugural event in Irish Protestant history. Catholic memory tends to lump the early modern together with that long phase of subjection before the first genuine articulation of the political will for independence, in 1798. It is true that Pearse facilitated, in 1916, 'the retrospective ordering of earlier rebellions into a cumulative

Reclaiming the early modern 13

sequence of inspirational defeats'[1] by declaring, famously, that 'the Irish people have asserted their right to national freedom and sovereignty ... six times in the past three hundred years',[2] but the pre-1798 rebellions to which this statement presumably referred – in the 1590s and the 1640s – never really took hold in the popular imagination. Since the sixteenth century is the formative period of the Protestant–Catholic divide in Irish culture, this neglect of the Renaissance in popular memory is all the more remarkable.[3]

It is also in marked contrast to the recent scholarly rediscovery of 'early modern Ireland' in cultural history and postcolonial studies. Historians as well as literary and cultural critics have focused on the events and ideological struggles especially in late sixteenth-century Ireland as one of the first genuinely 'colonial' encounters in England's imperial history. Of particular interest has been the prominent textual production of the 'savage' or 'wild' Irish in a range of contemporary texts, images and maps, and the attendant discourse of Irish 'barbarism' that enabled the positive self-image of English 'civility'.[4] Yet at the same time, this early colonial conflict, as it found textual articulation, is replete with the inherent difficulties and logical contradictions that threatened the project of establishing (in discourse) an essential difference between two neighbouring cultures where markers of sameness abounded and where both looked back on centuries of a common history.[5] Ireland was England's 'other', and, as in other encounter histories of this kind, the fear of cultural assimilation and subsequent loss of selfhood runs through the writings of many early modern English commentators who saw in Ireland 'the ghostly and substantial menace ... [that was] threatening to explode the desired unity of Britain and its attendant civilization'.[6]

Recent literature has not been silent on the watershed years of the late sixteenth century, though on the whole the topic is still only infrequently taken up in fiction. Of particular importance have been literary recreations of the poet Edmund Spenser, author of *The Faerie Queene* (1590/96), who spent most of his adult life in Ireland and who is in many ways a pivotal figure of Anglo-Irish cultural history in the early modern period. The critical assessment of Spenser's life and works has moved in recent years from emphasising his anti-Irish stance to seeing him more as a reluctant critic of Elizabethan policy in Ireland, an English exile working in the colonial administration of a neighbouring island who experienced head-on all the contradictions and tensions of early modern colonial rhetoric and practice. At the same time, the rigid dividing line between his poetry and his politics that once held sway in Spenser studies has been under considerable revision. It is hardly surprising, then, given this newly focused academic interest in Spenser, to see him emerge in a range of literary texts as a figure torn between the hesitant admiration for Irish cultural achievement and the exigencies of an officially sanctioned civilising mission.

Robert Welch: a divided Spenser

The image of Spenser constructed in the pages of Robert Welch's 1994 novel *The Kilcolman Notebook* roughly follows this agenda. Kilcolman was the name of the castle in County Cork where the historical Spenser lived, and which was razed to the ground in 1598 by the native Irish as Hugh O'Neill's country-wide rebellion spread gradually south. The novel comes in the form of a fictional journal written by Spenser in his study at Kilcolman Castle, describing a trip to London where he went to oversee the publication of *The Faerie Queene* (as indeed the real Edmund Spenser is known to have done). Together with his sometime neighbour in Ireland, Sir Walter Ralegh, Spenser is shown visiting the court and meeting the Queen in a series of private conferences.

The text is not intended as a historical novel in the tradition of Scott; despite several ironic gestures at authenticity and the presence of 'real' historical characters there is no sustained attempt, for instance, to recreate contemporary language or the finer details of everyday life. In a move of deliberate anachronism, the fictional explorations of the historical binaries central to the tale – Spenser/Ralegh; Spenser/Elizabeth; Ireland/England – are distinctly modern in tone and sentiment. The text's historical imaginings thus cluster less around its manifest content than around the dynamics we see unfold in three scenes where Spenser meets the Queen to discuss her dreams, the centrepiece of the tale.

Spenser, ironically addressed as the 'hermaneut' (59 *et passim*),[7] is called upon to explain these dreams, and one point of the exercise is to highlight the ambiguity of his position between the pretence of English 'civility', the presumed 'barbarity' of Ireland, and the undisputed centre of absolute power, the Queen, the revered object of Spenser's vast poetic undertakings. All of these dreams feature scenes of domination and subjection involving cross-gender fantasies and hermaphrodite identities as a foil against which the colonial politics of Spenser's Irish experience are to be read. As Andrew Hadfield has pointed out, Welch's book 'plays heavily on Spenser's supposed fear of becoming Irish', fashioning Ireland as 'a site onto which repressed English fears can be projected, and a desired space which threatens to paralyse the colonising English subject'.[8] Creatures of uncertain or indeterminate sexuality are presented as symbolic of Ireland's disruptive impact upon England's invariably masculine colonial identity. The Queen herself, in her role as Spenser's desired love object, instils fear and anxiety in her admirer and threatens to destroy the certainties of his male pose.

The tale is punctured by two deliberately pornographic scenes intended to serve as political allegories. On their way to England, as they wait to sail from Cork harbour, Ralegh and Spenser visit prostitutes in a local brothel; later at court Spenser is shown in an extended sadomasochistic ritual with the Queen. The first scene in the Cork brothel is fairly straightforward in its allegorical content. Ralegh is shown performing buggery on the mistress of the house, calling her 'my Hibernia, my Newfoundland' (23) – lines that clearly echo Donne's 'Elegy 19', in which the poet's 'roving hands'[9] that explore the female body serve as a metaphor of colonial appropriation. The implication here is not only that sexual and colonial conquest are analogous, and that masculine aggression enables both (analogies that are staples of early modern descriptions of colonial relations), but also that an essential likeness exists between the contemporary colonial projects in Ireland and the Americas (in Donne, the line reads 'O my *America*, my new found land').[10] Whether this latter comparison can be sustained historically is currently in dispute,[11] but a figure like Ralegh was obviously an active participant in colonising projects on both sides of the Atlantic.

The second sex scene – an elaborate sadomasochistic ritual at court involving the Queen as 'Mistress' – is more difficult to disentangle. This is the third dream session to which Spenser is summoned. He is confronted with one of his own creations, the iron man Talus, companion of Artegall, the Knight of Justice, who is the central character in book five of *The Faerie Queene*. Talus is the ruthless executor of Artegall's will, who metes out with clinical efficiency whatever punishment his master decrees. The human cost of this iron principle is what appeared to the Queen in her dream (in the form of an abandoned mother with her several children, all of whom Talus cruelly kills), and it leads to some troubled speculation about the application of justice in a colonial context.

During the 'private entertainment' (85) that follows the session, Spenser suffers in a specially devised torture chamber at the hands of his royal Mistress and her assistants. The point of the extended description of these fairly crude sex games is to dismantle the delusion that good and evil can ever be kept apart in a context that feeds on the (very material) analogy between sexual and colonial penetration, and where identities are formed in the shady area between different cultures, genders and sexual identities, complicated further by the troubling mixture of shame, desire, anxiety and longing. Aggression may be complicit with victimisation just as humiliation has its own erotics and punishment its secret pleasures. Politics is aggressively personalised and disturbingly interlinked with sexual power and self-discipline. The point is brought home more unambiguously in one of the following scenes, in which Spenser overhears a conversation about the Munster plantation on board the ship that is taking him back to Ireland. This colonising project, according to one of the unnamed speakers, proceeds on a logic of the ruthless enforcement of personal discipline: '[W]e master our Irishness by mastering the Irish. ... We master our blackness by mastering black Africa. There is no other way' (108). Justice, then, has little to do with the application of universal laws that clearly differentiate between good and evil. Justice is the harsh regime against the body that aims to eradicate in the external world those degenerative tendencies it most fears emerging within the self.

This is finally what this fictional Spenser has succumbed to: he has 'gone native' in body and soul. 'I wept in the room, aromatic with the scent of resin, for myself and for Christ. And, shockingly, searingly, for Ireland. My country. My home. My people in their rags and dirt and filth. ... I was now a native, even though I could never be accepted' (109). This contagion of the colonising mind with sympathy for the natives is – in the terms suggested by the defenders of the plantation project – the ultimate failure of masculine will, constituting the true threat to English civility that Ireland represents.

What all this amounts to in terms of the conception of 'history' which the novel espouses becomes clearer when we look at another detail from one of the Queen's dreams. The novel is packed with intertextual, even (to coin a phrase) interhistorical allusions. It frequently projects its images forward in time to evoke not only later textual interventions but also specific instances and episodes belonging to Ireland's subsequent history – such as, for instance, prominent images of hunger and starvation, a proleptic reference to the mid-nineteenth-century Irish Famine. There is no need here to unravel all the various intertextual references but the image that is evoked by the Queen at the end of her first session with Spenser goes some way, I want to suggest, towards explaining the historical framework to which the novel subscribes. Responding to Spenser's evocation of the future as a 'new age of Hermaphroditus, ... [a] killing time' (62), the Queen explains:

> I see a man ... standing in the whitewashed hovels of a windswept island off the western coast of the country in which you have your residence, Hibernia. He is dressed in black shabby clothes, his arms by his sides, as he stares out into the rainy light. Under a black hat the blue eyes are looking straight into the future and he is transfixed, frozen by fear. He sees the whole terror unfold out there in the sea-light. I do not know where I get the image from, but he is there, suddenly, in my mind. (62–3)

One possible source for this image is section nine of Walter Benjamin's 'Theses on the philosophy of history', in which Benjamin describes a Paul Klee painting, *Angel of history* – a piece so famous it does not require quoting at length. Importantly, Benjamin's (or rather Klee's) angel is caught in a storm which 'irresistibly propels him into the future to which his back is turned, while the pile of debris before him grows skyward'.[12] If Benjamin's angel of history is indeed the source for Welch's Irishman in 'black, shabby clothes', then the deliberate switch in the image from having the figure face the past to having him gaze into the future defines the whole of Irish history *since* the early modern moment of violent colonisation as that 'single catastrophe which keeps piling wreckage upon wreckage'.[13] It was set in motion by that psychosexual double bind which the novel suggests as the defining moment of modern Anglo-Irish history.

History itself, we can deduce from that, is an outward projection of the psyche which aims to force the external world into that violent symmetry of virtuous discipline in which the modern self is harnessed (the idea of moral education which Spenser's *Faerie Queene* is intended to promote). The violence of the colonial struggle is suggested as the necessary defence against the temptations that threaten to lure the self into the submission it seeks to escape, the dangerous sensuality represented by Ireland. That such a view of history as essentially a psychosexual condition is presented in prose – with its customary strength in attending to the internal development of individual characters within specific social and cultural confines – is no more surprising than the preference for basic binary patterns of historical conflict in drama, which repeats in the structural encompassment of its topic the classic theatrical triad of protagonist, antagonist and spectator.

Brian Friel and Frank McGuinness: a divided island

Among the more prominent dramatic treatments of the period in recent years are two full-length stage plays, Brian Friel's *Making History* of 1989 and Frank McGuinness's *Mutabilitie* of 1997. Both plays discuss similar themes yet differ markedly in their historical preoccupations. As its title indicates, Friel's play is principally concerned with the modalities of historical transmission; it is a long meditation on the problematic transfer of historical memory from the original agents of history to a curious and expectant 'posterity'. Friel's central character is Hugh O'Neill, the Ulster chieftain reared partly in England who has long been considered the last 'champion of Gaelic separatism'[14] on account of his (unsuccessful) rebellion in the 1590s intended to overthrow English colonial rule in Ireland. The decisive battle that sealed O'Neill's fate was fought at Kinsale, on the southern coast (historically in 1601), and Friel decided to structure his play around that military climax, dividing it into two scenes 'before' and two scenes 'after' Kinsale.[15]

The pre-Kinsale scenes show us a fictional O'Neill as mediator between two cultures – or, as he puts it, between 'two deeply opposed civilizations' (28). He caricatures the Anglo-Irish struggle as a confrontation between, on the one hand, '[i]mpulse, instinct, capricious genius, brilliant improvisation' and, on the other, 'calculation, good order, common sense, the cold pragmatism of the Renaissance mind' (28). This 'cliché history' (28) – which is owed largely to Matthew Arnold's nineteenth-century musings about the difference between 'Saxon' and 'Celt'[16] – serves well enough to describe his position (in the play) on the fence between loyalty to the English monarch, who had him raised among the English aristocracy, and tribal allegiance to his Gaelic background. Married to the daughter of an English settler but urged by local Gaelic chieftains to rise against England, he finally breaks into open rebellion after learning that Spain has agreed to support the Irish struggle against England. Act two of the play first shows the rebels in defeat after Kinsale (scene one) and then O'Neill as a bitter old man in Rome (scene two).

The play quite deliberately distorts historical fact in the interest of dramatic effect. Friel himself has defined the play as 'a dramatic fiction that uses some actual and some imagined events in the life of Hugh O'Neill to make a story. ... [W]here there was tension between historical "fact" and the imperative of fiction, I am glad to say that I have kept faith with the narrative.'[17] The first victim of this approach is chronology: the Battle of Kinsale, for instance, is shown to take place in 1593 rather than 1601; O'Neill's third wife, Mabel Bagenal, died not in 1593 (as the play has it) but in 1595; etc. But to object to Friel taking these liberties would be to apply the yardstick of historical accuracy to an imaginative text that simply cannot be measured along such lines.

Friel's most important reason for predating Kinsale is to have the ultimate defeat in battle coincide with the death of both O'Neill's wife Mabel and his newly born son in childbed. The symbolic meaning is obvious enough: the couple's offspring would have naturally combined in one person the two cultures, English and Irish, that O'Neill finds so difficult to reconcile in his own world. The failure of this fusion signifies both the military failure at Kinsale and the more general failure of Gaelic cultural survival that the play dramatises as a whole. Other historical inaccuracies concern curious anachronisms such as, for example, the frequent reference to England and Ireland as 'nation states' (it makes little historical sense to talk about early modern state formations in these distinctly nineteenth-century terms), and the evocation of a sense of privacy which goes against everything we know about the emerging public/private divide in the early modern period. More centrally, though, in his dramatisation of the early modern, Friel departs significantly from the conceptual framework of historical plausibility, especially in the positioning of O'Neill as a self-conscious mediator between Irish and English cultures.

The historical O'Neill occupied indeed an intermediary, even liminal position between England and Ireland but in terms other than Friel depicts on the stage. The play does make clear that O'Neill was raised in England not out of generosity but with the explicit aim to have him eventually installed as a loyal political leader in what was still considered the most remote and intractable part of Ireland, Ulster.[18] When O'Neill used his English knowledge against his former benefactors, he was not so much reverting to an earlier, 'native' state of his own ethnic self – as the play suggests – but drawing on all available personal resources which included the training and education received in England. That is to say, O'Neill did not simply switch back and forth between different codes but radically destabilised the English sense of national identity by '[drawing] on his formative experience among the English in manipulating to his advantage the sign system of English civility'.[19] O'Neill was thus 'straddling markers of English and Irish identities'[20] with the result that his own person and example threw into doubt the very possibility of any unambiguous categorising of national or ethnic identity. What Friel shows in full operation – recognisable patterns of national and ethnic definition – was in fact only beginning to emerge at this historical juncture.

The point is important because it shows that national identity is always to some degree a fabrication – an imposition, so to speak, *après la lettre* – rather than the a priori condition of any particular historical encounter. In early modern Ireland, the reality of national or ethnic allegiance was the existence of many 'varieties of Irishness',[21] not of any clear-cut antagonisms or binary divisions. In Friel's play, however, the English and Irish spheres are kept entirely separate from the start, and O'Neill is shown as the only person in the play who can master both ethnic registers: in his speech, he can switch from refined English to a Tyrone accent at the drop of a hat; he has no difficulty establishing emotional intimacy with his wife Mabel, the daughter of a New English settler; and he comments several times precisely on the difficulties of his role as a broker of cultural difference. There is in the entire play no moment of mixture, no in-between state where mutual contact might result in cultural change,[22] only the retrospective ordering of a range of ethnic elements in a predefined pattern of antagonism that was, historically, the *outcome* of the Anglo-Irish colonial struggle, not its cause.

Yet even such distortions may perhaps be brushed aside as irrelevant criticism of an imaginative text by pointing to the central topic of the play – which is, after all, precisely the question of how history is 'made'. From the start O'Neill is targeted by his biographer, Archbishop Peter Lombard, who intends to write O'Neill's history by '[i]mposing a pattern on events that were mostly casual and haphazard and shaping them into a narrative that is logical and interesting'. History, Lombard contends, is 'a kind of story-telling' in which 'truth' may not be the 'primary ingredient' (8): 'Maybe when the time comes, imagination will be as important as information. ... History has to be made – before it's remade' (9). This notion of history as a purely verbal construct that can assume many different shapes and that is intended principally to serve the needs of a particular readership is reinforced several times throughout the play. '[T]he life of Hugh O'Neill can be told in many different ways', Lombard explains, '[a]nd those ways are determined by the needs and the demands and the expectations of different people and different eras' (15–16). O'Neill himself notes in despair that in the writing of history, 'art has precedence over accuracy' (27). Finally, in the last scene of the play, when an old and embittered O'Neill has hit rock bottom in Rome, we can see Lombard's 'story-telling' in action (62–70). Easily rebutting a frustrated O'Neill who insists on the reality of shame and defeat, and on the centrality of historical agents in his life that Lombard intends to marginalise or even ignore in his account – such as his wife Mabel – the Archbishop is 'making history' by turning the tragedy of O'Neill's life into the story of an inspirational failure.

One problem with this final scene, as Sean Connolly has pointed out, is its logical incompatibility with Lombard's earlier theories about the shape-shifting nature of all historical discourse. If the past can be narrated in many different ways, no single account can lay claim to the notion of undisputed historical truth. But the last scene pits O'Neill's belief in the complete failure of his ambitions against the pretensions of his biographer that higher claims require his life to be presented instead – falsely – as a triumph. The implication here is that this history is not an alternative version but a deliberate distortion of the past, and when O'Neill insists that Lombard's account will 'embalm' him 'in a florid lie' (63), history is indeed reduced to the status of a simple untruth. As Connolly notes, that 'historians commonly distort the past in order to serve the needs of the present ... is undeniable, but also rather obvious'.[23] The real critical force of Lombard's position – that history is never either true or false but always a construction that serves particular interests – is entirely lost in this final exchange of the play.

The question it raises, then, is how the history that the play itself 'makes' is to be judged. One lesson seems clear enough: the past is always an elusive entity that will eventually frustrate all attempts at full recovery. Perhaps the principal point is simply to make us aware of the constructed nature of all historical discourse and the multiple 'other' stories that remain untold in any single account. But neither of these points can explain why Friel has decided to focus on events in the early modern period rather than on more recent or better known historical contexts. Fintan O'Toole has suggested that the particular historical time frame in any Friel play matters very little, since what the dramatist is really interested in is 'a time outside history, a personal time, the time of our lives'.[24] This goes some way towards explaining why, in many of his history plays, Friel always pushes hard to transcend any given historical context and arrive at general pronouncements about the human condition. But the starting point for his historical excursions is nearly always in concrete historical time, never in 'the time of our lives', and this cannot be explained away, in my view, as merely a random, uninformed choice.

I want to suggest that in turning to the early modern period in *Making History*, Friel subscribes to a vision of history as a violent clash of civilisations, a confrontation between two once equally powerful, equally self-respecting cultures – one of which will eventually, as if by necessity, be overwhelmed by the other. This is the history the play 'makes': it fashions the past in accordance with a dichotomy derived, ultimately, from the present, reading a contemporary understanding of cultural difference back into the past. The play is concerned with an erasure, a destruction – the cutting down to size of a civilisation unable to ensure its own survival. The later manipulation of the historical record of Gaelic culture merely serves to cover up its final demise. Friel turns to the early modern period precisely because of its general historical assessment as a 'threshold period' in which such confrontations were played out and in which, as the story runs, the foundations were laid for our own modernity.

Yet this view of the early modern moment as the eruption of an irreconcilable rift between the opposing paradigms of residual and emergent, ancient and modern – much as it draws on a tradition of scholarship that has presented the Renaissance in just these terms – was as out of date and unhelpful in 1989 as it is today. By relying on this (ultimately false) dichotomy, the history which the play 'makes' repeats the mistake of the history-making in the play: it plays off one account of the past (a clash of cultures) against another (its unrealised potential and opposite: peaceful coexistence) in much the same way that Lombard simply overwrites what he and O'Neill know to be the 'true' version of events with a therapeutic tale of heroic defeat.[25]

One alternative dramatic reading of the past that *Making History* chooses simply to overwrite is explored in Frank McGuinness's *Mutabilitie*, which also deals with Ireland in the 1590s. The play is clearly indebted to the recent tide of interest in early modern Ireland by cultural historians and new historicist critics, briefly referred to above. Unlike Friel's play, this kind of history-writing insists on the historical reality of mutual contact, exchange and interaction between different cultures, despite inequalities and lopsided power relations. McGuinness's title is a quotation from *The Faerie Queene*, more precisely from the two 'Cantos of Mutabilitie' – the one section of the long poem that was not only written but is also explicitly *set* in Ireland. Appropriately, Spenser – as 'Edmund' – appears as a central character in the play, together with a wayfaring actor from London in search of profitable employment, a certain 'William' – easily recognisable as Shakespeare.

This unlikely meeting of the two poets is not grounded in historical fact: although Spenser did indeed live in Ireland for the best part of his adult life, from 1580 onwards (with only a few interruptions), Shakespeare, to our knowledge, never set foot in Ireland. In the play, however, Shakespeare heads a group of London actors who come to the island in the belief that 'Ireland's opening up' (36)[26] and that the time may be ripe to establish a professional theatre there: 'It'll be a novelty, a first, you said', one of William's actor colleagues recalls their reasons for the trip, 'we'll clean up. A bit of money for the taking, and land there, you said, it's going a-begging' (36). This characteristic infusion of artistic endeavour with the economic profit motive points to the important discussion in the play of the role of poetry in both cultures (about which more in a moment).

At the opening of the play, the three English actors lose their way in the woods and are attacked by a band of native Irish; while William can escape with a leap into the nearby river, his two colleagues are captured. William is saved in the next scene by an Irish bard and wisewoman in

Edmund's service, the File (pronounced to rhyme with Chile). The rest of the play features on various historical and mythical levels the interaction and hostilities between the two parallel groups set up in this opening sequence of events: on the one hand the Irish 'aristocracy' around High King Sweney (now gone mad and out of touch with his people),[27] his queen Maeve, and several of their shattered retinue, together with their two English captives; on the other hand Edmund, his terrified wife Elizabeth, William, and two Irish servants, Hugh and the File (the only character in the play who crosses back and forth between both groups). This set-up resembles the basic constellation of Friel's play in its clear divide between English and Irish camps, but each ethnic group includes, significantly, two nominal antagonists in their midst: the two English captives among the Irish aristocracy; the File and Hugh (who are sent to spy on Edmund's household) among the English settlers. This arrangement leads almost automatically to discussions in both groups about proximity, coexistence and the complexities of cultural change.

The play deliberately works mythical elements into its multilayered plot to undercut the tendency of overpragmatic readings. For instance, the characters Sweney and Maeve are suggested by legend rather than by historical research. Mad King Sweeney of Dal Arie is the central figure of the Irish epic *Buile Suibhne* (which survives in a seventeenth-century manuscript),[28] in which he is transformed into a bird, and Maeve is the legendary warrior queen of Connaught who instigated the Cattle Raid of Cuailnge, the central tale of the ancient Irish epic *Táin Bó Cuailgne*.[29] The character of William similarly assumes mythical properties when he is welcomed by the native Irish as their long-awaited saviour, as the bard who 'shall come from the river ... gleam like a spear, like a fish' (2 *et passim*), and when later he does, in a sense, bestow the gift of theatre upon Ireland.

Instances of cross-cultural longing are emphasised in the opening sections often through recourse to sexuality: Sweney's daughter, Annas, attracts the attention of Richard, her captive (one of the English actors); William himself seeks the intimacy of the Irish servant Hugh (an articulation of homosexual desire that is clearly meant to be read as a liberating gesture). But, in general, the initial hopes and hints of mutual respect that counteract in these early encounter scenes the reality of capture and servitude soon give way to bleaker views. One reason for this is the play's heavy investment in the inevitability of historical change. The concept of mutability – the reality of constant change and the loss of both epistemological and material fixity – was a prime obsession of the European Renaissance, articulated famously in such examples as John Donne's lament over the new rule of contingency and the passing of order and stability – 'all coherence gone'[30] – or in the rise of the goddess Fortune to unprecedented representational prominence in image and text.[31] In Spenser's 'Two Cantos of Mutabilitie' the goddess Mutabilitie challenges the rule of Jove, king of the gods, and in a trial presided over by Nature demands to be instated in Jove's stead as the organising principle not only of the sublunary sphere but of the entire world: '*Times* do change and moue continually. / So nothing here long standeth in one stay: / Wherefore, this lower world who can deny / But to be subiect still to *Mutabilitie?*'[32]

Mutabilitie loses out to Jove only through an argumentative trick: although it is true that change is indeed the state of all things, 'that all things stedfastnes doe hate',[33] change as such is constant, and so reintroduces a condition of permanence into the world. Recent critical readings of Spenser's unfinished final cantos have suggested that one referent of the concept of 'mutabilitie' may be Ireland itself and the shifting, elusive character of Irish culture as perceived by contemporary English observers. In the play it is the File who embodies this principle: '[I]t is thinking which pays homage to the principle of change, and change controls this earth and its workings' (43).

But McGuinness's use of the concept of 'mutabilitie' is not limited, I suggest, to its historical applicability to early modern Ireland. Instead it is widened to stand as a figure for a central condition of cross-cultural contact. Change is not to be equated exclusively with defeat, loss and exile. Rather, change affects and governs all participating elements in that great system of interlocking forces and mutual influences that constitutes the cultural encounter. Perhaps the central encounter in this play of many encounters is the meeting of the three poets – William, the poet–playwright; Edmund, the poet; and the File, the bard. Each poet represents a different tradition that determines in turn their individual fate.

The File most clearly recognises that she must change her song and that the old bardic lore no longer suffices to deal with the pressures of the moment. Like Edmund's poetry in *The Faerie Queene*, hers is a tradition of king worship and excessive flattery, as Maeve points out: 'Your English master, Edmund, he is no different to you. He serves his queen as you served your king. He writes exalted verses to her as she sits in glory upon her throne' (31). But the File's poetry, focused as it once was on a high royal centre now in visible decline, has lost its object of praise, and before the play ends Edmund too loses faith in his own combination of poetry and politics. William's 'modern' brand of poetry – which is, of course, the literary model for McGuinness's own work – has a different direction and purpose. In the play's central act of conjuring (in act four), a re-enactment of the fall of Troy, William, in response to the File's pleadings, applies his poetic gift to revitalise Gaelic culture and stage an imaginative counter-attack on the English colonisers. This dream sequence in which the spirits of Troy are summoned to 'rise from out of their graves' (78) blends imperceptibly with Edmund's vision of the Irish as 'ghosts crying out of their graves' (79), but whether Edmund's rushed exit – signifying, as it might, the temporary departure of the coloniser – is the result either of successful Irish pressure or of Edmund's fevered imaginings is deliberately left unclear. The success is short-lived in any case. William takes his art elsewhere in the end, and, though he will continue to side with the losers, his faith operates in terms other than the File had hoped. As she realises, words will not rescue a dying culture. William's gift was but 'a dream, a fantasy' (93). It did not bring salvation. Poetry will not finally revert the process of historical change.

At one level of the plot, the English and Irish camps mutually besiege each other: Edmund, inhabitant of the 'castle', is concerned with the extension of English rule in Ireland, with making Ireland governable; the Irish aristocracy spy on the castle in order to resist the forces of English invasion. The spatial locations of the play reflect its apocalyptic scenario: the 'castle' – a place of fortification, colonial power and military resolve – is surrounded by an unspecific 'outside', a generic 'wilderness', where the native Irish have gathered after the devastation of 'these late wars of Munster' (12 *et passim*), referred to several times in the play as the reason for Ireland's current state of famine and starvation.

Like Edmund's memory of the Irish 'ghosts crying out of their graves' and several other passages in the play, the reference to 'these late wars of Munster' is a direct quotation from a sixteenth-century political reform tract, *A View of the Present State of Ireland*, written by the historical Edmund Spenser in 1596, two years before the action of the play.[34] This tract with its recommendations for pacification bordering on genocide has become notorious as an instance of Ireland's ruthless political suppression at the hands of the ruling English elite. What prompts its usage in the play is not the attempt to quote a few authentic soundbites but the curious poetic quality of some of its more graphic passages. As in the juxtaposition quoted above – where the dead spirits of Troy rise alongside the Irish ghosts from their graves – the unsavoury political imaginings of the *View* are lifted to a level of myth where historical fact is overwritten by the poetic imagination. History, in this play, is probed not for its factuality but for the semantic multiplicity of the cultural poetics contained in its often elusive textual traces. Central to this poetic metamorphosis is the Janus-faced figure of Edmund, who (mis)uses his creative powers to further political goals that run counter to the spirit of his art. At the end of the play, the castle in which he resided in Ireland and the 'castle' of his poetic imagination merge into a single funeral pyre (98–9).

There are two ways of reading the outcome of this violent encounter staged in the play as a whole. The first would emphasise the inevitability of the catastrophic ending implied by the explosive mix of mutual suspicion: at the end of the play, the castle goes up in flames, Edmund flees in obvious distress, mad King Sweney and Queen Maeve are killed by their own people, who also cruelly murder their English captives.[35] The second reading would foreground the signs of a brighter future in the midst of all this destruction: the killing of Sweney and Maeve actually liberates the next generation of native Irish by relieving them of the need to re-establish the old order, Edmund leaves behind his child who in the very last scene of the play teams up with the remaining Irish in an image of possible future union. In a public statement on the play, McGuinness has implicitly favoured this latter reading by emphasising that the Gaelic culture – which he describes as 'extraordinarily rich, strange, and archaic' – 'was not capable of renewing itself [or] finding new directions for itself. ... [I]n the face of this extraordinary colonial power [i.e. the English] the structures of the Gaelic world collapsed and we went into the serious confusion that typified our history from the 1600s right through to the 1900s.' The important point is that neither side was unaffected by this confrontation: 'It's very clear from looking at Ireland's history that England has had a major part in the shaping of what we are, but it's equally true that England's relationship to Ireland has very deeply affected it and defined it.'[36]

This is finally a reading of history that runs directly counter to the basic condition of cultural irreconcilability posited in Friel's *Making History*. McGuinness is never given to downplaying the violence and the bloodshed of Anglo-Irish history – he is in fact far more uncompromising on this point than Friel – but he structures his exploration of early modern Ireland around the knowledge of mutual contact and the very real changes that have resulted from centuries of a common history. Where *Making History* defines the historical process as a struggle for survival, where only one side can claim ultimate victory, the governing figure of history in *Mutabilitie* is the reality of inevitable, if violent, change. This finally redeems both parties implicated in the cultural encounter and opens for both a new horizon of possibility.

There is much in *Mutabilitie* that makes it a problematic, possibly unsuccessful play – the cheap points scored by making Shakespeare both gay and a Roman Catholic; cryptic passages in the dialogue; its heavy mythologising – but in stressing the relevance of the mixing and fusing of cultures, of exchange and contact, it offers a necessary corrective to static visions of history as a morality tale wrapped up in a rhetoric of finality, fatality and irrecoverable loss. *Mutabilitie*, by contrast, shows the defeat of a civilisation to be never fully an erasure: something always survives, can be recovered, continues to exert influence.

John Montague and Seamus Heaney: divided times

Although they resolve the conflict differently, both these plays rely in their aesthetic structure on the figure of the *agon* by pitting two alternative world views against each other. Poetry, as it turns to the same thematic material, opts for yet another deep structure of historical representation. What I want to show with my two final examples is how the lyric mode transcends linear time by suggesting extra-temporal alignments in the juxtaposition of images, movements and thought patterns from nominally separate but subliminally linked moments of historical experience.

John Montague's *The Rough Field* (1972) operates visibly in a dual time frame which aims to contrast the present – the poet's present – with various selected moments in historical time. For instance, the first of the book's ten sections comes in two columns of print: the poems that occupy the centre of each page are flanked in either the left or the right margin by prose quotations in smaller type. These quotations come from a variety of different sources – mainly official documents and letters – that take as their general theme the Nine Years War and the Ulster plantation of the late sixteenth and early seventeenth centuries. (The margins in other sections cite still other historical documents – religious pamphlets, newspaper clippings, hymns, etc.) The early modern moment is further evoked by prefacing each section with reproductions of late sixteenth-century woodcuts taken from John Derricke's savage anti-Irish diatribe *The Image of Irelande* (1581), a long pamphlet in doggerel verse intended to celebrate the then Lord Deputy Sir Henry Sidney's campaign against the Irish at the end of the 1570s.

The volume is in its entirety based on this duality of temporal reference. It records in verse the impressions and memories of the poet during two return trips to his home town of Garvaghey (from the Irish *Garbhachadh*: 'rough field', hence the volume's title) in County Tyrone.[37] Memory, activated by topography, is the defining trope of the book. As the poet revisits the scenes of his childhood and early youth, he observes on at least two levels 'the pattern history weaves':[38] he is '[m]arching through memory magnified' (53) on both a personal and a communal level. In terms of the latter framework, the history of place and people that he weaves into his long *poème fleuve* constitutes, as Robert Garratt has observed, 'a narrative of regional Ulster history from the Elizabethan wars to the civil-rights marches in Derry'.[39] Perhaps this is going slightly too far, for Montague's aim is not to compile a comprehensive chronology but a poetic jigsaw of selected moments of crisis, watershed events perhaps, that have significantly shaped the history of the province. (That he should do so in the early 1970s under the impact of social disintegration in Northern Ireland is hardly surprising.) Pride of place in this narrative is awarded to the early modern restructuring of the social and political landscape of Ulster. In view of the considerable critical attention that *The Rough Field* has already received in recent years, I want to focus here on just two aspects: the topographical focus of the poem's historical reconstructions and the nature of the link between past and present it detects in the operation of history.

Topography – the writing of place – is as important to Montague as it has been and continues to be to other Irish writers.[40] Landscape – in its social sense as a human investment in space – is frequently evoked as a formative site of memory and identity, and any poetic reference to the loss of topographical knowledge often has critics expounding on theories that read spatial transformation not as a sign of natural change but as the loss of a general sense of history. In the words of one such critic, '[p]oets who deal with a colonial past often see landscapes as the embodiment of a repressed past', and the language and stories recorded in place-names they see 'as a vessel for lost traces and fossils of history and consciousness'.[41] A sense of loss clearly pervades *The Rough Field* in which the Irish landscape is equated with 'a manuscript / We had lost the skill to read, / A part of our past disinherited' (35). '*Had* lost', it is important to emphasise, for now 'No rock or ruin, dun or dolmen / But showed memory defying cruelty / Through an image-encrusted name' (35). Memory seems to have at least partially returned (it is precisely this work of recovery that the poem undertakes) and it is a sense of the landscape as a palimpsest of multiple historical meanings – native and stranger – which now gives Ireland, and especially the poet's native Tyrone, both meaning and purpose. Landscape only becomes important because it is assumed to reveal underneath the scars inflicted by a fragmentary and discontinuous colonial past the traces of an earlier culture of which it is a mute spatial witness, the near-mystical remnant of an organic dreamtime *before* the invaders arrived on the scene.

Montague is actually less given to this romanticising than some of his critics (the occasional spurts of nostalgia notwithstanding). One way of avoiding the slip into romance is to make historical references specific rather than general. Montague suggested in an interview in 1980 that this was indeed his project, leading a critic to argue that in contrast to the 'ahistorical qualities' of Patrick Kavanagh's 1942 poem *The Great Hunger*, Montague's own 'sequence deliberately engages history, especially political history, and the past'.[42] The Kavanagh comparison is Montague's own; as he explains, the 'frustration' in the older poet's work 'is not historic. ... The historical dimension didn't exist for him. It's the difference between *The Great Hunger* and *The Rough Field*. ... One important aspect of my work ... is that it is mediumistic, in so far as it is letting older generations speak through me.'[43] This poetic ventriloquising of the writer as 'medium' implies an unusual proximity to the 'real' agents of history but also an oddly passive stance of the poetic voice. Taking the position seriously, we may ask what the political history of the Ulster plantation and the Elizabethan wars leading up to that moment are actually made to signify in *The Rough Field*.

On one level, as Montague has explained in another interview, they signify quite simply the 'origins of the Northern problems' which he locates in 'a classic colonial situation crossed with religion when England became Protestant'.[44] The poem indeed works its way from the sixteenth-century colonial moment towards an anatomy of the present situation of civil conflict in Northern Ireland, but, put in such general terms, this is little more than any standard account of Irish history would offer as a gloss on the historical origins of the current Ulster crisis. The purpose of poetry in times of war, Montague thinks, is to introduce people to the reality of the world of 'violence and pain', and to 'give [them] a glimpse of why what is happening is happening, why the bombs are going off'.[45] Does this imply that the poet is merely a better, more eloquent historian, who can embellish the historical record but not add anything to it? My own feeling is that Montague does indeed run the danger of doing little more than repeat well-known historical causalities in verse. The early modern is, at this level of the poem's historical consciousness, presented in terms of a teleological inevitability, leading directly towards contemporary civil conflict – a view which should be taken for what it is: a particular choice of historical reading, not a necessity.

Montague's most common poetic strategy is to start with a personal memory and then widen it into a particular historical background, which can produce exciting associative strings of images but conflates sometimes too quickly perhaps the personal and the political. Section IV, 'A Severed Head', the part of the poem that most directly engages the early modern transformation of Ulster, shows this procedure quite clearly. The section begins with three quotations in the margins (two of them from contemporary texts)[46] that map out the interplay of authority and resistance in the political landscape of Ulster around 1600. The actual poem starts with the speaker taking a walk along a mountain road where his 'former step' quickly echoes in his mind, and he sees himself again as the child he was, 'driving cattle / To the upland fields' (33).

The next move of memory is to evoke first the former inhabitants of the valley, and then the 'shards / Of a lost culture': the slopes 'strewn with cabins, deserted / In my lifetime' (34). These reflections prompt the metaphor of the landscape as a manuscript that is difficult to read (quoted above), before the poet sets out on an imaginative recovery of that landscape. Having now arrived in the deep time of history, he recalls in a series of historical flashbacks three of the sixteenth-century O'Neill chieftains – Con Bacach, Shane and Hugh (whom we have already met in this chapter) – in confrontation with representatives of the English crown. After these three vignettes we are first taken through Hugh's submission after the defeat at Kinsale, and then through a poetic rendering of the Flight of the Earls, before Irish schoolchildren of later centuries are shown struggling with the English language – one result of the Tudor conquest, the sequence implies, is the loss of the native language. (It is interesting and rather telling to see that the common people – here the schoolchildren – only enter the poem in a state of political oppression, while any earlier glory of Gaelic culture is entirely the preserve of the ruling local elite.)

Up to this point in the section, the poetic narrative expounds a history of decline and a gradual slide into disinheritance and loss. But the final passage hints, if not at a complete reversal, then at least at a redirection of this trajectory by implying the possibility of a new communality that none of the previous history would have allowed us to expect. In the final five stanzas of the section, no fewer than eighteen local place-names are evoked

– some of planter origin, some of Gaelic origin, some going back even further in time – suggesting a new social order of mixed ethnic and cultural affiliation. That this order is currently (at the time of publication in 1972) not a peaceful one is part of what the poem aims to show, but the verbal cartography also works towards an image of hopeful coexistence: '[And what of] Names twining braid Scots and Irish, / Like Fall Brae, springing native / As a whitethorn bush?' (40) It is in such passages that the violent early modern conflict between two opposing cultures implies not only a continued state of native subjection but also a new matrix of historical possibility, a 'neighbourhood', in the full sense of the term, rather than an ongoing state of siege. More so, the colonisers themselves do not remain untouched by the unbridled spirit of place: 'even the English in these airts / Took a lawless turn' (40).

The sixteenth-century woodcuts that introduce each section, if read against the grain, can be seen to be doing something similar. Nominally, these woodcuts (which are important documents in their own right, given the otherwise scant visual evidence we have of early modern Gaelic culture) repeat the colonial gaze of disapproval and deprecation. They show the 'wild Irish' as the English saw them: defecating at table, hiding in impenetrable woods, wearing their notorious 'glib' and mantle, practising 'Papism'. They are also records of the full scale of colonial violence done in Ireland: severed and impaled heads, burned dwellings, devastated landscapes. Yet in order to represent Gaelic culture as wild and barbaric, the anonymous artist of these woodcuts first had to record it in detail, and this moment of contact implies already a transformation. As McGuinness's *Mutabilitie* would also seem to argue, there is no colonial encounter that does not affect and change both sides implicated in it.

The continuous presence of the historical in the landscape is paradigmatically circumscribed in what is one of Montague's best-known poems, 'Like dolmens round my childhood, the old people' – a poem first published in 1961, which here finds a new home in the sequential survey of *The Rough Field*. The poem is another example of Montague's characteristic conflation of the personal and the political. A series of eccentric local characters he recalls from his childhood days are reimagined through the grown man's mature sense of self. In the final stanza, however, these figures break through the confines of a personal landscape of memory to be recruited in the name of a national theme:

> Ancient Ireland, indeed! I was reared by her bedside,
> The rune and the chant, evil eye and averted head,
> Fomorian fierceness of family and local feud.
> Gaunt figures of fear and of friendliness,
> For years they trespassed on my dreams,
> Until once, in a standing circle of stones,
>
> I felt their shadows pass

> Into that dark permanence of ancient forms (15).

The poetic drive of this stanza is curiously ambiguous. Line 3, for instance, jars so heavily that the rhythmically uneven conjunction of 'fear' and 'friendliness' hardly allows the alliterative sound pattern to establish itself in the ear. Is the historical condition described here oppressive or benign? Some critics resort to a merely descriptive level of analysis: '[T]he only way to remember this Ireland [the 'strangeness and waywardness of Ancient Ireland'] is to cast it in stone, to visualize it as dolmens: The past can only survive when it dies a peculiar kind of death, a death which leaves traces in form or art.'[47] Perhaps, but does 'the dark permanence of ancient forms' suggest stifling fossilisation or a protective alliance? Are dolmens massive obstacles blocking access to the future or an inspirational source of energy? I want to suggest that Montague's poetic history suffers from this state of doubtful indecision. It presents history as a collage of isolated moments that most frequently lock the present into a cycle of inevitable repetition, while only occasionally suggesting the possibility of new departures. The aesthetic congruence and symmetry of 'ancient form' he discovers in landscape clearly have an impact on the present, but in forms left oddly unresolved by the poetic 'medium'.

My final example in this chapter – a handful of poems by Seamus Heaney – offers a few scattered images rather than a sustained historical survey comparable to *The Rough Field*. I shall look at Heaney's historical metaphor of the bog as a form of topographical memory in some detail in Chapter 4; here I only want to turn briefly to the few explicit references to the early modern period in his work of the 1970s. Important for both its view of a divided landscape and a possible repossession of disputed ground is the poem 'Belderg' from the 1975 volume *North*. Heaney – much like Montague – has frequently turned to the history of place-names as repositories of legend and memory; in 'Belderg' he subjects the name of his own birthplace, Mossbawn (in County Londonderry) to a critical etymology:

> So I talked of Mossbawn,
> A bogland name. 'But *moss*?'
> He crossed my old home's music
> With older strains of Norse.
> I'd told how its foundation
>
> Was mutable as sound
> And how I could derive
> A forked root from that ground
> And make *bawn* an English fort,
> A planter's walled-in mound,
>
> Or else find sanctuary
> And think of it as Irish,
> Persistent if outworn.[48]

Heaney has elaborated in one of his critical essays on the historical point he was making here.[49] Partisan history would always capitalise on just one element that has gone into the historical fusion that produced modern Ulster; here the landscape is represented as a meeting-place of several different cultures – English, Scots, Irish, 'Norse' – wide apart in time, space and religion. The home as tree (a reference also to the 'world tree' of Norse mythology) is a prominent metaphor in 'Belderg', with the poet studying the 'growth rings' accrued by that home, as they reveal layer upon layer of successive inhabitants. The linguistic fusion in 'Mossbawn' – with its 'forked root' reaching into the dual history of planter and Gael – articulates the reality of a century-long coexistence, a mutually shared landscape, that remained a mere suggestion in *The Rough Field*.

The (hesitant) optimism of this historical vision is not consistent throughout Heaney's early volumes. Two other poems revisit what are by now familiar figures in this chapter, Spenser and Ralegh. In 'Bog Oak' from the 1972 collection *Wintering Out*, Heaney 'meditates on that familiar Irish building material, oakwood retrieved from bogland, and derives from it a colonial history' in which Spenser 'is heavily implicated'.[50] The poem recalls rural figures such as the carters or the 'moustached / dead' whose 'hopeless wisdom'[51] strikes a note of sadness that pervades several of the countryside poems in *Wintering Out*. Ultimately, these rural labourers – whose lives are far removed from mystic '"oak groves"' or the druidic 'cutters of mistletoe / in the green clearings'[52] – are descendants of their Elizabethan forebears who were reduced to misery and starvation during 'these late wars of Munster' waged by the English planters:

> Perhaps I just make out
> Edmund Spenser,
> dreaming sunlight,
> encroached upon by
>
> geniuses who creep
> 'out of every corner
> of the woodes and glennes'
> towards watercress and carrion.[53]

Here Spenser, the 'dreaming' poet of *The Faerie Queene*, whose poetic calling Heaney to some extent followed, figures centrally in a history of dispossession that robbed Ireland of its dignity and Celtic mystique. The last stanza carries again direct quotations from Spenser's *View of the Present State of Ireland* in which Irish woods and bogs were demonised as breeding-places of rebels and impenetrable strongholds of 'barbarism'.

A later poem implicates Spenser's neighbour at Kilcolman Castle, Sir Walter Ralegh, even more deeply in a relationship of colonial suppression. 'Ocean's Love to Ireland' from the volume *North* takes its title from the nearly six hundred lines extant of Ralegh's five 'Cynthia' poems, presumably written in honour of the Queen (who was known in one of her many mythical identities as Cynthia, the moon goddess, while she is known to have addressed 'Sir Walter' as 'Water' or 'Ocean'), the last of which contains the phrase 'Ocean's Love to Cynthia' in its title.[54] Heaney pinches the title and combines it with another detail of Ralegh's life, his abuse of one of his maids of honour, as reported by the seventeenth-century biographer John Aubrey. According to Aubrey, Ralegh got the maid 'up against a tree' and proceeded to rape her, whereupon 'she cryed in extasey, Swisser Swatter Swisser Swatter'[55] (i.e. 'Sweet Sir Walter'). Heaney, making the maid Irish (Aubrey is silent on her origins), uses these and other details for an extended allegory of the political relationship between Britain and Ireland:

> Speaking broad Devonshire,
> Ralegh has backed the maid to a tree
> As Ireland is backed to England
>
> And drives inland
> Till all her strands are breathless:
> 'Sweesir, Swatter! Sweesir, Swatter!'[56]

The allegory works on several levels (language, sexuality, social standing, etc.), the most important of which for my purposes is the idea that the birth of modern Ireland is the result of a political 'rape' (a conceit Heaney also uses in another poem of the same volume, 'Act of Union'). The sexual act of violence against the maid is aligned with the military acts of violence during the historical massacre at Smerwick (1580) in which Ralegh was implicated (and which Spenser mentions in the *View*), where the ground was 'sowed', as the poem reports, 'with the mouthing corpses / Of six hundred papists'. The 'ruined maid', in her metaphorical identity as Ireland, finally 'fades from their somnolent clasp' into politicised myth: 'ringlet-breath and dew, / The ground possessed and repossessed'.[57]

We can see in these two poems an imaginative use of history which borrows specific details from the historical record – a quotation here, an unverified anecdote there – and inserts them into wider cultural circuits of meaning: reading the currently depleted state of the Irish countryside as a direct result of the 1580s campaign against the Irish in Munster, reported by Spenser, or defining the political double bind between Britain and Ireland in terms of male sexual violence. In scope and ambition, this use of history moves far beyond the retelling of major events through verse (the strategy adopted in *The Rough Field*) and will find its culmination in the bog metaphor Heaney deployed to considerable poetic effect in *North*. Yet both poems, by looking back to the early modern moment as the instigator of a history defined in terms of oppression, as the manifestation of brute force, cannot quite encompass a view of the past that acknowledges its semantic multiplicity, its potential richness of possibility and vision. This, I want to suggest, is finally achieved by the imaginative

Reclaiming the early modern 33

evocation of history recorded in my last example, the 1972 poem 'Traditions'.

The poem is one of a number in *Wintering Out* that play on the theme of linguistic imperialism: 'Our guttural muse / was bulled long ago / by the alliterative tradition'.[58] The conflict here is not only an oral one between 'guttural' and 'alliterative' (a reference to the technique of alliteration in Anglo-Saxon poetry, also employed by Spenser in *The Faerie Queene*) but also a conflict between the earthy, tribal fidelities of Irish legend and the heady intellectualism of English poetry. 'Bulled' here repeats the sexual overtones of rape and masculine imposition that we saw articulated in the Ralegh poem, creating 'a linguistic–sexual metaphor for Ireland's traumatic colonial history'.[59] Shakespeare, whose *Othello* is quoted in the first section of the poem, is ironically evoked in section II, where some of the contemporary results of that early modern linguistic 'bulling' are noted in the local variety of English spoken in Northern Ireland: 'some cherished archaisms / are correct Shakespearean'.[60] It is in the final section of the poem that the stanzas move in quite a different direction:

> MacMorris, gallivanting
> round the Globe, whinged
> to courtier and groundling
> who had heard tell of us
>
> as going very bare
> of learning, as wild hares,
> as anatomies of death:
> 'What ish my nation?'
>
> And sensibly, though so much
> later, the wandering Bloom
> replied, 'Ireland', said Bloom,
> 'I was born here. Ireland.'[61]

In the space of twelve short lines, Heaney here assembles and creates a dense dialogic network between two Irish literary characters (MacMorris, Leopold Bloom), three canonical English and Irish authors (Shakespeare, Spenser, Joyce) and three texts dealing partially or centrally with Ireland (Shakespeare's *Henry V*, Spenser's *View*, Joyce's *Ulysses*). The lines suggest that MacMorris's question 'What ish my nation?', enigmatic and unanswerable (unanswerable in 1599, when *Henry V* was written), may have been informed by Spenser's description of the starving, 'nation-less' and wandering Irish as 'anatomies of death'[62] (another direct quotation from the *View*), and links the scene to the passage in the Cyclops chapter of *Ulysses* where Leopold Bloom – the wandering Irish Jew, 'nation-less' on account of his religion – is accosted by the anti-Semitic and nationalist 'Citizen' to affirm with 'assertive dignity'[63] his birthright to call Ireland his home: 'Ireland. ... / I was born here. Ireland.'

This cross-historical dialogue is more than a mere collage of a few juicy quotations from centuries of literary history. Heaney's mini-pantheon of legendary characters includes several historical varieties of Irishness: the demonised wild Irish, a central colonial fiction in early modern England, who appear here in a state of near starvation as 'anatomies of death'; the Irishman in Britain, who has achieved status and recognition but who continues to be the target of racist and nationalist hostilities (MacMorris); and the internal exile (Bloom), whose personal history undermines the supposed homogeneity of European nation states, and who quietly claims for himself the right to a multi-ethnic Irish homeland.

These are indeed (as the title proclaims) 'traditions' of national identification, and they suggest a continuous history of exile, marginalisation and political dispossession. But what their imaginative juxtaposition also amounts to is a history of redemption: over three centuries may have passed before Macmorris's question was finally answered, but the late response confirms that nothing is ever lost from the annals of history. In view of the poem's linguistic preoccupations, the reference to *Ulysses* also emphasises the finding of a distinct national voice in what was once the colonial tongue; and the link between the date of *Henry V* – 1599 – and the publication of *Ulysses* – 1922 – spans the centuries of political oppression from the Tudor reconquest to the founding of the Irish Free State. The redemptive and, indeed, liberating construction of this dialogue across time can find, even in a history of subjection, moments of Irish self-assertion and agency.

Conclusion

The discussion so far bears out, I hope, my claim that the uses of history in recent Irish writing can indeed be diverse and complex, even if often contradictory and divided in their ideological commitment. In the textual samples I have covered in this chapter, the historical dynamics of the Tudor reconquest have been imagined in strikingly different terms: as a psychosexual double-bind of pain and desire, as a clash of cultures, as a continuous mechanism of violent change, as a form of compulsory repetition, and as a metatemporal, transhistorical dialogue. The three main chapters that follow will open the scope of historical conceptualisations still further as the dialogue with forms of history-writing and historiographical theories is intensified and taken to a higher level of intermedial reflection.

Unlike the present chapter, which is intended more as a representative survey of different generic possibilities, those that follow are all genre-based: they will deal exclusively (and in that order) with the novel, with drama and with poetry. This focus on genre does not only, as I have already pointed out, follow the material; it also to some extent suggests a congruence between the internal structure of specific historical events and the expressive possibilities of each literary genre. The historical undercurrent of the novel responds to the course of events played out over time; it employs most frequently a temporal pattern of anticipation and deferral in which to ground its particular choice of plot. It is not surprising, then, that novels rather than poems or plays have served as the principal aesthetic forum for the representation of the Famine and its slow but hardly irresistible slide into the state of utter cultural annihilation.

Drama, by contrast, is most directly concerned with the decisive moment of confrontation: the open stage drags into visibility what the historical record suggests as opposing and often irreconcilable paradigms. The playwright's interests most frequently focus on the point where this constellation reaches its climax, hence the significant plot choice (as we shall see) of structuring the dramatic action around a battle, a rebellion or some other form of military encounter. Poetry, finally, in its relative independence from spatial and temporal constraints, has to offer perhaps the most wide-ranging conceptual alternatives to traditional, linear models of historical causality. The technique of metaphorical juxtaposition, for instance, is often employed to suggest a simultaneity of different temporalities or an imaginative concurrence and correlation of ideas and images unavailable to other modes of historical description. Seen in context, all three genres make important and dynamic contributions to current forms of historical thought, and one central concern of what follows is to acknowledge this vital role of literature in the construction of our modern historical selves.

Notes

1 Ian McBride, 'Memory and national identity in modern Ireland', in McBride (ed.), *History and Memory in Modern Ireland* (Cambridge: Cambridge University Press, 2001), 1–42: 35.
2 *Proclamation of the Irish Republic (Poblacht na hÈireann)*. Quoted from the reprint in Seamus Deane (ed.), *The Field Day Anthology of Irish Writing*, 3 vols (Derry: Field Day Publications, 1991), vol. 3, 733–4: 733.
3 Even McBride's excellent collection on *History and Memory in Modern Ireland* includes only one essay on a pre–1798 topic: Alan Ford's analysis of Irish Catholic martyrology.
4 A selective list of recent collections and book-length studies in the field would include Patricia Coughlan (ed.), *Spenser and Ireland: An Interdisciplinary Perspective* (Cork: Cork University Press, 1989); Brendan Bradshaw, Andrew Hadfield and Willy Maley (eds), *Representing Ireland: Literature and the Origins of Conflict, 1534–1660* (Cambridge: Cambridge University Press, 1993); Andrew Hadfield, *Edmund Spenser's Irish Experience. Wilde Fruit and Salvage Soyl* (Oxford: Clarendon Press, 1997); Christopher Highley, *Shakespeare, Spenser, and the Crisis in Ireland* (Cambridge: Cambridge University Press, 1997); Willy Maley, *Salvaging Spenser: Colonialism, Culture and Identity* (Basingstoke: Macmillan, 1997); Mark Thornton Burnett and Ramona Wray (eds),

Shakespeare and Ireland (Basingstoke: Macmillan, 1997); and Andrew Murphy, *But the Irish Sea Betwixt Us: Ireland, Colonialism, and Renaissance Literature* (Lexington, KY: University Press of Kentucky, 1999).

5   The issue of English–Irish 'proximity' – understood in both geographical and cultural terms – is especially well explored in Murphy, *But the Irish Sea Betwixt Us*.
6   Hadfield, *Edmund Spenser's Irish Experience*, 199.
7   Robert Welch, *The Kilcolman Notebook* (Dingle, Co. Kerry: Brandon, 1994). All page references in the text are to this edition. To my knowledge, the only research article on this novel is David Gardiner's 'A view of Elizabeth's Ireland(s): Robert Welch's *'The Kilcolman Notebook'*, *Notes on Modern Irish Literature* 10 (1998), 4–17. Thanks to David Gardiner for providing me with a hard copy of this essay.
8   Andrew Hadfield, 'The trials of Jove: Spenser's allegory and the mastery of the Irish', *Bullán* 2, no. 2 (1996), 39–53: 39; 40.
9   John Donne, 'Elegy 19: To his Mistress Going to Bed', *The Complete English Poems*, ed. A. J. Smith (Harmondsworth: Penguin, 1971), 125.
10 Ibid. (My italics.)
11 The case for an Ireland–New World analogy was most forcefully argued by Nicholas Canny who suggested that those Englishmen involved in the colonising projects in the Americas first served 'years of apprenticeship' in Ireland. See *The English Conquest of Ireland: A Pattern Established* (Hassocks, Sussex: Harvester, 1976), 159. The model has since been questioned; see, for instance, Hiram Morgan, 'Mid-Atlantic Blues', *The Irish Review*, no. 11 (1991/92), 50–6.
12 Walter Benjamin, 'Theses on the philosophy of history', trans. Harry Zohn. Quoted from the reprint in Tamsin Spargo (ed.), *Reading the Past* (Basingstoke: Palgrave, 2000), 118–26: 121. I shall have occasion to return to Benjamin's 'Theses' in Chapter 3.
13 Ibid.
14 J. C. Beckett, *The Making of Modern Ireland, 1603–1923* (London: Faber, 1969), 22.
15 See the stage directions in the front matter. I am quoting throughout from Brian Friel, *Making History* (London: Faber, 1989). All page references in the text are to this edition.
16 See his influential work *On the Study of Celtic Literature* (1867).
17 Programme notes to *Making History*. Quoted in Sean Connolly, 'Translating history: Brian Friel and the Irish past', in Alan J. Peacock (ed.), *The Achievement of Brian Friel* (Gerrards Cross: Colin Smythe, 1993), 149–63: 158–9.
18 However, the most recent historian of the Nine Years War casts doubt on the thesis that O'Neill was educated in England (in the Sidney household), calling the assumption of his English upbringing '[o]ne of the most persistent myths about Hugh O'Neill': Hiram Morgan, *Tyrone's Rebellion: The Outbreak of the Nine Years War in Ireland* (Woodbridge, Suffolk: Boydell Press, 1993), 92. Nevertheless, Morgan concedes that O'Neill would have visited the English court several times in his career, so we can safely assume that he was exposed to English culture for long stretches of his life.
19 Murphy, *But the Irish Sea Betwixt Us*, 103.
20 Ibid., 100. For a recent reassessment of O'Neill's rebellion, see Morgan, *Tyrone's Rebellion*. Friel based his character less on historical research than on the imagi-

nation of the Irish novelist Sean O'Faolain. In his 1942 novel *The Great O'Neill*, O'Faolain was one of the first to attack the myth of O'Neill's Irish patriotism and to emphasise the pragmatic aspects of his self-fashioning as an Irish chieftain. O'Faolain's preface contains a passage that might have inspired Friel to write the play: 'If anyone wished to make a study of the manner in which historical myths are created he might well take O'Neill as an example, and beginning with his defeat and death trace the gradual emergence of a picture at which the original would have gazed from under his red eyelashes with a chuckle of cynical amusement and amazement. Indeed, in those last years in Rome, the myth was already beginning to emerge, and a talented dramatist might write an informative, entertaining, ironical play on the theme of the living man helplessly watching his translation into a star in the face of all the facts that had reduced him to poverty, exile, and defeat.' Sean O'Faolain, *The Great O'Neill. A Biography of Hugh O'Neill, Earl of Tyrone, 1550–1616* (London: Longmans, Green and Co., 1942), vi; see also Connolly, 'Translating history', 160. Another precedent for Friel's treatment of O'Neill (and earlier response to O'Faolain) was Thomas Kilroy's 1966 play *The O'Neill*, published for the first time in 1995 (Oldcastle: Gallery Press).
21 The phrase is Roy Foster's. See his *Modern Ireland, 1600–1972* (Harmondsworth: Penguin, 1989), 3 (title of 'Prologue').
22 A similar tendency to exaggerate contrast and to play down or ignore commonality mars Friel's earlier play *Translations* (1980), as I argue in Chapter 3 below.
23 Connolly, 'Translating history', 163.
24 Fintan O'Toole, 'Marking time: from *Making History* to *Dancing at Lughnasa*', Peacock (ed.), *The Achievement of Brian Friel*, 202–14: 202. See also p. 116, n. 22, for more comments on this essay.
25 For a related criticism of the play see Hiram Morgan, 'Making history: a criticism and a manifesto', *Text & Context* 4 (1990), 61–5.
26 Frank McGuinness, *Mutabilitie* (London: Faber, 1997). All page references in the text are to this edition.
27 For a survey of the uses of the Sweeney figure in modern Irish writing, see Neil Corcoran, *After Yeats and Joyce: Reading Modern Irish Literature* (Oxford: Oxford University Press, 1997), 19–25.
28 See the English translation by Seamus Heaney, *Sweeney Astray* (London: Faber, 1983).
29 Translated by Thomas Kinsella as *The Táin* (Oxford: Oxford University Press, 1970).
30 John Donne, 'An Anatomy of the World: The First Anniversary', *The Complete English Poems*, 276, line 213.
31 On Fortune, see Klaus Reichert, *Fortuna oder die Beständigkeit des Wechsels* (Frankfurt am Main: Suhrkamp, 1985).
32 Edmund Spenser, *The Faerie Queene*, ed. A. C. Hamilton (London: Longman, 1977), Book 7, Canto vii, stanza 47, lines 6–9.
33 Ibid., stanza 58, line 2.
34 The most accurate edition is still *A View of the Present State of Ireland*, ed. R. F. Gottfried, *The Works of Edmund Spenser: A Variorum Edition*, ed. Edwin Greenlaw et al., 10 vols (Baltimore, MD: Johns Hopkins University Press, 1949), vol. 10: 'The Prose Works', 40–231. More accessible is the following edition, based

on the first printed (and lightly censored) version of Spenser's text, which did not appear until almost forty years after composition: Andrew Hadfield and Willy Maley (eds), *Edmund Spenser: A View of the State of Ireland. From the First Printed Edition (1633)* (Oxford: Blackwell, 1997).

35 The programme notes to the London premiere of the play (Royal National Theatre, Cottesloe, premiered 20 November 1997) extended this cycle of violence into the twentieth century by following up the explanatory section on the 'Munster Wars' with photographs and images illustrating Irish history from the 1590s to the current crisis in Northern Ireland.

36 Interview with Frank McGuinness by Deborah Ballard in *GCN* (September 2000), 45.

37 The literal subtext of the poem is spelled out briefly but helpfully by Seán Lucy in 'John Montague's *The Rough Field*: an introductory note', *Studies* 63, no. 249 (1974), 29–30.

38 John Montague, *The Rough Field* [1972] (Oldcastle: Gallery Press, rev. edn 1989), 53. All references in the text are to this edition.

39 Robert F. Garratt, 'John Montague and the poetry of history', *Irish University Review*, John Montague issue, vol. 19, no. 1 (1989), 91–102: 94.

40 The issue will come up again in my discussion of Brian Friel's *Translations* (Chapter 3) and Seamus Heaney's *North* (Chapter 4).

41 Elmar Schenkel, 'Embodying the past: history and imagination in John Montague's *The Rough Field*', in Hans-Ulrich Seeber and Walter Göbel (eds), *Anglistentag 1992 Stuttgart: Proceedings* (Tübingen: Niemeyer, 1993), 102–110: 107. For a related argument, see Elizabeth Grubgeld, 'Topography, memory, and John Montague's *The Rough Field*', *Canadian Journal of Irish Studies* 14, no. 2 (1989), 25–36. Grubgeld argues that 'the poem seeks the recovery of a place' (29).

42 Garratt, 'John Montague and the poetry of history', 91.

43 Timothy Kearney, 'Beyond the planter and the Gael: interview with John Hewitt and John Montague. On northern poetry and the Troubles', *The Crane Bag* 4, no. 2 (1980), 85–92: 89; 91.

44 Dennis O'Driscoll, 'An interview with John Montague', *Irish University Review*, John Montague issue, 58–72: 60–1; 66.

45 Kearney, 'Beyond the planter and the Gael', 88.

46 The quotations are not always very reliable. For instance, 'Tyrconnell' is changed to 'Tyrone' in the letter from Sir John Davies that Montague quotes; the year of this letter is incorrectly given as 1612 rather than 1609; and the subtitle of Derricke's poem, 'A discovery of woodkarne', is offered as its main title. These silent changes are presumably intended to heighten the topical relevance of the quotations.

47 Schenkel, 'Embodying the past', 106.

48 Seamus Heaney, 'Belderg', *North* (London: Faber, 1975), 14.

49 Seamus Heaney, 'Belfast', *Preoccupations. Selected Prose, 1968–1978* (London: Faber, 1980), 28–37. 'Our farm was called Mossbawn. *Moss*, a Scots word probably carried to Ulster by the Planters, and *bawn*, the name the English colonists gave to their fortified farmhouses. Mossbawn, the planter's house on the bog. Yet in spite of this Ordnance Survey spelling, we pronounced it Moss bann, and *bán* is the Gaelic word for white. So might not the thing mean the white moss, the moss of bog-cotton? In the syllables of my home I

see a metaphor for the split culture of Ulster' (35).
50 Neil Corcoran, *The Poetry of Seamus Heaney: A Critical Study* (London: Faber, rev. edn 1998), 31.
51 Seamus Heaney, 'Bog Oak', *Wintering Out* (London: Faber, 1972), 14.
52 Ibid., 14.
53 Ibid., 14–15.
54 Cf. *The Poems of Sir Walter Ralegh. A Historical Edition*, ed. Michael Rudick (Tempe, AZ: Arizona Center for Medieval and Renaissance Study/Renaissance English Text Society, 1999), 46–66.
55 *Aubrey's Brief Lives*, ed. Oliver Lawson Dick (London: Secker and Warburg, 1950), 255–6.
56 Seamus Heaney, 'Ocean's Love to Ireland', *North*, 46.
57 Ibid., 47.
58 Seamus Heaney, 'Traditions', *Wintering Out*, 21.
59 Corcoran, *The Poetry of Seamus Heaney*, 39.
60 Heaney, 'Traditions', *Wintering Out*, 21.
61 Ibid., 22.
62 Historically, this is very unlikely, as the *View* circulated only in a few manuscript copies during Shakespeare's lifetime.
63 Corcoran, *The Poetry of Seamus Heaney*, 40.

2

FACT INTO FICTION: NOVELS OF THE IRISH FAMINE

While much contemporary Irish literature suggests to many critics a continuing, perhaps obsessive, concern with historical consciousness in modern Ireland, no such assumptions were current in the nineteenth century. The mere suggestion that the Irish have any kind of historical memory at all would have made many Victorian commentators shake their heads in disbelief. Some equated the Irish outright with Nietzsche's cattle: '[T]he Irish, on their scanty farms', wrote J. Veneday in 1844, 'will only do that which is absolutely necessary … Systematically they "live from hand to mouth;" … Neither the Irish landed proprietor, nor the Irish farmer, confide or believe in any continuance of the relations between them. The consequence is, that both think only of the present moment.'[1]

Veneday was attacking the system of land tenure in Ireland whereby thousands of tiny plots were held by peasants who had to fear eviction if they decided to improve their lands and thus make them more profitable, an investment rewarded either by loss of land or higher rents. Hence, any concern with the future seemed positively suicidal to Ireland's landless peasants. In retrospect, Veneday's comment that the Irish 'think only of the present moment', and that they have, as a consequence, no historical consciousness, looks more than just stunningly wrong; in view of its timing, it is an almost uncanny premonition made on the eve of the Irish Famine of the 1840s, which was not only the greatest social disaster of nineteenth-century Europe, but to this day proves the hardest challenge yet to the public forms of a collective national memory in Ireland.

The causes of the Great Famine may be subject to continuous reinterpretation but the salient facts are pretty much beyond dispute. In Ireland, from 1845 onwards, the potato crop failed four years out of five, a blight caused by a then unknown fungus, *phytophthora infestans*, which had only recently crossed the Atlantic. Similar blights were also recorded in other European countries – most notably in Scotland and Belgium – but only in

Ireland, where the potato was the staple crop of the rural poor, did it have truly devastating consequences. It is now estimated that out of a population of slightly over eight million in the early 1840s, one million died of starvation and famine-induced diseases, while between one and two million were forced into emigration.

Ultimately, the cost of the Famine cannot be measured even in these imposing figures. Materially, it forced a violent programme of modernisation on Ireland's economic and social structure; politically, it radicalised public opinion in Ireland, feeding the nationalism of later decades; linguistically, it dealt a death blow to the Irish language; and psychologically, it traumatised a society that had to watch its poorest members starve while failing to take action on their behalf. To this day, the Famine stands as the signifier of spiritual depression, of demoralising helplessness, of degrading victimisation.[2]

This seismic upheaval of Irish society also disrupted the spatial and temporal parameters of the Irish historical experience. 'Part of the horror of the Famine', Terry Eagleton writes, 'is its atavistic nature – the mind-shaking fact that an event with all the pre-modern character of a medieval pestilence happened in Ireland with frightening recentness.'[3] Eagleton's key word here – 'atavism' – imagines Irish history in terms of temporal disjunction and archaic anachronism, a violent clash of timeframes. Part of my aim in this chapter is to ask how Irish novelists, from the mid-nineteenth century to the present, have dealt with such a disjointed image of their own past; specifically, I want to consider how – in view of the historical rupture of the Famine experience – the 'Famine novel' has been able to sustain (or not) its own ideal of narrative coherence.

The Famine: ruptures and continuities

I want to begin with the juxtaposition of two recent, highly public acts of Famine commemoration, Sinéad O'Connor's pop song '"Famine"', released in 1994, and the Famine Museum in County Roscommon, which opened in 1995. At first hearing, Sinéad O'Connor's song might appear more concerned with forgetting than commemoration. Although it deals explicitly with the Irish Famine of the 1840s, the word 'Famine' is apostrophised because the stability of its historical referent is drawn into doubt: in this song, the Famine never actually happened.[4] Given the huge upsurge of historiographical interest in the Irish Famine in recent years, and the widely held belief that the event constitutes nothing less than a 'watershed in Irish history',[5] these are puzzling lyrics. How are they meant to be read?

Writing about the discursive processes that turn the raw material of history – the unstructured, diffuse and unconnected series of mere occurrences – into recognisable textbook 'events', one critic has recently argued that '[l]ike all past events the Famine is primarily a retrospective, textual creation. The starvation, the emigration, and the disease epidemics of the late 1840s have become "the Famine" because it was possible to inscribe those disparate but interrelated events in a cohesive narrative.'[6] These are by now familiar reservations about the ideological dangers attendant on the uncritical acceptance of historical master narratives, but the sense in which, for Sinéad O'Connor, the 'Famine' never actually happened, is hardly owed to such advanced theorising.

The reasons for her dismissal of the Famine as a historical incident clearly relate to the connections she establishes between past and present. The song diagnoses a rupture, a sudden loss of history after the Famine, that has left – in a questionable analogy that will recur in this chapter – the Irish nation like a hurt, helpless child. Impeded by injury and unable to 'grow up', Ireland suffers from an inability to come to terms with the event, and this mental blockage has fatally delayed the process of growth and maturation that would enable the very formation of historical memory. This is, at root, a psychological argument: 'Like malfunctioning adults who have been sexually, physically or psychologically abused, the Irish are said to malfunction because of their traumatic experience of Famine.'[7] So the 'Famine' never actually happened because no one can properly remember it.

The argument that contemporary Ireland has fatefully neglected its past and hence owes a pressing debt of memory to the thousands of ancestors who perished during the Famine enjoys more widespread currency. Countless contributions – popular, journalistic, academic, artistic, etc. – to the Famine commemorations in the 1990s, during the 150th anniversary of the Great Hunger, argued that the failure to confront the full extent of the outrageous human loss had impeded the onset of modernity in Ireland. Not infrequently, many ills of the present were blamed on the reluctance or even downright refusal to come to terms with the cultural legacies of the Famine period:

> We [the Irish] are blind to the manner in which, through song and story and nod and wink and walk and glance, we have handed the trauma on from father to daughter, mother to son. The violence of our past is present in our present, enacted again and again in the fruitless conflicts which beset Southern society and the violence which has haunted the North for more than twenty-five years.[8]

If there was an element of escapism in such pronouncements (locating the scapegoat across the water) there was also the tacit acknowledgement that the difficult work of cultural memory would have to be a steady, if troublesome, progress through the generations.

In the same year that Sinéad O'Connor released her Famine song, a new museum opened in Ireland, dedicated exclusively to the memory of the Irish Famine. The Famine Museum is situated in the Strokestown Park estate, County Roscommon, the former residence of the Mahon family.

The site gained notoriety in 1847, when Major Denis Mahon, master of the estate in the 1840s, was assassinated (on 2 November of that year), presumably as a reprisal for his part in the programme of enforced emigration and eviction that operated on his estate. His death, and the fact that reference to it comes so easily, highlights the biased operation of historical memory which the museum intends to rectify. Major Mahon's death is remembered and discussed even today, but of the thousands of Famine victims – several hundred of whom died on the Atlantic passage that the Major had financed – hardly a name survives. The Famine Museum, the official website proclaims, 'was designed to commemorate the history of the Great Irish Famine of the 1840's and in some way to balance the history of the "Big House".'[9] It uses the archival material that was discovered on the estate to preserve for history not only the chronology of the Mahon family but also an account of the living conditions of the tenants resident on their lands during Famine times, people of whom 'nothing of a physical nature has survived to commemorate their lives'.[10]

Such a project, another official publication explains, had finally become possible in the 1990s after decades of neglect because 'a number of present experiences, national and global, return us to a consideration of the past'.[11] Having failed – so far – to learn from its own troubled past, Ireland can now recover 'the meaning of its history'[12] through an attention to similar social disasters in the Third World. The dangers of transcultural and transhistorical alignments of wildly different experiences might be only too apparent in such a pronouncement, yet the museum promotes just this sense of a transglobal family of historical victims: 'Now, 150 years after the Famine, emigration ... provides the sense of contact with a broader global community, a common identity and history with other groups and nationalities.' Oddly, the depth of local detail that the focus on individualised victims of the Famine promises is immediately threatened with elision by this unmitigated act of affective globalisation.

Whether the transhistorical analogy between the nineteenth-century Irish Famine and modern-day famines has, in fact, any relevance at all for contemporay Irish identity, is doubted by Cormac Ó Gráda, the foremost economic historian of the Famine. Commenting on the generous (nongovernmental) Irish help for the Third World, Ó Gráda thinks that it might indeed 'be argued that the more we [the Irish] have distanced ourselves from our own past and the more we have forgotten what really happened in the 1840s, the more generous we have become in the face of Third World disasters'.[13] Like Sinéad O'Connor, he diagnoses a rupture, a break, a loss of contact, just where the curators of the Famine Museum discover an essential continuity. For them, the link might, at this moment, still be buried and neglected, but it can be rescued as the point of contact between modern Ireland and the society that was swept away by the Famine.

Clearly, these two cultural appeals to historical memory – song and museum – are strikingly different in their readings of the relevance of the past for the present, yet they share a sense of historical urgency that is characteristic of much contemporary investment in the Famine period (particularly evident in the commemorations throughout the 1990s). Whether it is the event that directly leads up to the present day, on however bumpy a road, or whether it marks the point at which all contact with a previous Ireland was irretrievably lost, it is a historical moment that not only continues to fire the imagination but keeps resisting its smooth appropriation into official, community-building memory.

In terms of the conceptualisation of the idea of historical progress, thinking in models of either rupture or continuity might be understood to constitute mutually exclusive a priori assumptions about the course of history. Yet what I want to suggest in this chapter is that the cultural work of history focused on the Famine never really lives up to its own promise unless it holds both these moments in a kind of creative tension. This claim is informed by Paul Ricoeur's observation that in the 'memory of the horrible' (his point of reference is Auschwitz), 'historical explanation and the individuation of events through horror ... cannot remain mutually antithetical'. Ricoeur argues that the 'horror' that attaches to the victims of what he calls 'uniquely unique events' exerts 'a specific function of individuation within our historical consciousness': it isolates, refuses comparison, and resists its opposite, which he defines as the 'work of explanation that connects things together'. This latent conflict between individuation and explanation may develop into a damaging schism if accounts of the 'horrible' resort to only one of these strategies, resulting either in 'a purely emotional retort' or in a dry history that 'dissolve[s] the event in explanation'. By contrast, fusing their respective strengths in (fictional and/or factual) accounts of the 'horrible' means to 'elevate' both, 'each by means of the other'.[14]

To make the point in the detail required, this chapter traces the ways in which the memory of the Famine, since the 1840s, has been shaped and reshaped in a continuous dialogue between fictional and factual approaches to the past – especially in the novel, in which the fictional response to the Famine has found its most extensive articulation. Thus, although this study is largely concerned with Irish writing since the 1970s, I shall include in my survey of Famine novels a look at some nineteenth- and early twentieth-century works because it is only against this earlier literary record that more current fictional negotiations of the Famine begin to make historical sense. It will become clear very soon that the contrast we saw emerging above in the brief comparison between the memory of the Famine in song and museum – that the event is 'objectively' factual for history and elusively polysemantic for art – cannot be sustained when the dialogue between the imaginative literature and the historiography of the Famine is examined in terms that explicitly foreground their conceptual interrelations.

Early Famine novels: 1847 to *c.* 1900

The first literary response to the Famine came early, almost before the fact. William Carleton's novel *The Black Prophet* was serialised in 1846 in the *Dublin University Magazine* and then published in book form in the following year.[15] The novel is an exuberant Gothic tale of betrayal, double-dealing and revenge, structured around a twenty-year-old murder case that still haunts the community in whose midst it occurred. The moral outrage of the murder, committed during the year of rebellion (1798) by Donnel Dhu, or Donald M'Gowan – the titular 'black prophet' – functions as a blueprint for the experience of famine. Donnel Dhu devises a plot that aims to lay the blame for the old crime on an honest farmer, but he is eventually found out in an unexpected counter-plot. At the end of the novel, it is his own wife, freshly returned from America, who supplies the evidence which sends him to the gallows.

Rotten family relations are reflected in the moral depths to which the famine victims have fallen. 'During such periods, and under such circumstances', an intrusive narrator comments,

> the famished people, in general, live and act under antagonist principles. Hunger, they say, will break through stone walls; and ... it is not surprising that the starving multitudes should, in the ravening madness of famine, follow up its outrageous impulses, and forget those legal restraints, or moral principles that protect property under ordinary or different circumstances.[16]

In this landscape of misery and enforced lawlessness, people cannot develop their true human potential – such as, for instance, Sarah M'Gowan, daughter of the black prophet, whose energies are wasted and whose brilliance of mind and heart can be articulated only in an unaccommodated wildness of character.

The imagery of the novel advertises the gloomy appearance of land and people, both inside and out, on nearly every page. The black prophet lives in the black glen, hidden away in his black soul is the black deed – the pervasive signifier 'black' serves as an indication of vanishing moral standards and as a descriptive term for the material state of the country: 'The roads were literally black with funerals; and, as you passed along from parish to parish, death-bells were pealing forth, in slow but dismal tones, the gloomy triumph which pestilence was achieving over the face of our devoted country – a country that each successive day filled with darker desolation and deeper mourning.'[17] The key signifier is even evoked in the form of black humour: 'God knows, there's not upon the face of the earth a counthry where starvation is so much practised, or so well understood. Faith, unfortunately, it's the national diversion wid us.'[18]

The novel presents the Famine in all its horror but, because of the year of composition, there are none of the staples of later Famine narratives, such as the descriptions of relief measures: the public works, the soup kitchens, the relief committees, not even the poorhouses (which were not introduced to Ireland until 1838, almost two decades after the year in which the novel is set). The villains of the piece are the rapacious and immoral shopkeepers who thrive on other people's misfortunes, and the strong farmers who mercilessly push their weaker rivals out of the market. The predominant moral tone of the tale is that of social conservatism. The turn to open rebellion by younger males is explained as the response to injustice and exploitation, yet such acts of lawlessness are ultimately condemned, and the most striking representative of this group in the book eventually succumbs to the fever. It is not solely the violence of the politically motivated rebels which causes the narrator's unease but also the potential violence of the Famine victims themselves.[19] Hence, crowd scenes are ambiguously portrayed; at the same time as the narrator records the just cause for outrage on the part of the people, he fears their swift transformation into an angry and violent mob.

Descriptions of individual suffering tend to verge on the abstract: 'Their cadaverous and emaciated aspects had something in them so wild and wolfish, and the fire of famine blazed so savagely in their hollow eyes, that many of them looked like creatures changed from their very humanity by some judicial plague that had been sent down from heaven to punish and desolate the land.'[20] In such passages and elsewhere, the narrator takes his eye off the plot to inform the reader in general terms about the state of Ireland, the reasons for the recurring famines, and the precautions that should have been taken by the government, but that have been fatally ignored.[21] The inclusion of footnotes in the fictional text, containing statistics and recollections of previous famines, amply demonstrates how Carleton's 'didactic purposes obtrude themselves on the life of the novel'.[22] It also bears out his fear of being accused of exaggeration. The preface to the 1847 edition is explicit on both points:

> [S]uch a subject [famine] is one which involves the heart-rending consideration of life and death to an extent beyond all historic precedent ... [I]t occurred to [the author] that a narrative founded upon it, or at all events, exhibiting, through the medium of fiction, an authentic detail of all that our unhappy and neglected country has suffered, during *past* privations of a similar kind, might be calculated to awaken those who legislate for us into something like a humane perception of a calamity that has been almost perennial in the country ... [The reader] may rest assured that the author has not at all coloured beyond the truth. The pictures and scenes represented are those which he himself witnessed in 1817, 1822, and other subsequent years; and if they be false or exaggerated, there are thousands still living who can come forward and establish their falsehood.[23]

Even as the uniqueness of the event is affirmed – 'beyond all historic precedent' – the current famine is, ultimately, seen only as a repetition of earlier famines. All Ireland is locked in a deadly repetitive cycle of destitution, pestilence and starvation, which only a wiser legislature can bring to a hold. In a vain appeal to the politicians of the day, the book edition of *The Black Prophet* was dedicated to Lord John Russell, then British Prime Minister, whose dismal record in Famine relief was to have more disastrous consequences than even Carleton could have anticipated.

With many of these concerns – the vivid descriptions of Famine victims, the Gothic scenes of horror and death, the open appeals to public aid, etc. – Carleton's novel set both tone and precedent for many subsequent Famine narratives. His most prominent early successor as Famine novelist, however, opted for quite a different scenario. If *The Black Prophet* speaks out for a culture that is about to vanish, a society that had for years been situated on the brink of poverty and famine, the landless farm labourers in rural Ireland hardly even come into view in Anthony Trollope's Famine novel, *Castle Richmond* (1860). Here, the love story woven only sparingly into the fabric of *The Black Prophet* takes centre stage against the backdrop of a blackmail threat to the property of an old landed family, the Fitzgeralds of Castle Richmond.

That threat is eventually averted, but for much of the novel – set in Counties Cork and Kerry in the 'Famine Year' 1846–47 – the loss of property and title implies a shared experience of suffering between the Fitzgerald family and the Famine victims. The structural use of the Famine as an external reflector of the novel's main narrative shows that, for Trollope at least, the public disaster of the Famine could be ideologically contained in the analogy with private misfortune.[24] Like a personal crisis, it is seen as having a potentially cleansing effect. The Famine, Trollope explains, is like a 'disease' which, once past, 'has taught us lessons of cleanliness, which no master less stern would have made acceptable'. It is a harsh but necessary form of catharsis: 'A famine strikes us, and we again beg that that hand may be stayed ... But, lo! the famine passes by, and a land that has been brought to the dust by man's folly is once more prosperous and happy.'[25] The Malthusian reflex to rationalise famines as necessary 'checks to population'[26] is only too apparent in such statements, even though in this novel Trollope does not share without reservations the nineteenth-century obsession with political economy.

The Famine is also contained and sanitised by strategically displacing the hunger victims to the margins of the novel's main chronotopes. *Castle Richmond* characteristically spatialises its Famine references, grounding the plot in a topography of Big Houses.[27] Traffic between these locations is frequent and Famine victims appear, as a rule, only on the roads in between. They are literally a perverse form of roadside decoration, an instance of sad, degenerate worldliness soiling the landscape. One character notes how on his way to Castle Richmond in February 1847, 'the country was colder, and wetter, and more wretched, and the people in that desolate district more ragged and more starved *than when he had last crossed it*'.[28] Against this imagery of a wasted landscape, traversed by well-fed landowners, prospective brides and mischievous blackmailers, the novel cultivates an affective bond with landed property. A deep attachment to the land characterises, for instance, the longing of the protagonist, Herbert Fitzgerald, as he looks over the Castle Richmond estate for what he believes will be the last time, on the evening before he sets off for London in search of work (thinking at this point that he is stripped of his inheritance forever):

> Every tree about the place, every path across the wide park, every hedge and ditch and hidden leafy corner, had had for him a special interest, – for they had all been his own. ... None but those who have known the charms of a country-house early in life can conceive the intimacy to which a man attains with all the various trifling objects round his own locality; how he knows the bark of every tree, and the bend of every bough; how he has marked where the rich grass grows in tufts, and where the poorer soil is always dry and bare; how he watches the nests of the rooks, and the holes of the rabbits, and has learned where the thrushes build, and can show the branch on which the linnet sits.[29]

Trollope's engagement with the Famine, I suggest, has to be understood in terms of the clash between this dream of a romantic landscape of intimate property and a devalued terrain wasted by native mismanagement.

In his *Six Letters to the Examiner*, written a decade before the novel (1849–50), Trollope parroted the official government view, showing himself convinced of two things about the Famine: first, that it would prove a providential purge of a rotten economy and second, that the relief effort of the English government was exemplary.[30] Ten years later, his views were less assured – most notably, some of his characters wonder whether the doctrines of political economy are really to be upheld at all times – but acceptance of the political and economic forces responsible for the social disaster was still only hesitant and partial. Like Carleton, Trollope uses the novel as a forum for general reflections on the social implications of the Famine; unlike Carleton, he cannot find fault with the governmental measures implemented to halt its spread. There are further differences. For instance, if Carleton's novel is in many ways an anatomy of human behaviour faced with the extremity of absolute deprivation, Trollope's novel normalises the Famine by reducing the spectacle of starvation to a peculiarity of local scenery. Between them, they define a spectrum of possibility in contemporary attitudes to the Famine: the moral appeal to compassion and the willing surrender to market forces.

But despite such differences, *The Black Prophet* shares with *Castle Richmond* the difficulty of representation: descriptions of Famine victims or the effects of starvation, although vividly rendered in both texts, are largely unconnected to the main plot, despite the attempt in both novels at a metaphoric equation between the social disaster and the principal plot line. If formal coherence and the aesthetic integration of all its narrative elements are indeed among the chief aims of the nineteenth-century realist novel, fictional and historical registers are in conflict in both books –

a conceptual difficulty of writing Famine narratives that persists well into the later decades of the nineteenth century.

After Carleton and Trollope, there is a steady stream of Victorian Famine novels. Some of these come under the political, some under the comic rubric,[31] while others follow Trollope in exploring further the Big House genre.[32] Novels taking the form of fictionalised family chronicles have to meet the obvious generic demand to include references to the Famine in their chronologies, a requirement that troubles one prominent example in this category, Margaret Brew's *The Chronicles of Castle Cloyne* (1885), even more deeply than *Castle Richmond*. Brew intends to show how the Famine was 'impartial in its effects', bringing '[p]eer and peasant, landlord and tenant, the home of the great, and the cabin of the lowly ... under its terrible influence'.[33] In order to translate this historical insight into an aesthetic structure, Brew creates 'two different stories running side by side through the book, each having but slight connection with the other'.[34] One plot line concentrates on folk material and initially spins a traditional, rustic tale of romantic desire checked by material pressure, in which the faithful lady is betrayed by the disloyal gallant – a reckless love affair effectively contrasted with the exigencies of rural life.

Brew's popular fictional 'brew' of clashing passions and dancing peasants eventually turns sour when the Famine has a disruptive and unexpected impact on the fate of her heroine, Oonagh MacDermott. Her disloyal lover – who had earlier shunned Oonagh when she had to sell her father's farm as a result of economic pressure – dies of starvation and leaves behind a young boy. Oonagh 'adopts' the boy and devotes the rest of her life to seeing the father's ambition fulfilled in the son: to be ordained as a priest. Years later, on the final pages of the novel, she dies a happy mother on the day her adopted son reads mass for the first time in his own church. The second plot, structured not around the peasant population of the Castle Cloyne estate but around the Catholic residents of the local Big House, contrasts Oonagh's fate – the tale of one woman's fight for survival – with a story of political ambition thwarted by economic and dynastic disintegration. The Catholic Dillons of Castle Cloyne had for generations been subject to the Penal Laws until the 1829 Emancipation Bill restored them to their political rights. When the master of the estate finally achieves his lifelong ambition to be elected to parliament, the Famine puts the old landed family under such economic pressure that the entire property falls prey to the Encumbered Estates Act.

Only a handful of characters wander through both plots. The 'gaunt spectre of the great Famine',[35] however, is present in each, if to different effect: it adds a sense of purpose to Oonagh's life – she can now raise a child as a mother without actually having to go through the anxieties of courtship, marriage and pregnancy (the feminist surplus of this plot device is entirely wasted, though, in a figure made to epitomise all traditional female virtues) – and it brings down an old landed family that managed to survive the apartheid legislation of the Penal Laws but not the catastrophe of the Famine.

The novel is marked by a notable sense of unease in having to deal with the Famine at all, despite the conscious choice of integrating it into both plot lines. It is with a sigh of relief that Brew bids farewell to the topic at the appropriate point in her chronicle: 'Now both reader and author can draw breath freely, for we have come to the end of the Famine.'[36] Given this almost palpable discomfort with the topic, it is hardly surprising that only a few personalised characters are actually shown in the novel to be starving – most notably John Molloy (Oonagh's unfaithful lover) and his wife Susie – and that it is principally the dark, undifferentiated masses of 'the poor' who die 'like chickens that would have the pip'.[37] (In fact, the untimely demise of Oonagh's faithful dog – the topic of an entire chapter[38] – receives more attention than any human death by famine.) Oonagh's 'adoption' of her unfaithful lover's child – which rights a past wrong (her desertion by John Molloy) – could be seen as the attempt to introduce an element of narrative continuity that enables the undoing of the historical and personal rupture caused by the Famine – in contrast to the post-Famine Californian wealth of Hyacinth Dillon, 'the last of the old family',[39] who is not in any rush to buy back the family estate.

Brew, who was born in County Clare probably around 1850 (and hence no immediate witness to the Famine), worries – like Carleton – about the credibility of her Famine depictions: 'It may be said that I have painted the great Irish Famine in colours that are too gloomy, and in language that is too strong. But to this I answer that the story of the Irish Famine could not be told with a pen dipped in rose-water, even in a work of fiction.'[40] The claims of reality on fiction, Brew thinks, are excessive, and she makes a conscious distinction between the fragrant rose-water of the imagination and the murky slough of history. In the novel, her tone characteristically changes when the Famine is addressed directly – the relevant passages are either buttressed by statistics or supported with references to historical 'fact'.

An earlier Famine novel by David Power Conyngham, *Frank O'Donnell* (1861), operates on a similar division. In order to incorporate the Famine into his 'tale of Irish life', Conyngham has to interrupt the flow of his descriptions of an Irish 'Arcadia' – replete with images of 'the peasantry in their gay, light-hearted, holiday enjoyment'[41] – and switch to a different register. 'We must now draw the curtain over two years', he opens his reflections on the Famine, and then continues with a nationalist history lesson, culled straight from the writings of John Mitchel, the restless Young Ireland agitator:[42] 'This potato blight and consequent famine were powerful engines of the state to uproot millions of the peasantry, to preserve law and order, and to clear off surplus population, and to maintain the integrity of the empire.' As if to apologise for the intrusion of the historian or political campaigner into his tale, Conyngham adds a footnote: 'It is impossible to give in the pages of a novel, without detracting from its merits as a novel, a correct account of how the money, voted and given to relieve the famine, was squandered and wasted.'[43]

These recurrent formal disruptions point to the apparent impossibility, felt by these writers, of creating a convincing fictional plot from their Famine material. They might thus lend weight to the argument, advanced by Terry Eagleton, that the Famine 'strains at the limits of the articulable', that it 'threatens to burst through the bounds of representation as surely as Auschwitz did for Theodor Adorno', and that the Famine 'is truly in this sense an Irish Auschwitz'.[44] Eagleton could have solicited support for his argument from many contemporary commentators on the Famine who often concur in their verdict that 'the Famine cannot be described'.[45] Alternatively, he could have quoted Aubrey de Vere, writing in the latter half of the nineteenth century, who called into question the very morality of Famine poetry: 'why / Should grief from fancy borrow? / Why should a lute prolong a sigh, / Sophisticating sorrow?'[46]

But I am not convinced that this Irish version of Adorno's Auschwitz argument really holds. For one, the reasons given for shirking Famine descriptions are by no means always the same. Most frequently they oscillate between prudence (it *should* not be described) and impossibility (it *cannot* be described). One early twentieth-century Famine novel places them neatly side by side: 'It would be impossible to catalogue the filth in these dark holes, or enumerate the combined odours arising into one foetid cloud of intolerable horror – it would be unpublishable if the *true* picture of what Hunger had brought the unhappy fellow-creatures to, in these pestilent lairs, was painted accurately.'[47] The passage moves from the impossibility of representation to the impossibility of publication, but finally expresses little doubt that a 'true picture' or 'accurate painting' of the Famine, if attempted, might indeed be achieved.

That this is not just an empty claim is borne out by the simple fact that there *is* a substantial literature on the Famine, even if Eagleton cannot find it in Yeats or Joyce,[48] and the sheer force of this continuous literary interest in the Great Hunger makes Eagleton's confident assumption that the 'Famine is the threatened death of the signifier'[49] look rather wildly off target. Colm Tóibín has recently responded even more vehemently to this notion: 'It is possible that Eagleton himself knows that his last statement' – that the Famine 'is truly in this sense an Irish Auschwitz' – 'is not true "in this sense" or any other. No one was traumatised into muteness who did not witness the events.'[50]

Given that the great 'literary silence' of the Famine is in fact no silence at all but rather a loud roaring, other representational problems of Famine novels seem to me more urgently in need of attention – especially, in the case of the examples discussed so far, the conceptual problems emerging from the textual fusion of different epistemological registers, and the attendant difficulty of subsuming the Famine under the imperatives of plot structure. As we have seen, the most common reflex in these early novels is the almost natural impulse to hide behind footnotes, statistics or eye-witness claims that are expected to authenticate the aesthetic imagination. Much of this hesitancy is clearly owed to a sense of the enormity of the Famine, of the sheer scale of the human suffering involved, which might ultimately be denigrated by any 'mere' fictional treatment. The retreat to the protected terrain of 'facts and figures' suggests as much, in conjunction with the repeated assurances that the verbal recreation of the Famine is, if anything, less drastic than the reality, and never an exaggeration in historical terms. The Famine acts in all these novels as an intrusive and disruptive element, a dark, alien force that negates the very possibility of human survival, that keeps resisting its full narrative integration – and is hence singled out, demarcated, moved to the realm of extra-fictional discourse.

The reflex to turn to 'authentic' historical material that is such a notable feature of early Famine novels is thus largely a consequence of the novelist's need to balance the demands of a culture deemed worth preserving, against a nature run wild; put differently, the life principle of fictional imagination is at odds in these novels with the wholly destructive impact of a formerly congenial human habitat. 'History' was recruited by many of these writers as the rational code that allowed them to distance themselves from the Famine and its 'ravening madness' (Carleton) while keeping as close as possible to the actual human experience, reining it in to their imaginative tales in the form of factual footnotes or social reportage. Paradoxically, then, through its use in the Famine novel, history validates fiction even as it eases the pain of memory: novels call upon history not so much for the value of statistics but for the discursive authority of the historiographical voice, which alone is understood to enable adequacy of impression and address – while at the same time toning down the emotive effect.

Novels written at a temporal remove from the Famine of about two or three generations – that is, from roughly the end of the century onwards – tend to be less scrupulous about the appropriation of the Great Hunger for fictional or emotional purposes. One way of accounting for this change is to identify it, in the terminology suggested by Jan Assmann, as the shift from 'communicative' to 'cultural' memory.[51] Communicative memory (*kommunikatives Gedächtnis*) is defined by the everyday, it is unspecific, thematically variable, and generally unorganised. Its effect is the emergence of a sense of self that is constituted through the everyday exchange with other members of the social group; it is socially mediated and community-focused: its concern is a past still alive in talk and social communication, made possible through cross-generational contact.

The point at which Famine fiction achieved some form of fictional integrity coincides with the moment at which 'communicative' Famine memory drops below the horizon of the everyday, when an unordered, largely fragmentary array of images and personal recollections yields to more tightly structured and more purposefully arranged cultural narratives

– with the effect that in the closing decades of the nineteenth century we begin to find Famine references in fiction woven more closely into plots that advertise their structural cohesion. This is also confirmed by the gradual emergence of a relatively small but clearly recognisable 'archive of images', recently identified by Christopher Morash, that became available as structuring devices for these narratives: '[T]he Famine had become an increasingly potent element in the propaganda war which accompanied the struggle for land ownership, and as a consequence Famine images such as the "stalking spectre" and the green-mouthed corpse were repeated in magazines like the *Irish Monthly Magazine* until they had the boldly defined outlines of religious icons.'[52] Such imagery is also widely deployed in the novel where it increasingly comes to control not only the meaning but also the political usefulness of references to the Great Hunger.

It is striking how many of these early Famine images explicitly feminised the idea of starvation, capitalising on the ancient formula that equated land with the female body.[53] The image of a woman begging at Clonakilty, first published in the *Illustrated London News* on 13 February 1847, is one of the best known contemporary Famine illustrations: it shows a woman reduced to begging, clinging to her dead child.[54] The religious iconography of the image – the suffering look, the upturned eyes, the protective mantle, the dead child – fuses conventional representations of the Madonna and the pietá, suggesting the premature interruption of an unfolding cycle of salvation. Even better known is the image of Bridget O'Donnel, another Famine beggar, first published in the *Illustrated London News* on 22 December 1849: barefoot, clad in rags, with worn-out facial features, surrounded by her starving children.[55] Such images aimed visually to translate for London audiences the abstract notion of Famine into the bodily exhaustion of the individual.

But the extant visual imagery is rarely as committed as is the textual description to depicting the extremes of suffering. In Louisa Field's Famine novel *Denis* (1896), for example, the most striking image of a Famine victim occurs during the examination of a dead woman's body at an inquest: '[A]s they viewed the body', Field writes, the coroner's jury – 'tradesmen of Moyne' – began to wonder

> if it were indeed a body and not some ghastly preliminary sketch or model of a woman, a word which one associates with graciously rounded outlines, knees soft to nurse little ones, arm and breast softly padded for the repose of tired curly heads. *This* was a bony outline, over which was painfully dragged and stretched a casing of yellow leather, ghastly to behold. But they gave this Thing the name of a respectable widow who lived in a lonely hovel, and had children in heaven – and in America. Alas, there was a letter with a Philadelphian postmark for her at Moyne post-office this very day![56]

The scene is almost archetypal in its set-up: the female body is subjected to the inquisitive, voyeuristic gaze of several male observers. The horror of the visual appearance upsets the erotic undercurrent and leads to crude objectification: no remnant of humanity, no fading memory of former life, this is a mere 'Thing' – the capitalisation functioning as a further distancing device. The corpse is like an artist's unfinished model or preliminary sketch, lacking the refined features and rounded outlines of the fully developed form; it is not quite real. This body, a faint echo of femininity at best, does not even serve its 'natural' purpose any more – the nursing of children – rather, 'the ideal of motherhood … is rendered totally and painfully inadequate'.[57] This parallel in the lack of life-sustaining qualities between land and the female body explains the iconographic preference for what Margaret Kelleher has called the 'feminisation' of the Famine.

It is with a sense of shock that the text reinserts this 'ghastly' appearance in a social context, bestowing a name on it, affirming the existence of children and the proximity of a caring but helpless community. The now undeliverable letter in the post office is the textual affirmation of an interrupted cycle, the network of social relations, just as the scene as a whole epitomises the sheer difficulty of reading human meaning into a pile of bones wrapped up in 'a casing of yellow leather'. The scene is an instance of broken links, of missing connections, of violent disjuncture. But this break is intrinsic, plot-driven; it does not indicate any longer a structural inability to subject Famine images to larger concerns of aesthetic form and narrative coherence.[58] Rather, it is precisely this rupture that made the controlling images of Famine texts – around the end of the nineteenth and into the first decades of the twentieth century – available for the specific cultural sign system of Irish nationalism, indicating the gradual shift in Famine references from living memory to deadly signifier. '[A]s the century progressed', Melissa Fegan notes, 'the Famine as a literary subject became loaded with political issues. … [T]he Famine was a political tool, a complex metaphor which became a shorthand for violence and oppression.'[59] The 'metaphor' was ubiquitous, politically useful, and readily available for chronological streamlining. Nationalists could integrate the Famine into a coherent narrative, despite its unsettling and devastating impact (which – in an unexpected alliance – hardly bothered political economists either, who could explain the Famine within a teleological pattern of progress[60]), because its destructive power could serve as a causal element in the metanarrative of national liberation.[61] This political emplotment of the Famine largely replaces the earlier plot we have seen emerging in the Big House novels and folk tales that contained a varying mixture of romance and mystery ingredients.

Writing the Famine in literature and history, 1910 to the 1980s

The scene from *Denis* raises the emotive stakes, and a similar turn to heightening the affective dimension of Famine narratives by amplifying the

Fact into fiction: novels of the Irish Famine 55

emotional appeal to the reader is a feature of novels such as Mildred Darby's *The Hunger* (1910) and Liam O'Flaherty's *Famine* (1937). Darby's book announces itself in the subtitle as *Realities of the Famine Years in Ireland*; the novel is perhaps less interesting for the fictional plot which the author constructs around these 'realities' than for the rationale behind its historical address to the reader. In the introductory chapter, Darby laments the disappearance of readable traces of the past in the Irish landscape, and offers to rescue with her novel the last remnants of a 'communicative' Famine memory:

> There is little in the well-stocked, well-farmed fields of Erin to-day to recall the catastrophe which befell the country in the years between 1845 and 1848, or to suggest to the mind's eye a picture of the same lands lying untilled and derelict, because the beasts of burden to draw the plough had long since been sold or devoured, and the men to follow it lay rotting unburied corpses by the roadside ... Ruined villages and overcrowded graveyards can but dumbly hint at past calamities, but in the cabins, still occupied, in the substantial farmhouses built on the site of the fallen hamlets, in presbyteries and rectories nestling near the Churches and Chapels, in the mansions and castles dominating each neighbourhood are yet to be found men and women who themselves lived through the catastrophe. Their tongues can tell, each its own version of the facts to which those ruined houses are monuments, and of the reasons *why* those roofless cabins were emptied of their inmates. Only by thus reviewing both sides, and all versions, of the same tale, can a clear mental picture be formed of the years still called by the peasants the 'Hunger Years'.[62]

This is a spirited plea to acknowledge the plurality of experience and the value of oral history as the only lead into the 'realities of the Famine years' – realities of memory that are deemed to cut deeper than surface facts in the same way that Aristotle thought poetry was more 'philosophical' and 'serious' than history.[63] Yet much of Darby's novel relies on straightforward historical documentation: paragraphs explaining contemporary economic conditions and processes, the system of land tenure, social legislation, etc., and above all a continuous narrative of the Famine years based on 'typical' scenes and attitudes – hunger riots, ascendancy ignorance, the organisation of relief, etc. – form the framework of the plot; the occasional infusion of oral testimony is rare and inconsequential.

Much of the force of the novel is owed to the effective juxtaposition of contemporary actions and thought patterns – such as the memorable chapter on 'Feasting and Famine' which contrasts a luxurious dinner party at the Big House with stark incidents of starvation. Most of the plot is actually concerned with what the author considers to be, after Famine and pestilence, the 'third terror' of those times: 'threatening Anarchy'[64] – by which she means instances of armed rebellion. The original voices which Darby claims to have 'verified from the many public records of those years of famine'[65] are colourful illustrations rather than historical acts in their own right. And yet Darby's method would allow her to discard the political altogether and represent the Famine entirely as a 'history of mentality': a defence of idiosyncratic memory, both personal and collective. That she ultimately fails to do so in *The Hunger* does not render the conceptual approach any less relevant. Darby is the first novelist of the Famine to point to a radically alternative historiography as a potential imaginative resort of the genre.

Where Darby still falls short of her own precepts, Liam O'Flaherty ostensibly succeeds. His novel *Famine* is commonly considered the crowning achievement of the first century of Famine fiction.[66] In print to this day, the novel is perhaps the most striking literary instance of the historical explanation that promoted a link between the Famine and Irish national self-definition in terms of active political resistance: it was published, significantly, in the same year as the Irish constitution, in 1937. The narrative of national tragedy and the pursuit of national sovereignty are inextricably linked at this historical juncture.

The plot of *Famine* hardly warrants much praise. It records a downward spiral of inevitable decay and disintegration. The rain that drowns the countryside on page 1 is deemed by one character the 'ruin of the Valley',[67] a dark prophecy that will ultimately be fulfilled when the Famine sweeps the valley clear of all its former inhabitants.[68] Often noted for its epic touch,[69] the novel is relentless in its forward drive, and in its cold, merciless unfolding of cruel tragedy. One commentator has praised the book for its 'narrative approach – direct, documentary, matter-of-fact ... without either sentimentality or a note of falseness',[70] but this aspect of style is remarkable only when measured against the (in the case of a Famine novel, absurd) expectation of pastoral bliss. O'Flaherty's writing can, in fact, be clumsy, laboured, even verging on the naive: 'At this moment, Michael appeared from the bedroom. Immediately, the atmosphere became strained and there was a silence except for the grunting of the pigs, which were on their way to the door after finishing their meal.'[71] This personification of the porcine is no isolated slip, but there are enough passages whose clinical simplicity make up for some involuntary dips into bathos.

Two central characters – Brian Kilmartin, the 'honest peasant' and domestic tyrant, and his daughter-in-law Mary – are pitted against each other in a crowded plot. Brian clings fiercely to tradition and a farmer's cult of hard work, but dies of exhaustion on the final page of the book as he attempts to bury his wife: 'He tried to spit on his hands, but there was no moisture on his lips. Then he thrust the point of his spade at the frosty earth, put his naked foot on the haft, and pressed with all his force. The point did not penetrate.'[72] It is hard to miss the symbolic point here: the Irish soil, dry and frozen after two years of Famine, will neither yield food nor receive the dead. Life is erased, stripped away, reduced to the utter stillness of death. Mary, by contrast, exudes the will to live. She is set apart from the rest of the Irish peasant population by her origins – her father was English – and by her constructive, 'unfemale' energies, which earn her the epithet 'virago' when she too is finally affected by the 'imminence of famine'.[73] Her activities, such as her decision to start a vegetable garden, are contrasted with the 'general apathy' prevailing in the valley. This does not keep Brian from denouncing her innovations as 'revolutionary and dangerous'.[74] Brian and Mary are opposing principles – stubborn attachment to tradition versus the rational decision for change – and it is the woman who will eventually break the Famine-induced 'stupor of indifference'[75] by securing a passage to America for herself, her child and her rebel husband.

Where the novel succeeds most is in its representation of the complex social dynamics of nineteenth-century rural Ireland. The novel projects its plot, like Trollope's *Castle Richmond*, on to a social, commercial and political topography, a topography, here, of disaster. The Black Valley as the site of abject poverty functions like a photographic negative of at least three other locations: the village and manor of Crom (the commercial circuit), the nearest town of Clogher (the political centre) and the local Big House (the seat of cultural and economic power). Thus the Black Valley simultaneously signifies, first, the failure of commercial exchange – hunger is only the most potent sign of this; second, the rejection of British rule – some Famine victims from the valley become political rebels; and third, the underside of affluence – it is the poverty of the Black Valley that enables the wealth of the absentee landlord. In addition, the local Big House is a site of multiple corruption: politically, it stands for the exploitation of Ireland by Britain, perpetuated through the Union; economically, it epitomises all the faults of the land system and the abuse of absenteeism; socially, it is the place of residence of the corrupt land agent whose immorality is translated from the economic to the sexual sphere. Within his fictional framework, O'Flaherty keeps close to his characters and achieves a highly personalised depiction of Famine victims which lends the novel much of its emotional force. The 'powerful immediacy'[76] of the narrator's wandering gaze – the strongest point of the novel – is what Darby would have wanted to preserve for posterity with her oral history programme: the Famine experience from the point of view of the ordinary victim, with all the attendant emotional investments of the solitary individual engulfed in an incomprehensible tragedy.

In writing *Famine*, O'Flaherty drew on a range of sources,[77] among them the first sustained narrative history of the Famine by Canon John O'Rourke, first published in 1875. O'Rourke gives much the same reasons as Darby and other novelists for embarking on this project:

> Several reasons occurred to [the author] why such a work [putting together 'the leading facts of the Great Irish Famine'] should be done: the magnitude of the Famine itself; the peculiarity of its immediate cause; its influence on the destiny of the Irish Race. That there should be no unnecessary delay in

performing the task was sufficiently proved ... by the fact, that testimony of the most valuable kind, namely, contemporary testimony, was, silently but rapidly passing away with the generation that had witnessed the Scourge.[78]

To recapture this testimony O'Rourke sent questionnaires all over Ireland in order to collect information from the last survivors of the period. He then produced a long-winded political history that is interspersed with data culled from 'living memory'. In terms of its historical analysis, O'Rourke's book is now largely outdated (and it is also, in its tiring attention to mere trifles, often a tedious read)[79] but it constitutes a significant departure from the uses made of the Famine in earlier nationalist propaganda.

It is worth recalling how John Mitchel, the Young Irelander and radical editor of *The United Irishman*, who was later deported to Australia before escaping to the US, thought and wrote about the Famine:

[T]he potato blight, and consequent famine, placed in the hands of the British government an engine of State by which they were eventually enabled to clear off, not a million, but two millions and a half, of the 'surplus population' – to 'preserve law and order' in Ireland (what they call law and order), and to maintain the 'integrity of the Empire' for this time. It was in the winter of 1846–47 that proceedings began to be taken in a business-like manner ... for the Last Conquest of Ireland, (Perhaps).[80]

We have already come across a version of this sentence in Conyngham's 1861 Famine novel *Frank O'Donnell*, and its appearance there is just one sign of the pervasive influence of Mitchel's genocide theory on popular nationalist opinion in nineteenth-century Ireland and beyond. Graham Davis has recently claimed that the 'Mitchel thesis' – strangely watered down from the genocide theory to the charge of 'starvation amidst plenty' – has been a standard theme in Famine historiography ever since it was first pronounced.[81] This shorthand argument hardly does justice to the substantial work produced recently by post-revisionist Irish historians (such as Christine Kinealy, whom Davis includes in his charge) but it serves to sum up, more or less, the ideological position of O'Rourke, who wrote about a decade after Mitchel.

In his own – deliberately naive – understanding, O'Rourke aims to supply no more than a chronology of political events, and he concludes his long, document-based narrative by appealing to '[e]very reader [to] form his own views upon the facts given in this volume; upon the conduct of the people; the action of the landlords; the measures of the Government', anticipating that 'those views may be widely different'.[82] This appeal to the autonomy of the reader only pretends, of course, to debunk the authority of O'Rourke's speaking position, but it is important to see that emphasis on the ideology of a historiographical text can obscure the extent to which the writing of history may serve causes other than the grand political vision under which it sails.

O'Rourke may have shared with Mitchel the conviction that the Irish

Fact into fiction: novels of the Irish Famine 59

were starving in the midst of plenty but the very form of his own historical intervention tells a different story, at least in rudimentary form. While Mitchel uses the Famine almost exclusively as a weapon in a propaganda war against Britain, O'Rourke aims to recapture the experience of human suffering. Mitchel focuses, essentially, on himself – the *Jail Journal*, after all, is generically an autobiography – while O'Rourke's indiscriminate approach to documents leads him, unintentionally perhaps, but no less thoroughly for that, to foreground the common people, who occur in Mitchel's writings only as an undifferentiated mass of peasants, an abstract figure: 'two millions and a half'. By contrast, each single voice which O'Rourke includes in his account points to the plurality of the historical experience. In one paragraph he can switch from the perspective of the detached narrator – 'The blight of 1845 was noticed in Ireland about the middle of September. Like the passage birds, it first appeared on the coast, and, it would seem, first of all on the coast of Wexford. It soon travelled inland' – to the anxious voice of a 'Meath peasant': '"Awful is our story; I do be striving to *blindfold them* (the potatoes) in the boiling. I trust in God's mercy no harm will come from them."'[83]

O'Rourke is not an early proponent of oral history. But coming to the early historiography of the Famine via the route I have taken – down a series of novels – brings out rather clearly the difference in textual and conceptual terms that sets him apart from Mitchel and other propagandists who have seized on the Famine as an easy prey of nationalist discourse: the inclusion, on the part of O'Rourke, of a plurality of voices; his need to broaden the evidence to encompass social complexity; his willingness (in order to meet his own standards of 'objectivity') to abandon the dominance of a single narrative perspective. None of this is spelled out or theorised at any length, nor does O'Rourke have a conception of oral history that goes beyond a general belief in the value of eyewitness testimony. But the need in Famine historiography to take account of folk memory – so urgently felt by modern Famine historians – has one of its origins in this book. The novels by Darby and O'Flaherty discussed above – which tell their Famine stories not from the Big House perspective but from the point of view of the ordinary peasant – clearly do something very similar: they deploy their structural form in the service of a cultural memory that wishes to preserve a socially meaningful image of the past.

This conceptual proximity of Famine historians and Famine novelists (or, more frequently, mythmakers) became an anxious concern for the historiographical camp in the second half of the twentieth century.[84] The first two important postwar works of Famine historiography – *The Great Irish Famine. Studies in Irish History, 1845–52*, edited by R. Dudley Edwards and T. Desmond Williams in 1956; and *The Great Hunger: Ireland 1845–9*, published by Cecil Woodham-Smith in 1962 – have often been compared to each other by contrasting them indirectly with the presumed emotional appeal of the novel. Edwards and Williams took as their measure of achievement the degree to which a rigorous scholarly analysis might supplant the dominance of popular Famine myths. Their explicit targets were '[t]he political commentator, the ballad singer and the unknown maker of folk-tales' – such as, for instance, John Mitchel, the 'political commentator' most directly at odds with the professional historian: 'There was no conspiracy to destroy the Irish nation.'[85] In their attempt to rationalise and demystify the Famine, Edwards and Williams relied on statistical, document-based historical research – which in Edwards's own view ran the danger of producing a bureaucratic, 'dehydrated'[86] account of an 'ordinary' crisis: a mere exercise in archival discipline.

The Great Famine can now be seen as an early outing of revisionist thinking, designed to set the record straight on the 'uniqueness' of the Famine as a historical event. The extraordinarily difficult genesis of this first comprehensive scholarly account of the Famine published in the twentieth century – the book took over ten years to see the light of day[87] – illustrates more than anything the status of the Famine as the historical site where the battle over the meaning of the Irish past is fought. To claim that the volume ignores the human suffering at the heart of the Famine 'story' seems unjust[88] but has always appeared convincing when compared to Woodham-Smith's potboiler, *The Great Hunger*.[89] In this bestselling account of the Famine – still in print after over forty years[90] – Woodham-Smith follows her own advice to aspiring biographers: 'Keep the story moving.'[91] The book is a continuous story of the Famine years which relies on pronounced value judgements, conceptual completion of its narrative, suggestive biographical sketches, and a range of fictional devices: emplotment (the Famine told as tragedy), personalisation (the villains are Lord John Russell and Charles Trevelyan), stylistic flourish, the use of cliff-hangers,[92] delayed decoding, and explanation by metonymy.

The adoption of literary techniques maximises rather than lessens the historical impact of the book, which is why the hostile 1960s history exam question at University College Dublin – '*The Great Hunger* is a great novel. Discuss'[93] – misses the point by accusing Woodham-Smith of what she does deliberately, and does well. Ricoeur's insight – which deflates the premise on which this question is based – that '[o]ne and the same work can … be a great book of history and a fine novel'[94] acknowledges that in works such as *The Great Hunger* history and fiction are not in conflict with each other but actually converge in their ways of 'seeing' the past. Woodham-Smith's success with the general reading public illustrates the power of narrative over the construction of Famine memory: if the ultimate signifier of the Famine is death, then this zero point of human experience fails to produce any meaning at all in a representational mode that allows contextualisation of its possibility but never actually addresses the emptiness at its core. Woodham-Smith's reputation as a historian is growing again,[95] and her power as a narrator was eloquently praised in an early review by Steven Marcus:

Fact into fiction: novels of the Irish Famine

> In Mrs. Woodham-Smith's hands, abstract statistics come alive as human beings, as she paradoxically undoes the usual effect of statistics, which is to impersonalize, average out, and distance our response to concrete experience. *The Great Hunger* is a work of unusual distinction, informed at every point by the knowledge that facts alone do not amount to history unless we include among them the fact of consciousness.[96]

This is perhaps the best description of the conceptual gap between *The Great Famine* and *The Great Hunger*: the refusal on the part of compartmentalised, detached academic historiography to acknowledge its role in the formation of consciousness, illustrated also by the respective choice of titular keyword: an abstract, almost technical phenomenon – 'famine' – on the one hand, and a reminder of immediate, individualised bodily suffering – 'hunger' – on the other.

The conceptual differences between these two historical works now seem like a prelude to the wider debate over 'revisionism' in Irish historical writing that preoccupied the academic scene in the 1980s and 1990s (and which considerably influenced, as we shall see below, Famine novels written towards the end of the twentieth century). The impact of Woodham-Smith's mode of history-writing on Irish writers is evident from playwright Tom Murphy's statement that the 'Famine is racial memory'.[97] To see the history of the Famine as the foundational historical experience of the modern nation is almost by necessity to request sympathy for the victims; Murphy's own play *Famine*, premiered in 1968, deals with the reverse side of this statement: the anxieties of survivor guilt.

The play is a complex statement on the question of national heritage. Drawing explicitly on Woodham-Smith's book,[98] it constructs an image of the Famine as the survival of the fittest and thus evokes a version of national history difficult to accept. On one level, Murphy presents the variety of practical and emotional responses to famine and deprivation: piety, armed resistance, inwardness, despair, etc. The character at the centre of the plot, John Connor, the 'village leader',[99] fails to live up to the calling expressed in his name, both in spiritual and political terms: that of the old Irish chieftain, leader of his people. But when he proceeds to kill his own wife and his son at the end of the play, he is finally ready to accept one terrible truth of the Famine: that in order for some to survive, others have to die.[100] The play aims more directly than other treatments of the topic to test the commitment of the present to the memory of a troubling past – a memory of individual responsibility in times of mortal crisis that may be as divisive as the rhetoric of those nationalists who have turned this memory into the grand narrative of *communal* suffering. Murphy's play must rank as one of the few 'high literature' treatments of the Famine, and it shares with another such example – Patrick Kavanagh's long poem *The Great Hunger* (1942)[101] – an understanding of the Famine as a form of spiritual and emotional hunger. The same holds true for John Banville's fragmented, postmodern Famine narrative *Birchwood* (1973), which slips backwards in time to recover a '[r]eality [that] was hunger', only to concede that '[i]t was not hunger that was killing us, but the famine itself'.[102] The Famine here aspires to a complex cultural condition, irreducible in meaning to instances of bodily exhaustion or clinical pathology.

The more immediate fictional dwellers in the historiographical terrain surveyed by Edwards/Williams and Woodham-Smith, however, are the authors of historical novels. Walter Macken (*The Silent People*, 1962), Elizabeth Byrd (*The Famished Land*, 1972) and Michael Mullen (*The Hungry Land*, 1986) have all presented testimonies of suffering that draw on the wider social context explored by the volumes discussed above, inheriting the sense of tragedy from Woodham-Smith and a descriptive framework from Edwards/Williams. One of the authors – the only non-Irish writer of the trio, the American-born Elizabeth Byrd – explicitly acknowledges Edwards and Williams's *The Great Famine* as a source, calling it 'the definitive book about those tragic years'.[103] What all three novels are attempting to do is to fill in the broad historical outline with specific, localised detail. In the process, they construct differently nuanced versions of an imaginative Irish homeland that aims to define and contain the 'racial memory' of the Famine.

In *The Famished Land*, Byrd chooses as her heroine Moira McFlaherty, aged 16 at the beginning of the plot in 1845, who manages to survive the Famine through a combination of instinctive cunning and spectacular good luck. Through the course of the novel, Moira, her family and the entire village pass through the whole destructive cycle of crop failure, half-hearted Famine relief operations, desperate fund-raising, failure to pay the rent, and eventual eviction, accompanied by deprivation, hunger and, ultimately, death. Throughout the novel the focus is on the Mayo village of Ballyfearna and its residents, even though Moira at one point has to abandon her home and take to the road in an unsuccessful attempt to connect with her wayward lover.

Famine sufferers from outside the village blur into an indistinct mass of 'roadlings' or into wailing crowds outside the poorhouse. In the larger scheme of the novel, the parochial omphalos is under threat of erasure but the tenacity of the country people ensures its continued existence, even though in a much diminished form. The Famine is seen as a fatal, but ultimately only temporary, disruption of the pastoral idyll of the Irish countryside – as the Yeatsian image of 'hills purpled with twilight'[104] (reiterated twice, both on the first and on the final page of the novel) affirms – and of the innocent pastimes of the country people, who follow age-old rhythms of life, love and labour. The novel begins and ends with a traditional wake, contrasting the socially meaningful experience of death with the senseless slaughter of the Famine. As Byrd attempts to breathe life into the scorched countryside and a morally depleted populace, she insists on the possibility of inherent renewal: in this novel the escape route of the transatlantic passage is denied the characters, who have to draw sustenance from the spirit of the land and its stoic endurance of continued oppression.

Ten years earlier, Walter Macken also had his central character reject emigration as a mode of survival in his 1962 novel *The Silent People*. The book is an attempt to put the Famine into historical perspective by following the life of Dualta Duane, a surprisingly well-read but hot-tempered peasant, from about the year 1826 through to the Famine. Dualta epitomises the plight of the common people: he is on the run from almost the first page of the novel, simply for defending his personal dignity against an abusive landlord. The patterns of honest, rural existence which he embodies are contrasted with several forms of high living: that of the wealthy Protestant ascendancy, but also that of the Catholic middle classes and the career of the single outstanding individual – in this case Daniel O'Connell, the Liberator, whose path crosses Dualta's several times.

Ultimately, though, the hope of achieving liberty through political agitation is rejected as Dualta, who early on is tempted by organised forms of armed resistance, decides to opt for the private life of hard work and domestic bliss. Tellingly, when O'Connell last appears in the book, it is as a weak old man, 'speaking in a cracked voice',[105] his passion spent, his magic gone. The potential politicisation of Irish life remains a tantalising suggestion in this novel: always just visible on the horizon, it is realised only in the embryonic form of O'Connell's 'voice', the single most remarkable attribute of the 'great man'. When this voice is 'cracked' – physically, morally and politically – the silence that ensues is the condition of both land and people; not now the stoic silence of passive endurance but the soundless horror of utter annihilation. Macken's title is programmatic in this respect – the great silence follows on from the great hunger and locks the whole of Ireland in a relentless cycle of apathy and destruction: 'The two sounds you would always associate with the land, the bark of the dog and the crow of the cock, were no longer to be heard. [Dualta] would always remember the silence. It was so profound that he could not have heard anyhow the sound of the other horseman who rode ahead of him.'[106] At the end of the novel, Dualta, having already secured a passage on an emigrants' ship for himself and his wife, turns back down the road towards his old home. For him, survival is finally not a material fact but a purely mental condition.

The image of a fully politicised Ireland, only half glimpsed in Macken's novel, comes finally into its own in Michael Mullen's *The Hungry Land* (1986).[107] This exuberant adventure tale of romance and rebellion locates 1840s Ireland both geographically and politically between revolutionary France and the now fully independent American states. This makes for a broader geographical sweep than in the tales by Byrd and Macken who both focused on the isolated village in the valley. At the beginning of *The Hungry Land*, the flamboyant young hero arrives from France with heady plans for revolution, midway through the novel he and his fellow rebels cross the Atlantic to purchase arms in New York, and even in Ireland, as characters move around freely between the main venues of the story, there is far less sense of immobility or stifling narrowness than in previous novels. With this choice of plot structure, Mullen reverses the perspective which had dominated the Famine novel since O'Flaherty: the story is not told through the eyes of the starving but from the angle of those characters who are not immediately affected by hunger and starvation.

The moral centre of the tale is occupied by old Michael Barrett, the modern equivalent of the old Irish chieftain, who has amassed a considerable fortune with his shipping fleet. His strongest link to the Ireland of old is through his patronage of the poet Gill, with whom he entertains a kind of love–hate relationship. Gill is abused throughout the novel as a bad poet but eventually fulfils his promise of reciting a final poem at Michael Barrett's deathbed. Gill, 'rake and poet',[108] is the image of contemporary Ireland in dejection, constantly drunk but still spiritually in touch with a heroic past. The many additional subplots need no detailed summarising here. There is plenty of romance and rural cunning, and Mullen knows who the villains are: the brutal colonel in charge of the military garrison; the tyrannical land agent; the corrupt butler of the local Big House. One by one this evil trio will eventually fall, but without handing final victory to the heroes of the tale: the peasants, the rebels and the selfless, heroic women. Attribution of blame for the tragedy of the Famine is complex, as Irish and English, high and low, share in both compassion and cruel neglect.

Part of the point of the tale, which sets it apart from other examples of the genre, is the attempt to restore agency to Famine Ireland: 'better to hang than to starve' is a motto repeated several times, and the funeral pyre of Barrett House which the dashing rebel and his red-haired Irish rose watch from the ship as they leave Ireland at the end of the novel is an image that captures the spirit expressed in this phrase. Even if the outcome of rebellion, assassination and emigration is only further destruction and continued political oppression, these are ways of overcoming the apathy and indifference associated with the Famine victims. Hence the fiery rebels and belligerent peasants are offered as models of Irish pride and opposition. This novel, then, principally commemorates the heritage not of those who starved but of those who resisted and survived the Famine.

'Survival' is the common theme of all three of these popular novels, even if only Mullen emphasises the active part played by the Irish people in stemming the tide of death and starvation. If the fictional webs spun around the theme of survival are, to a large extent, historical dreamwork, they increasingly reflect the impact of, and dissatisfaction with, a historiographical tradition intent on making discontinuity its overriding theme. The emphasis on the Famine as a historical watershed is shared by Woodham-Smith and (to a lesser extent) by Edwards/Williams, and one way of reading the Famine novels that have been spawned by their work is to see them as exercises in affirming the reality and continuity of human experience against the historiographical rhetoric of disruption, finality and structural reorganisation. Thus, if it was one of the objectives of the Edwards/Williams volume to substitute a blurred form of memory with sound academic history, then this categorial division is actively reinforced at this temporal juncture in the 1980s when novelists trace (or invent) the coherence of human biography, and historians divide nineteenth-century Irish history into temporal segments 'before' and 'after' the Famine. This neat but, in its tacit assumption of a divided consciousness, artificial distinction between memory and history, between folk and fact, will be increasingly challenged in the 1990s.

Contesting boundaries: Famine fiction in the present

In 1997 Michael Mullen published a second Famine text, *The Darkest Years. A Famine Story*, which is all the more remarkable for coming from the pen of the same writer whose earlier Famine novel was so deeply steeped in the romantic tradition of the adventure tale. The conceptual difference between the two texts can be taken as indicative of changes in the historical approach to the Famine at large, demonstrating, in this instance, a revised attitude towards the use of source material. The little book is a history of the Famine in Castlebar, County Mayo, told entirely through contemporary newspaper reports in the *Connaught Telegraph*.[109] Such evidence is necessarily selective and fragmentary – 'unreliable' perhaps – but it tells its own fascinating story: that of the slow movement of perception and rationalisation as the local people come first to realise and then to resist – unsuccessfully – the terms of the tragedy played out in their midst. The book is not a major instance of Famine commemoration; its implied audience is outside the academy and the wider book market. Nevertheless, the conceptual idea behind the project points to the increasing value attached to direct, unmediated reportage of the Famine years.

A keen interest in eyewitness accounts was also demonstrated by the media hype over the 'Famine Diary' in the early 1990s. A 'Famine Diary' should be seen as both a genre and a desire for authenticity, expressed in the alleged national need for a testimony of suffering that might compare to the diary of Anne Frank. The three 'Famine Diaries' that came on the market in the 1990s differ both in reliability and purpose. The most recent of the three is a reprint of a well-researched weekly column in *The Irish Times*, written by Brendan Ó Cathaoir and originally published from 1995 to 1997 as a contribution to the 150th anniversary commemoration of the Famine. The book is in essence a more ambitious version of Mullen's, encompassing not only one city and one newspaper but the national press and 'the areas of highest excess mortality: the then densely-populated western seaboard, most of Connacht, parts of Munster, the midlands and south Ulster'.[110] It proceeds by summarising for each week the reports on the Famine published in Irish and English papers and magazines, a method that allows Ó Cathaoir to convey a sense of the relentless, week-by-week onward march of the Famine and the slow comprehension of contemporaries, while never losing sight of local nuances and the details of human suffering – thus making readers 'sense, indeed feel, at first hand, the anguish, the consternation, the incredulity, the despair, of the victims'.[111]

Two other 'Famine Diaries', published in the early 1990s, were presented as the 'real' diaries written by single individuals during Famine times, and both were texts that had as their main theme a transatlantic voyage in a 'coffin ship'. *Famine Diary. Journey to a New World* was described as a 'fictionalised retelling'[112] of the voyage by the Sligo schoolteacher Gerald Keegan, on whose authentic diary the editor claimed to be drawing. In fact, the book was based on the 1895 tale 'Summer of Sorrow' by the Scottish–Canadian writer and journalist Robert Sellar.[113] Sellar's tale follows all the conventions of Victorian memoir novels in which a manuscript is rescued from a dying man's hand at the last possible moment and later published by a third party. 'Save the book', the dying man, Gerald Keegan, says to the narrator, 'it will tell those now unborn what Irish men and women have suffered in this summer of sorrow.'[114] The 'book' that will supply posterity with this authentic account turns out to be Gerald's diary in which the fictional Sligo schoolteacher describes his voyage in a coffin ship from Famine-stricken Ireland to Grosse Ile, Quebec, and his subsequent service (up to his death) in the quarantine station there. It is appended to the section in Sellar's tale describing 'how the book was got'.[115] The biblical ring of this subheading is quite deliberate: the diary is treated like a sacred testimony of intense nervous distress and mental anguish.

Famine Diary is thus not a diary but 'a work of historical fiction based on an earlier work of historical fiction'.[116] As an authentic record, it is a hoax, but once no longer assumed to be original it is an interesting attempt to dust off the archival record and bring the experience of the Famine closer to contemporary readers. The fake diary is, at core, an exercise in empathy, designed to touch a raw nerve in modern-day Ireland and its diaspora. According to Morash, it 'attest[s] to a need to have *real* memories of the Famine. The Famine – those thousands of lost lives and ways of life, those thousands of experiences of suffering beyond imagination – call out for some sort of memorial, much as the Holocaust does in the Jewish experience.'[117] What made the book so effective was less the rehearsal of a well-worn ideological position – essentially the Mitchel thesis – but the quality of the voice that appeared to be doing the talking: first hand, rather than reported. I would add to Morash's point only that the topical choice of the transatlantic passage is equally significant. Portraying the futility of overseas emigration – the only hope of survival thwarted – heightens and internationalises the tragedy, and allows the diasporic Irish to share more directly in contemporary Famine commemoration.

In 1994, another fictional Famine Diary was published (by the same editor), entitled *Robert Whyte's 1847 Famine Ship Diary. The Journey of an Irish Coffin Ship*, which complements the first diary's story of the emigration of a Catholic schoolteacher with the highly polished shipboard record of 'a Protestant gentleman of education and position'.[118] The attempt here is clearly not only to supply yet another 'real Famine memory' but also to counterweigh accusations levelled at the possible bias of the Keegan testimony. The tragedy played out on board the coffin ship, and later at the quarantine station of Grosse Ile, Quebec, is no different whether seen through Catholic or Protestant eyes, whether recorded by commoner or gentleman.

Elsewhere the desire to stay close to the victims, to recover as much as possible of their original voices – or, failing that, the voices of actual eyewitnesses – has taken more acceptable forms regarding the scholarly credentials of individual projects; the phenomenon as such has to be seen in the light of the 'revisionist' debate in Irish historical studies, already briefly referred to in the introduction. If much revisionist writing was regarded as dry, overly rhetorical and lacking in emotional investment, hiding instead behind the sanitising walls of academe and the sophisticated turn of phrase, the dramatic reiteration of nationalist sentiment – with its occasional equation of Famine and Holocaust[119] – increasingly fell into the same trap of ignoring the people at the core of the historical experience. It has led some recent Famine historians to reject altogether the imperatives of wider ideological debates and concentrate instead on the recovery of 'real' biographies, or fragments of such. Thus the drive towards local history as a more convincing narrative structure than the national frame of reference has opened up possibilities of new imaginative approaches to the actual experience of poverty and hunger. The local is the space of touch and intimacy, of the lived space of the body, not the mental and purely formal abstraction of the national or global.

The spate of publications compiling contemporary documents that go beyond folk memory – diaries, newspaper reports, letters, travelogues, etc.[120] – has similarly achieved a new quality of debate. It is now almost customary for new general books on the Famine period – at least for those addressed to a wider readership – to present themselves as cross-disciplinary accounts that fuse economic, social, political and memorial patterns of historical explanation, thus giving equal attention to the living conditions in the past and to the function of memory in the present.[121] Oral testimony has also had something of a revival in recent years,[122] although evidence of this kind – like folk memory more generally – is still often dismissed as unreliable historical evidence. But the idiosyncracies of individual memory – evidenced in selective amnesia, metonymic generalisations, and (sometimes deliberate) factual distortions – are clearly now being weighed against the didactic advantages of oral history: its vividness, attention to local detail, narrative richness, generous humanity and emotional appeal.

This is not simply a matter of separating fact from fiction but of holding an academically sterile vision of the past against the energy of living memory. As Colm Tóibín reminds us, '[t]he Famine only comes close when you bring it close: when you read about it, when you see a list of names, or when you start thinking about evictions of half-naked people on the decks of ships being soaked by the waves, or when you hear a song about it, or see a mass grave, or a road built during those years, or read some soundbite by an English administrator or politician'.[123] As recent history-writing reveals, this desire to retrieve the Famine experience as an imaginative reality, and to acknowledge its shaping power on the formation of national consciousness, is now no longer seen as the exclusive domain of the literary. Still, current Famine novels with their explicit foregrounding of a transhistorical dialogue between past and present have perhaps responded even more directly than recent historical works to the sentiment expressed by Tóibín. The three most recent Famine novels to have come out of Ireland, Seán Kenny's *The Hungry Earth* (1995), Nuala O'Faolain's *My Dream of You* (2001) and Joseph O'Connor's *Star of the Sea* (2002), are all, in their different ways, attempts to translate this dialogue into aesthetic form.

The first two of these novels, significantly, have amateur Famine historians as their protagonists. Kenny's novel has not fared well with critics – Fegan calls it (not without justice) a 'laboured attempt at a morality play'[124] – but it does allow an insight into the troubled status of the Famine as national heritage in the mid-1990s. In the novel, the successful Dublin accountant Turlough Walsh is confronted simultaneously with the corrupt ethics of his working life and the claims of the past on his own sense of self. His job is to maximise the resources of his company, which invariably involves pushing weaker competitors out of the market and into unemployment, thus causing considerable social distress. The point of the novel is to draw out the connections between Turlough's doings in the 1990s and the ruthless pursuit of profit during the Famine.

Turlough begins to see these connections when he unexpectedly inherits a cottage in the west of Ireland. Bumping his head against the cottage door activates a kind of surreal flashback device which allows Kenny to have his protagonist slip into the past and wake up – with his late twentieth-century consciousness intact – in the midst of the Famine horrors of the 1840s. Realising the extent of his own ignorance about the past leads to a radical reorientation in the present: the successful accountant gives up his job and his middle-class home, moves to the west of Ireland and starts a local history society dedicated to the commemoration of the Famine. The moral lesson is brought home on the last page of the novel when Turlough finds out that he is a direct descendant of one of the most reprehensible characters he met during his time journeys, a self-proclaimed rebel who burns landlords out of their estates only to buy up their lands cheaply afterwards – 'a cannibal who ate his neighbours to survive the Famine'.[125]

Fact into fiction: novels of the Irish Famine

Kenny's novel capitalises on the insight that Catholic Ireland at the time of the Famine was as class-divided in itself as it was culturally separated from the ruling Protestant elites. In terms of its approach to the question of memory, it suggests the existence of a widening gap between past and present that can be bridged only through new forms of historical remembering – essentially practical empathy rather than clinical, detached scholarly analysis. This is made most obvious at the point in the novel when Turlough Walsh – now 'Potato-famine Walsh'[126] – appears on radio together with a feminist historian from University College Dublin. The encounter is a camouflaged duel between revisionist and nationalist historians. The feminist endorses a view of the Famine as an essentially beneficial watershed that allowed Ireland to correct the ills of the past and develop into a modern society with a bourgeois middle class as its driving force. Lest we miss the absurdity of this position, Queen Victoria is presented as a proto-feminist whose visit to Famine-stricken Ireland in 1849 was – in the view of the feminist historian – 'a fantastic display of leadership ... [which] ultimately brought about the development of democracy and women's rights in this country'.[127]

Turlough rails against these crass distortions (as he sees them), accuses his antagonist of twisting the facts to suit her own agenda, and insists on his position by enlisting the child analogy we have already come across in Sinéad O'Connor's famine song: '[T]his whole society we have today is like a person who has been horribly abused as a child, betrayed in every possible way. ... This child, brutally beaten, grows up and unwittingly becomes just like the parent. Without knowing it, we ourselves have become as bad as our old oppressors.'[128] The infantilising child analogy is given another twist here, as centuries of British colonial rule over Ireland are claimed to have produced present-day Irish brutalisation. Elsewhere Kenny has called the Famine a national 'trauma' which has been largely ignored but which can still be healed;[129] the novel which has Turlough trading on the idea of a fictional Famine museum thus advertises its proximity to the real Famine Museum by suggesting that a continuity of social experience between past and present can indeed be recovered, once all the psychic debris piled up in a century and a half of self-denial is cleared away.

Nuala O'Faolain presents differently nuanced speculations about history in her novel *My Dream of You*. The heroine of the tale, the fifty-year-old travel writer Kathleen Burke, returns to her Irish homeland for the first time in thirty years in order to pursue two projects that bring into tension her public and private sense of the past: one is to come to terms with her own childhood and youth in Ireland, the other is to research a divorce case that happened in the west of Ireland just a year or so after the Famine. Both investigations have a bearing on the concept of cultural memory advocated by the novel. In the first instance, her historical research fails to find the emotional and material reality behind the facts of the divorce. In the course of the novel, three possible explanations are on offer, each of which it is impossible ultimately to verify. This leads to the realisation that all attempts to reimagine history are controlled by the pressures not of the past but of the present – the story Kathleen finally decides to believe about the divorce is in essence the story of her own trip to Ireland, motivated by the desire to read history in terms of female empowerment. The link with the past is exposed as an imaginative tangent, rather than a direct road.

Kathleen's second project – the journey into her own private past – revolves around the fate of her mother. In 1970, when her mother was in her late forties and five months into a late pregnancy, she was suddenly diagnosed with cancer of the womb and hospitalised in a Catholic institution. Because of the constitutional ban on abortion, the doctors refused to treat the cancer in any way that might harm the foetus. In effect, this meant sacrificing both the mother *and* the child on the altar of religious beliefs, when at least the mother could have been saved. The Famine analogy is almost self-evident: the rural poor in the 1840s were equally sacrificed on the altar of political economy, and the realisation that the Irish government of the 1970s follows in the footsteps of the English colonial rulers of the 1840s not only complicates the attribution of blame but also affirms a historical continuity of a rather different kind than that suggested by the Famine Museum: essentially, now, a continuity of guilt and oppression, rather than of passive suffering. Taken together, the two central plots in the novel – the reconstruction of the Famine divorce case and Kathleen's journey into her own past – imply that history is available in terms of both rupture and continuity: the truth behind the divorce is forever elusive, while the story of Kathleen's mother's death affirms the permanence of patriarchal power. From this perspective, the point of the novel is perhaps to suggest that hope lies not in linearity and continuity, but in the willing acceptance of historical ruptures.

Both these novels make the construction and possible distortion of historical memory their central theme. As we have seen, earlier twentieth-century Famine novels are principally historical novels, with a plot set entirely in Famine times. By contrast, Kenny and O'Faolain both set their stories in the present, and their protagonists struggle with the extraordinary claims of the past on their own, late twentieth-century lives. Kenny perhaps too quickly imagines that the dedicated historical amateurism of his protagonist can somehow revitalise the psychic intensities of an earlier age. O'Faolain's Kathleen has more serious problems with her forays into a society removed from her own by a century and a half. Speculating about the 'trauma' of the Famine that 'must be deep in the genetic material of which I was made',[130] Kathleen makes several conscious attempts to bring the Famine figures back to life. For instance, trying to imagine the physical effects of hunger, she compares elusive Famine victims with images of more recent atrocities stored in her head: in contrast to her own disguise as a Famine child in a school pageant, 'real famine children would have been like the ones that come running towards the camera from napalm bombs and strafing and earthquakes – children with runnels of snot and sores at the corners of their lips, on faces tense with fear and hatred'.[131]

This implicit comparison with Vietnam war photographs raises the question of the extent to which it is possible to form an adequate visual impression of the scale of suffering during the Famine. For obvious reasons, photographs are absent from the historical record, and the drawings of hunger victims, evictions and various scenes of distress that appeared in London and Dublin magazines are stylised depictions that codify conventional pictorial forms of outrageous poverty. In her fictive biography of the woman involved in the divorce case (fragments of which are interspersed throughout the descriptive sections of the novel) Kathleen includes an image of dead children whose 'stomachs were hugely distended'.[132] Clearly, the attempt here is to relate the purely 'intellectual' knowledge of history to some kind of residual, contemporary reality of extreme bodily suffering.[133]

Kathleen's powers of historical reconstruction are exposed as painfully inadequate when she is taken on a tour of the bog surrounding the Talbot estate (the site of the historical divorce case), a narrow, depopulated stretch of ground that was once a crowded living space: 'Three hundred people, in just this corner. It was as crowded as Bangladesh.'[134] In order to make sense of this reality, Kathleen the travel writer has to resort to the memory of a visit to an isolated village in Mali – which is as much as saying that historical memory, when confronted with a cultural void such as depopulated bogland in the west of Ireland, works only by fracture and dissociation: by temporal and spatial displacement.

This is in essence to admit that a historically specific social and cultural dynamic is irretrievably lost. From the experience of this absence of any material links with the past, Kathleen formulates her own private doctrine of historical truth: 'I could *choose* what to believe about the Talbot scandal [the divorce case]. I *would* choose what to believe.'[135] She chooses in fact a version of the story that saves the few verifiable 'phenomena' of the case, so this is no plea for a simple distortion of the truth. But it is a refusal to bow to the strictures of traditional historiographical practice: the absence of archival records or other remains that allow a full reconstruction of the 'ordinary' Famine experience do not relieve Kathleen of the burden of having to affirm the truth of that experience. Like Kenny, O'Faolain creates a character on a crusade against an oblivious modernity; both novels see the Famine past principally as a moral challenge of the present.

This moralising reflex is largely absent from the latest Famine novel to be considered here, Joseph O'Connor's *Star of the Sea* (2002), which tells the story of the transatlantic voyage of a coffin ship in November/December 1847. Formally, the novel is a fragmented narrative that relies for its aesthetic effect on montage and polyphony; it is told entirely through a collation of various texts and documents – biographical reflections, newspaper clippings, dialogue transcriptions, logbook entries, quotations from original letters, song lyrics, etc. This technique approximates the kind of experimental multiple-viewpoint narrative (still lacking in Famine historiography) that Peter Burke has recommended as a form of history-writing that keeps in balance the many different perspectives on, and prevailing attitudes in, the past;[136] an approach that sharpens historical awareness by requiring readers constantly to negotiate between different habits of thought and historical speaking positions, thus placing them in a receptive disposition marked by the permanent interplay of proximity and distance.

The focus of the novel is largely on the passengers in First Class but this does not mean that the Famine victims are completely invisible. For instance, one of the central characters is a modern Irish trickster, a balladeer and murderer, who eventually talks his way out of steerage into First Class. The novel also pays homage to the many passive victims of starvation by naming all the individual dead in the extracts from the Captain's logbook, 'that terrifying ledger of human suffering'.[137] In terms of its aesthetic structure, the novel takes literally the metaphor of the coffin ship by evoking steerage as that dark, gloomy underbelly of the living microcosm of the ship, which enters the consciousness of First Class principally through sound and smell – disease is rampant below deck, a permanent stench and unsavoury 'odours' constantly rise to the cabins above. The 'strange and horrible smell', 'quite pestilential',[138] that the Captain records on day thirteen of the voyage is identified days later as the smell of putrefaction emanating from the decomposing corpses of two teenage stowaways. Famine is like a contagious disease that spreads round the entire boat from the anonymous hull of the ship and finally infects – metaphorically – even the central character of the tale, the ruined Anglo-Irish landlord, whose growing physical discomfort is eventually diagnosed as syphilis. Steerage – like famine – is a dark, unspeakable truth, suppressed and denied by First Class.

The novel accepts the Famine as historical fact; it does not engage in speculations about causes, or attribute blame to a particular party. No individualised character is free from guilt; all play their part in the unfolding tragedy. Moral uncertainty is mirrored by the uncertainty of representation. The novel passes itself off as a Victorian travel account containing 'Notes of London and Ireland in 1847', collected by the fictional editor of the book, an aspiring American writer and journalist, who is also a First Class passenger on board the *Star of the Sea*. One biographical chapter about him describes his failure as a novelist: 'Nothing had prepared him for it: the fact of famine. The trench-graves and screams. The hillocks of corpses. The stench of death on the tiny roads'.[139] Faced with the reality of the disaster, he doubts the validity – the very possibility – of an aesthetic response: 'The Famine could not be turned into a simile. The best word for death was death'.[140] And yet, '[t]o remain silent ... was to say something powerful: that it never happened: that these people did not matter'.[141] The compulsion to speak about the Famine even though there is no 'truthful' way of doing so, is a dilemma he shares with modern-day Famine historians. The solution offered by O'Connor is to make his editor-figure complicit with the events he narrates: the journalist is both part of the story and outside it. The possibility that a false version of events – of fraud, fabrication, lies – 'hover[s] over any account of the past' is the editor's final insight: the relevant questions are 'whether the story may be understood without asking who's telling it; to which intended audience and to what end'.[142] This is, finally, what haunts all fictional and factual representations of the Famine: its availability for any number of ideological purposes, necessitating an awareness of the present uses to which its memory is being put.

Conclusion

Given that *Star of the Sea* continues a tradition of novels about the Famine that has been a pressing concern in Irish writing for over a century and a half, it is astonishing to see that prominent reviews of the book in 2003 repeated the mistaken notion that there is a dearth of imaginative writing about the Famine.[143] Perhaps there is no thematic genre such as 'the Famine novel' (*pace* my own tacit assumptions in this chapter) but there is certainly a persistent return to the topic in Irish fiction, and that fiction has consistently widened its imaginative frame of reference in remarkable proximity to the debates and developments within Irish historical studies. One reason for the impression of a literary 'silence' about the Famine may be the expectation that a tragedy of such national importance should produce a literary work of suitably epic scale. Most imaginative writing about the Famine would be classified as popular – perhaps trivial – literature, to which I have paid more attention in this chapter than might be customary in academic monographs. But the existence of this large body of writing affirms more than anything the continuing challenge that the historical cataclysm of the Famine poses to the modern nation.

To Irish society, this challenge has been moral and political, to Irish novelists it has been representational – as I hope has become clear in my review in this chapter of a century and a half of Famine fiction. The initial challenge to writers was quite simply to enlist the Famine as the realistic referential groundwork on which the principal plot line could be superimposed. The generic shape of the early Famine novels – folk tales and family chronicles – relies on a steady background stream of uninterrupted life, the cyclical up and down of human biography, exemplified in individual lives and specific social relationships. The Famine as the zero degree of human experience was not readily amenable to this purpose, although this does not imply that either genre as such is adverse to the idea of disaster. The chronicle especially feeds on the principle of declined fortunes, but even here the Famine proved to be a disruption it could not easily accommodate. Many writers resorted to a view of the Famine as a dark and hostile but essentially natural force, threatening to overthrow human society – witness Trollope's characterisation of the Famine as a 'disease'. Carleton's lead (in the preface to *The Black Prophet*) to deal with the Famine in political terms was not really followed until later in the century by writers of fiction, when the event had long been discursively appropriated by nationalist historians and agitators, and just when the social experience of the Famine was slipping out of the reach of 'communicative' memory.

If history and fiction are still treated as separate truths in the early novels – the former required to control the potential excess of the latter – this false opposition is laid to rest in novels appearing from about the end of the century onwards. A monolithic conception of political history is now pried open to organise the literary image of the Famine around a multitude of voices and the plurality of experience. Perhaps the most characteristic aspect of this shift was the replacement of the view from the Big House with the view from below, which has held sway over Famine fiction to this day.[144] In the twentieth century, Famine novels are characteristically set among the rural poor and incorporate the perspective of the gentry only as a contrastive foil. As a result, Famine representations were more directly politicised, first in the interest of an explicitly nationalist agenda, later as a test of survival and endurance. At the same time, the image of the Famine victims as those 'unwashed, illiterate, barefoot peasants who had not the wit to buy a fishing rod to save themselves'[145] yields to a celebration of human dignity *in extremis*.

More recently, the challenge of the Famine for writers of fiction has been to make its literary image an invention that engages rather than ignores the dynamic of history and its representation, and which does not succumb to the power of prevailing ideologies. This has led both to a privileging of the first-hand or eyewitness perspective, and to a foregrounding of the psychic and discursive obstacles that stand between us and the past we wish to engage, and has generally raised consciousness of the transient nature of historical memory. The various attempts at the recovery of original or authentic voices – in literature as well as historiography – is the result of a more recent interest in the history of mentalities, and may even be to some extent the sign of a backlash against the poststructuralist account of reality as nothing more than yet another 'text', characteristic also of the unease generated by the privileging of textuality over truth in holocaust studies. To fashion Famine memory as 'true' invention, the most successful fictional forms have relied on a technique which never ignores our own position in respect to the past we intend to reconstruct or remember (and thus essentially to appropriate for our own purposes).

Fact into fiction: novels of the Irish Famine 75

The Famine novel has always progressed in tandem with new historiographical concerns, and neither discourse has ever fully emancipated itself from the other. Nor should they perhaps: both are close neighbours in scope and ambition. Famine novels have sometimes been written to 'supplement' but rarely to counter or contradict the historian's tale; rather, authors of fiction as well as historians have always freely borrowed from each other (if with little mutual acknowledgement). In this sense history and fiction have, in Ricoeur's phrase (quoted above), elevated 'each by means of the other', yet this close proximity may also explain why in epistemological terms, many Famine novels are written around an absent centre, why they hardly ever venture beyond a commitment to factual truthfulness regarding the historical events that come under the rubric 'The Famine'. Chronologies reign undisturbed and largely undistorted – except perhaps in Banville's *Birchwood* – and few imaginative reservoirs are tapped beyond the rich fountain of popular memory. What the poet Eavan Boland has written about the spatial 'limits' of maps, which she thinks can never fully visualise the emotive and bodily truth of the Famine – cartographic lines that describe the landscape but not the human suffering caused by that landscape[146] – applies also to the creative limits of the historical novel.

If genre, as Bakhtin and Medvedev argue, shapes reality for us rather than yielding to a structure already inherent in it,[147] then this (relative) imaginative restriction of the Famine novel is owed as much to the inescapably moral implications of the topic as to the ideal of narrative coherence formally promised by both the (realist) novel and the writing of (linear) history. But for the novel to accept as its orbit of fictional possibility the epistemological terrain charted by historiography means leaving its truth claims largely unchallenged, even when specific ideologies are attacked or experimental methodologies adopted. By contrast, contemporary dramatic and poetic negotiations of Irish history, as we shall see in the chapters that follow, have frequently ventured beyond such limits and in turn produced more assertive, certainly more unsettling, literary readings of the past.

Notes

1. J. Veneday, 'Ireland and the Irish during the Repeal Year, 1844', quoted from the extract in John Killen (ed.), *The Famine Decade. Contemporary Accounts, 1841–1851* (Belfast: Blackstaff Press, 1995), 21–3: 22.
2. For a brief survey of the broader cultural impact of the Famine, covering religion, sport and dance, see Kevin Whelan, 'The cultural effects of the Famine', in Joe Cleary and Claire Connolly (eds), *The Cambridge Companion to Modern Irish Culture* (Cambridge: Cambridge University Press, 2005), 137–54.
3. Terry Eagleton, 'Heathcliff and the Great Hunger', in Eagleton, *Heathcliff and*

the Great Hunger. Studies in Irish Culture (London and New York: Verso, 1995), 1–26: 14.
4 Sinéad O'Connor, '"Famine"', *Universal Mother* (London: Ensign Records, 1994). The song lyrics are printed in the leaflet accompanying this CD.
5 Cathal Póirtéir, 'Introduction', in Póirtéir (ed.), *The Great Irish Famine: The Thomas Davis Lecture Series* (Dublin: Mercier Press, in association with RTE, 1995), 9–17: 9.
6 Christopher Morash, *Writing the Irish Famine* (Oxford: Oxford University Press, 1995), 3.
7 Jim MacLaughlin, 'Commemorations, memories and myths', *Irish Reporter* 19 (1995), 3–5: 4. The whole of this issue is devoted to the topic of the Famine. Entitled 'Famine is a lie! The politics, history and portrayal of famine in Irish and global history', the issue argues that '[w]hat made the Great Famine so remarkable [in view of the fact that famines were a regular occurrence in nineteenth-century Europe] was the fact that Irish nationalists ... were to the forefront in attacking this naturalisation of famines by declaring that famines had socio-political and not just natural causes' ('Editorial', 2). The issue is the attempt to add a class critique to the nationalist perspective.
8 John Waters, 'Confronting the ghosts of our past', *Irish Times* (October 1994), reprinted in Tom Hayden (ed.), *Irish Hunger: Personal Reflections on the Legacy of the Famine* (Boulder, CO: Roberts Rinehart, 1997), 27–31: 29–30.
9 See www.strokestownpark.ie/intro/html (accessed 17 January 2001).
10 Ibid.
11 Stephen J. Campbell, *The Great Irish Famine: Words and Images from the Famine Museum, Strokestown Park, County Roscommon* (Strokestown, Ireland: Famine Museum, 1994), 54.
12 Ibid.
13 Cormac Ó Gráda, 'The Great Famine and today's famines', in Pórtéir (ed.), *The Great Irish Famine*, 248–58: 249.
14 Paul Ricoeur, *Time and Narrative* [1983–5], trans. Kathleen McLaughlin and David Pellauer, 3 vols (Chicago and London: Chicago University Press, 1984–88), vol. 3 (1988), 187–8.
15 Other early fictional accounts of the Famine include two anonymous tracts: *A Tale of the Irish Famine, in 1846 and 1847. Founded on Fact* (Reigate: William Allingham, 1847); and *The Widow O'Leary; A Story of the Present Famine* (Cork: G. Nash, 1847). The latter tract opens as a letter from an Irish writer to 'dear Edward' in England, responding to the query 'whether the accounts which have reached England of the present state of distress of the Irish' (3) are exaggerated or not; the book thus follows the conventions of the Famine traveller's report. For examples of this genre, see Lord Dufferin and G. G. Boyle's *Narrative of a Journey from Oxford to Skibbereen* (1847) – available online at http://vassun.vassar.edu/~sttaylor/FAMINE/Journey/Frontispiece.html (14 December 2005) – and the American traveller Asenath Nicholson's writings on 1840s Ireland, recently republished as Asenath Nicolson, *Annals of the Famine in Ireland*, ed. Maureen Murphy (Dublin: Lilliput Press, 1998). For a good and wide-ranging selection of contemporary accounts see Killen (ed.), *The Famine Decade*; for a survey of folk memory of the Famine, containing excerpts from the returns of the Folk Commission's Famine questionnaire in 1945, see Cathal Póirtéir (ed.), *Famine Echoes* (Dublin: Gill and Macmillan, 1995).

16 William Carleton, *The Black Prophet: A Tale of Irish Famine* (London and Belfast: Simms and M'Intyre, 1847), 214.
17 Ibid., 212. See also Benedict Kiely, *Poor Scholar: A Study of the Works and Days of William Carleton (1794–1869)* (London: Sheed and Ward, 1947), 151.
18 Carleton, *Black Prophet*, 348.
19 See Margaret Kelleher, 'Irish Famine in literature', in Póirtéir (ed.), *The Great Irish Famine*, 232–47: 234.
20 Carleton, *Black Prophet*, 250.
21 See ibid., 248–9.
22 Timothy Webb, 'Introduction', in William Carleton, *The Black Prophet: A Tale of Irish Famine*, facsimile of 1899 edition (Shannon: Irish University Press, 1972), v–xix: xii.
23 Carleton, *Black Prophet* (1847 edn), 'Preface', iv–vii.
24 In a recent article, Margaret Kelleher tentatively suggests the same alignment, only to then warn her readers of the limits of such a view. But the moral economy of the novel does enable this analogy, however incongruent or unacceptable it might seem. See Margaret Kelleher, 'Anthony Trollope's *Castle Richmond*: Famine narrative and horrid novel?', *Irish University Review* 25, no. 2 (1995), 242–62: 247.
25 Anthony Trollope, *Castle Richmond* [1860], The World's Classics (Oxford: Oxford University Press, 1989), 66. Compare also the comments of Charles Trevelyan, then Assistant Secretary to the Treasury, in *The Irish Crisis* (1848): '[W]e think that we may render some service to the public by attempting thus early to review, with the calm temper of a future generation, the history of the great Irish famine of 1847. Unless we are much deceived, posterity will trace up to that famine the commencement of a salutary revolution in the habits of a nation long singularly unfortunate, and will acknowledge that on this, as on many other occasions, Supreme Wisdom has educed permanent good out of transient evil.' Quoted from the excerpt in Killen (ed.), *The Famine Decade*, 175–82: 175.
26 See Thomas Malthus, *Essay on the Principle of Population* (first version 1798; several revised and extended versions over the following decades).
27 For an imaginative reading of the social landscape constructed by the architecture of these houses, see Morash, *Writing the Irish Famine*, 35.
28 Trollope, *Castle Richmond*, 232 (my italics).
29 Ibid., 383–4.
30 Anthony Trollope, *The Irish Famine: Six Letters to the Examiner 1849/1850*, ed. Lance O. Tingay (London: Silverbridge Press, 1987). Trollope had good knowledge of Irish affairs and lived in Ireland from 1841 to 1859. His attitude towards Ireland is notably coloured by this experience, and his views on the Famine should be seen in context. For a recent reassessment of Trollope and Ireland, see Melissa Fegan, 'The subtext of Trollope's famine novels', in Fegan, *Literature and the Irish Famine, 1845–1919* (Oxford: Oxford University Press, 2002), 104–30. For a later Famine novel written from an English perspective with a rather more representative attitude towards Ireland than that displayed by Trollope, see Edward Newenham Hoare, *Mike. A Tale of the Great Irish Famine* (London: Society for Promoting Christian Knowledge, 1890).
31 For representative examples, see Elizabeth Hely Walshe, *Golden Hills: A Tale of the Irish Famine* (London: Religious Tract Society, 1865) and its portrayal of

agrarian outrages and attempted assassinations, and David Power Conyngham (pseudonym 'Allen H. Clington'), *Frank O'Donnell: A Tale of Irish Life* (Dublin: James Duffy, 1861) with its quixotic panorama of Irish culture to which the 'strange and fearful crisis [ie, the Famine] has supplied new material' (xi).

32 See for instance, Anne Keary, *Castle Daly: The Story of an Irish Home Thirty Years Ago*, 3 vols (London: Macmillan and Co, 1875).
33 Margaret Brew, *The Chronicles of Castle Cloyne; or, Pictures of the Munster People*, 3 vols (London: Chapman and Hall, 1885), vol. 1, 'Preface', viii.
34 Ibid., vol. 1, viii.
35 Ibid., vol. 2, 161.
36 Ibid., vol. 3, 107.
37 Ibid., vol. 2, 265.
38 Ibid., vol. 3, chapter 5 (57–79).
39 Ibid., vol. 3, 285.
40 Ibid., vol. 1, vii.
41 Conyngham, *Frank O'Donnell*, 126; 125.
42 See below for the origin of this passage in Mitchel's *The Last Conquest of Ireland (Perhaps)* (1861) and a brief discussion of Mitchel's place in Famine historiography.
43 Conyngham, *Frank O'Donnell*, 193–5.
44 Eagleton, 'Heathcliff and the Great Hunger', 12–13.
45 Cf. Steven Marcus, 'Hunger and ideology' [1963], in Marcus, *Representations. Essays on Literature and Society* (New York: Random House, 1975), 3–16: 10.
46 Aubrey de Vere, 'Ode: After One of the Famine Years', in Christopher Morash (ed.), *The Hungry Voice: The Poetry of the Irish Famine* (Dublin: Irish Academic Press, 1989), 88–9, lines 73–6.
47 Mildred Darby [pseudonym 'Andrew Merry'], *The Hunger: Being Realities of the Famine Years in Ireland* (London: Andrew Melrose, 1910), 235.
48 Eagleton asks: 'Where is the Famine in the literature of the Revival? Where is it in Joyce?' ('Heathcliff and the Great Hunger', 13). Margaret Kelleher's criticism of this claim cuts deep, and it is with justified sarcasm that she writes: 'The extent to which Irish literature contains references to the famine depends, very simply, on where one looks' (Margaret Kelleher, *The Feminization of the Famine: Expression of the Inexpressible?* (Cork: Cork University Press, 1997), 4). This book and the two further recent book-length studies of Famine literature by Christopher Morash (*Writing the Irish Famine*) and Melissa Fegan (*Literature and the Irish Famine*) should dispel once and for all the myth that there is no imaginative literature about the Famine.
49 Eagleton, 'Heathcliff and the Great Hunger', 11.
50 Colm Tóibín, *The Irish Famine* (London: Profile Books, 1999), 66.
51 See Jan Assmann, 'Kollektives Gedächtnis und kulturelle Identität', in Assman and Tonio Hölscher (eds), *Kultur und Gedächtnis* (Frankfurt: Suhrkamp, 1988), 9–19.
52 Christopher Morash, 'Literature, memory, atrocity', in Morash and Richard Hayes (eds), *'Fearful Realities'. New Perspectives on the Famine* (Dublin: Irish Academic Press, 1996), 110–18: 113.
53 Margaret Kelleher looks at this issue in *Feminization of the Famine*, arguing that the focus on starving women in Famine depictions depoliticises the Famine by associating it with the domestic sphere. The argument is perceptive but

Fact into fiction: novels of the Irish Famine 79

  also problematic, both because it runs the danger of marginalising the representation of male hunger victims and because it is unclear, as Fegan asks, 'why Famine authors should want to avoid the political sphere' (Fegan, *Literature and the Irish Famine*, 211).
54 The image can be found online at http://vassun.vassar.edu/~sttaylor/FAMINE/Master/Beggar.html (14 December 2005).
55 See http://vassun.vassar.edu/~sttaylor/FAMINE/Master/BridgetODonnel.html (14 December 2005).
56 Louisa Field, *Denis: A Study in Black and White* (London: Macmillan and Co., 1896), 291–2.
57 Kelleher, *Feminization of the Famine*, 73.
58 Morash thinks otherwise: he argues that these iconic Famine fragments are 'rarely [used] ... as causal elements in the plot' ('Literature, memory, atrocity', 114).
59 Fegan, *Literature and the Irish Famine*, 9.
60 See Scott Brewster and Virginia Crossman, 'Re-writing the Famine: witnessing in crisis', in Brewster et al. (eds), *Ireland in Proximity: History, Gender, Space* (London: Routledge, 1999), 42–58: 45.
61 For instance, the Famine acts as an immediate incentive to political action in Louis Walsh's *The Next Time: A Story of Forty-Eight* (Dublin: H. Gill and Son, 1919). In this novel, the protagonist identifies images of hunger and starvation as the key reasons that made him turn to radical politics: 'the "Famine" scenes had produced in his heart a feeling of sacred wrath. Like so many others at the time, he had begun to feel that he could endure the horrible spectacle no longer' (182).
62 Darby, *The Hunger*, 2–3.
63 The reference is to section nine of Aristotle's *Poetics*.
64 Darby, *The Hunger*, 339.
65 Ibid., 1.
66 Eagleton considers *Famine* 'a magnificent novel' ('Heathcliff and the Great Hunger', 13); Kelleher thinks it is 'one of the most important of all Irish famine narratives' (*Feminization of the Famine*, 110); and Seán O'Faoláin's 1937 review of the novel was even more hymnic: 'It is tremendous. It is biblical. It is the best Irish historical novel to date' (quoted in Kelleher, 'Irish Famine in literature', 241).
67 Liam O'Flaherty, *Famine* [1937] (London: Four Square Books, 1966), 6.
68 It is more, in fact, than a prophecy, as rain and a generally wet climate greatly increased the spread of the fungus that was responsible for the potato blight. This knowledge was not generally available until the end of the nineteenth century.
69 See, e.g., Paul A. Doyle, *Liam O'Flaherty* (New York: Twayne Publishers, 1971), 106.
70 Ibid., 99.
71 O'Flaherty, *Famine*, 17.
72 Ibid., 382.
73 Ibid., 286.
74 Ibid., 97–8.
75 Ibid., 319 *et passim*.
76 Kelleher, *Feminization of the Famine*, 136.

77 For a survey of O'Flaherty's sources, see Kelleher, *Feminization of the Famine*, 136.
78 Canon John O'Rourke, *The History of the Great Irish Famine of 1847, with Notices of Earlier Irish Famines* (Dublin: McGashlan and Gill, 1875), vii.
79 No wonder, then, that when the book was recently reissued by Veritas Publications (Dublin) in 1989 it was reprinted only in an abridged version.
80 John Mitchel, *The Last Conquest of Ireland (Perhaps)* [1861] (Glasgow: Cameron and Ferguson, 1874), 82–3. Mitchel's influential writings on the Famine, especially in his seminal *Jail Journal* (1854), were frequently copied; the sentence quoted here appears, for instance, almost verbatim in David Power Conyngham, *The O'Donnells of Glen Cottage: A Tale of the Famine Years in Ireland* (New York: Kennedy, 1903), 275. In 'Making memories: the literature of the Irish Famine', in Patrick O'Sullivan (ed.), *The Meaning of the Famine*, The Irish World Wide: History, Heritage, Identity, vol. 6 (London and Washington: Leicester University Press, 1997), 40–54, Christopher Morash makes a similar point to the one he made in 'Literature, atrocity, memory', using Conyngham's novel to show how Mitchel's interpretation of the Famine 'as bureaucratic genocide' (47) was recycled by later writers and used for new ideological purposes.
81 Graham Davis, 'The historiography of the Irish Famine', in O'Sullivan (ed.), *The Meaning of the Famine*, 15–39: 16; 17.
82 O'Rourke, *History of the Great Irish Famine*, 522.
83 Ibid., 51. This use of folk memory sets O'Rourke apart from the other nineteenth-century account of the Famine, W. P. O'Brien's *The Great Famine in Ireland and a Retrospect of Fifty Years, 1845–95, with a Sketch of the Present Condition and Future Prospect of the Congested Districts* (London: Downey and Co., 1896), which relied principally on 'the elaborate and careful compilation of the facts then made by Sir Charles Trevelyan, who had in the preparation of it official access to all the best and most authentic sources of information existing on the subject' (83–4).
84 On Famine historiography generally, see the excellent discussion by Melissa Fegan, 'Faction: the historiography of the Great Famine', in Fegan, *Literature and the Irish Famine*, 10–34.
85 R. Dudley Edwards and T. Desmond Williams, 'Foreword', in Edwards and Williams (eds), *The Great Irish Famine. Studies in Irish History, 1845–52* [1956] (Dublin: Lilliput Press, 1994), vii–xvi: xi.
86 The expression is Edwards's own, as noted in his diary when the volume was in preparation. Quoted in Cormac Ó Gráda, 'Making history in Ireland in the 1940s and 1950s: the saga of the Great Famine', *The Irish Review* 12 (1992), 87–107: 101; reprinted in Ciaran Brady (ed.), *Interpreting Irish History: The Debate on Historical Revisionism, 1938–1994* (Dublin: Irish Academic Press, 1994), 269–87.
87 Ó Gráda's 'Making history' tells the whole story in detail.
88 See Fegan, *Literature and the Irish Famine*, 12–14.
89 Cecil Woodham-Smith, *The Great Hunger: Ireland 1845–1849* [1962] (London: New English Library, 1977). Frequent reprints.
90 The book is in fact the most commercially successful Irish history book ever.
91 Quoted in the entry on Woodham-Smith in the *Dictionary of National Biography, 1971–1980*.

92 See Tóibín, *The Irish Famine*, 69. As an example, Tóibín quotes the final sentence of Chapter 1, devoted to the prehistory of the Famine: 'Meanwhile, in 1844, a report was received that in North America a disease, hitherto unknown, had attacked the potato crop' (Woodham-Smith, *The Great Hunger*, 32).

93 Quoted in Fegan, *Literature and the Irish Famine*, 22–3.

94 Ricoeur, *Time and Narrative*, vol. 3, 186.

95 Eagleton writes: 'It has been fashionable among Irish historians to scorn Cecil Woodham-Smith's *The Great Hunger* as a popular tear-jerker; but although the book has its crop of errors and exaggerations, it is remarkable how much of its account is confirmed by the recent findings of James S. Donnelly, Jr. [who wrote most of the Famine essays for the *New History of Ireland, vol. 5: Ireland Under the Union I, 1801–70*, ed. W. E. Vaughan (Oxford: Clarendon Press, 1989)] whom nobody could accuse of either amateurism or Anglophobia' ('Heathcliff and the Great Hunger', 24). Ó Gráda is sceptical at first – 'Woodham-Smith's book has many weaknesses' (he is thinking mainly of her personalising of the tragedy and of the lack of economic context in the book) – but then sees the popular success of *The Great Hunger* rooted not only in its style but also in its historiographical value: 'Woodham-Smith was a formidable researcher. Much of her work is based on previously unused archival material' ('Making history in Ireland', 99; 106, n. 36).

96 Marcus, 'Hunger and ideology', 5.

97 Tom Murphy, 'Introduction', *Plays One: Famine* [1968], *The Patriot Game* [1991], *The Blue Macushla* [1980] (London: Methuen, 1992), xi.

98 The book provided Murphy with the 'facts of the Irish Famine' and led him to expect 'a half-dozen plays on the subject' ('Introduction', x) which never materialised. There is, however, a considerable body of stage plays about the Famine: Hubert O'Grady represented the Famine as melodrama in *The Eviction* (1879), *Emigration* (1880) and *Famine* (1886); Yeats's play *The Countess Cathleen* (1890) is arguably a Famine play; Maud Gonne wrote *Dawn: A Play in One Act and Three Tableaux – Sunset, Night and Dawn* in 1904 but the play was never staged, unlike Padraic Colum's *The Miracle of the Corn*, which was staged in 1908, as was Gerald Healy's *The Black Stranger* in 1945. Since Murphy's *Famine*, notable Famine plays include Eoghan Harris, *Souper Sullivan* (1985); John Banville, *The Broken Jug* (1994) – a version of Kleist's *Der zerbrochene Krug*; Joe O'Byrne, *The Last Potato* (1994); and Terry Eagleton's radio play *God's Locusts* (1995). Eagleton comments on the writing of *God's Locusts* in 'Staging the Famine', *Irish Reporter* 19 (1995), 12–13. On melodrama and the Famine, see Julia William and Stephen Watts, 'Representing a "Great Distress": melodrama, gender, and the Irish Famine', in Michael Hays and Anastasia Nikolopoulou (eds), *Melodrama. The Cultural Emergence of a Genre* (Basingstoke: Macmillan, 1996), 245–65; for a discussion of O'Grady's *Famine*, and the Yeats and Murphy plays, see Christopher Morash, 'Sinking down into the dark: the Famine on stage', *Bullán* 3, no. 1 (1997), 75–86.

99 Murphy, *Famine*, 3 (list of characters).

100 See also Kelleher, *Feminization of the Famine*, 150.

101 Patrick Kavanagh, 'The Great Hunger', in Paul Muldoon (ed.), *The Faber Book of Contemporary Irish Poetry* (London: Faber, 1986), 26–55.

102 John Banville, *Birchwood* [1973] (London: Minerva, 1992), 144; 153.

103 Elizabeth Byrd, *The Famished Land: A Novel of the Irish Potato Famine* [1972] (London: Pan Books, 1974), 'Acknowledgements', 7.
104 Ibid., 9; 301.
105 Walter Macken, *The Silent People* [1962] (London: Pan Books, 1988), 293.
106 Ibid., 286–7.
107 Michael Mullen, *The Hungry Land* [1986] (London: Corgi Books, 1988).
108 Ibid., 475.
109 Michael Mullen, *The Darkest Years: A Famine Story* (Castlebar: Cavendish House, 1997).
110 Brendan Ó Cathaoir, *Famine Diary* (Dublin: Irish Academic Press, 1999), xiii.
111 Joe Lee, 'Foreword', ibid., xi.
112 Gerald Keegan, *Famine Diary: Journey to a New World* (Dublin: Wolfhound Press, sec. edn 1991), back cover. The book appeared earlier under the title of *The Voyage of the Naparima: A Story of Canada's Island Graveyard* (Quebec: Carraig Books, 1982).
113 Robert Sellars, *The Summer of Sorrow, Abner's Device, and Other Stories*, Gleaner Tales, Part 2 (Quebec: Huntingdon, 1895), 341–462. The hoax of the *Famine Diary* is exposed in Jim Jackson, 'Famine diary – the making of a best Sellar', *The Irish Review* 11 (1991/2), 1–8. See also Jacqueline Kornblum, 'Mixing history and fiction', *Irish Literary Supplement* 11 (spring 1992), 10.
114 Sellars, *Summer of Sorrow*, 364.
115 Ibid., 347.
116 Morash, 'Making memories', 52.
117 Ibid., 53.
118 James Mangan, *Robert Whyte's 1847 Famine Ship Diary: The Journey of an Irish Coffin Ship* (Dublin: Mercier Press, 1994), 10. Doubts over the authenticity of this 'diary' are equally warranted.
119 Brendan Bradshaw described the Irish historical record as 'seared ... by successive waves of conquest and colonisation, by bloody wars and uprisings, by traumatic social dislocation, by lethal racial antagonisms, and, indeed, by its own nineteenth-century version of a holocaust' ('Nationalism and historical scholarship in modern Ireland' [1988], in Ciaran Brady (ed.), *Interpreting Irish History*, 191–216: 201).
120 See, for instance, Ó Cathaoir, *Famine Diary*; Killen (ed.), *The Famine Decade*; Nicolson, *Annals of the Famine in Ireland*; David Fitzpatrick, *Oceans of Consolation. Personal Accounts of Irish Migration to Australia* (Melbourne: Melbourne University Press, 1995).
121 See, for instance, Cormac Ó Gráda, *Black '47 and Beyond in History, Economy, and Memory* (Princeton, NJ: Princeton University Press, 1999).
122 See, for instance, Pórtéir, *Famine Echoes* – a compilation of excerpts from the returns of the Famine questionnaire circulated by the Irish government in 1945 – and the enduring popularity of Peadar Ó Leoghaire's (b. 1838) autobiography, *My Own Story* [1915], trans. C. T. Ó Céirin (Cork: Mercier Press, 1970).
123 Tóibín, *The Irish Famine*, 65.
124 Fegan, *Literature and the Irish Famine*, 238.
125 Seán Kenny, 'A nightmare revisited', in Tom Hayden (ed.), *Irish Hunger*, 181–90: 184.
126 Seán Kenny, *The Hungry Earth* (Dublin: Wolfhound, 1995), 197.

127 Ibid., 198.
128 Ibid., 202–3.
129 Seán Kenny, 'A nightmare revisited', 181; 190.
130 Nuala O'Faolain, *My Dream of You* (London: Michael Joseph, 2001), 65.
131 Ibid., 64.
132 Ibid., 144.
133 It is interesting to note in this context that many TV 'documentaries' of the Famine incorporate footage showing the victims of modern-day famines in Africa and elsewhere. Such problematic comparisons across time and space foreground the extent to which, for late twentieth- and twenty-first-century viewers, historical empathy appears to depend on the suggestive impact of visuals.
134 O'Faolain, *My Dream of You*, 69.
135 Ibid., 435.
136 See Peter Burke, 'History of events and the revival of narrative', in Burke (ed.), *New Perspectives on Historical Writing* (University Park, PA: Pennsylvania State University Press, sec. edn 2001), 283–300.
137 Joseph O'Connor, *Star of the Sea* (London: Vintage, 2003), 396–7.
138 Ibid., 153.
139 Ibid., 130.
140 Ibid., 129.
141 Ibid., 130.
142 Ibid., 404.
143 See Judith Palmer in *The Independent* (4 January 2003) and Terry Eagleton in *The Guardian* (25 January 2003); the reviews are available on line at http://enjoyment.independent.co.uk/books/interviews/story.jsp?story=365979 and http://books.guardian.co.uk/review/story/0,12084,880838,00.html (both accessed 20 August 2004).
144 Terry Eagleton's 1995 Famine play *God's Locusts*, which features a delegation of Irish radicals in negotiation with Famine relief officers and is set 'in the Treasury in mid-Victorian London' (Eagleton, *St Oscar and Other Plays* (Oxford: Blackwell, 1997), 173, stage direction), is perhaps the only exception.
145 Kenny, 'A nightmare revisited', 185.
146 See Eavan Boland, 'That the Science of Cartography Is Limited', *In a Time of Violence* (Manchester: Carcanet, 1994), 5.
147 See M. M. Bakhtin and P. N. Medvedev, *The Formal Method in Literary Scholarship. A Critical Introduction to Sociological Poetics* [1928], trans. Albert J. Wehrle (Baltimore, MD and London: Johns Hopkins University Press, 1978), chapter 7: 'The elements of the artistic construction' (129–41).

3

STAGING HISTORY IN CONTEMPORARY IRISH DRAMA

The 'Irish history play [is] a genre', Claire Gleitman writes in a recent article, 'which contemporary Irish writers have ... made their stock in trade'.[1] Plays about Ireland's past are indeed at the forefront of dramatic activity in Ireland; they are not only among the most popular contemporary additions to the repertoire in the Irish theatre and beyond, they also belong to the critically most challenging literary treatments of history. Some examples of the genre have already made a brief appearance in the previous chapters: Frank McGuinness's evocation of late sixteenth-century Gaelic Ireland in *Mutabilitie* (1997); Brian Friel's reconstruction of Hugh O'Neill's defeat at Kinsale in *Making History* (1989) – a play that builds on Thomas Kilroy's earlier handling of the same theme in *The O'Neill* (1966) – and Thomas Murphy's *Famine* (1968), to which could have been added the many Famine commemoration plays written in the mid-1990s.[2] The list could easily be extended: for example, Friel dramatised Bloody Sunday 1972 in *The Freedom of the City* (1973); Tom Paulin satirised the Anglo-Irish Agreement of 1985 in *The Hillsborough Script* (1986); Sebastian Barry wrote about the pivotal year 1922 through the perspective of 1932 in *The Steward of Christendom* (1995).

This overwhelming attention to history has been written off by some critics as a sentimental exercise in navel-gazing – 'Too many contemporary Irish plays bleat plaintively of old wounds'[3] – while others are busy dividing the plays up into what seem analytically sterile 'thematic categories'.[4] My aim in this chapter differs from these critical concerns. Like Claire Gleitman, I am interested in how the plays negotiate 'the ideological and psychological imperatives which control the ways in which history is remembered, transmitted and employed'.[5] Specifically, I want to investigate the radical historical 'methodology' adopted in three of the dramatically (and commercially) most successful Irish history plays of the 1980s, all written and produced within five years of each other: Brian Friel's *Transla-*

tions (1980), Stewart Parker's *Northern Star* (1984) and Frank McGuinness's *Observe the Sons of Ulster Marching Towards the Somme* (1985).

'Methodology' may be too pompous a word for the imaginative ease that characterises the historical address of these plays, but I use it here to emphasise my continuing critical concern with the link between literature, history and historiographical practice – a link that informs my discussion of the dramatic interchange between past and present throughout this chapter. In contrast to the previous chapter, I focus here on a narrow selection of texts rather than on (more or less) the whole of a tradition. My reason for this selective approach is that this particular triad of plays map out between them the most advanced conceptual possibilities of the modern Irish history play. Given the overwhelming praise that at least two of them have received since they were first written (the Friel and McGuinness plays), this is hardly a contentious position. What has been lacking in the general appreciation of these plays, in my view, is a sustained consideration of the extent to which their historical imaginings are the product of a fruitful participation in continuing critical debates, across the disciplines, about the very nature of the historical enterprise.

Their critical edge does not, of course, make these three plays necessarily representative of the concerns of the Irish history play as a whole, and certainly not of Irish drama more generally.[6] Nor do they share with each other more than a general thematic focus on events in Ireland's past, and perhaps nothing but a broad generic category such as 'history play' would provide a suitable heading under which their divergent dramatic interests could be contained. But from a temporal distance of more than two decades, significant structural similarities do now come into view: for instance, the use of the past not simply as an 'explanation' of the present, but as one of its constituent elements; the highly ambiguous nature of all cultural negotiations of divisive historical legacies; the pressing responsibilities of posterity to account for all facets of the past. The moral urgency of these plays clearly has its roots in the post-1968 Northern crisis – which was into its second decade of prolonged violence when the plays were written – even if only two of the writers are actually from the North, and neither play is set during the modern phase of the Troubles.

The writing of these plays in the 1980s was also enabled by new cultural ventures intended in some measure as an antidote to the stark realities of civil conflict. Prominent among these was the Field Day Theatre Company, founded in 1980 by playwright Brian Friel and actor Stephen Rea.[7] Field Day owes its existence as a company more to short-term financial pressure than to long-term planning: to stage the new play *Translations*, Friel and Rea needed Arts Council funding, which was only granted to existing regional companies.[8] Despite these mundane beginnings, Field Day developed into a major forum for cultural debate in Ireland in the 1980s, a neutral 'fifth province' of the imagination beyond politics and sectarianism, which soon provided one (though by no means the only) outlet for theatrical experiments with theme and genre. Field Day was perhaps a decisive factor in breaking the formal mould of O'Casey's Dublin trilogy of the 1920s, whose characteristically irreconcilable tension between public politics and private grief had established itself as a blueprint for the modern Irish history play.[9] Two of the plays considered here (by Friel and McGuinness) were originally written for Field Day, even though *Observe the Sons of Ulster* was eventually premiered at the Peacock in Dublin. Although Field Day was based in the North (throughout the 1980s new Field Day productions were first shown at the Guildhall in Derry) the company still 'bore all the traces of attempting to bear the burden of representing an entire nation',[10] and its various projects and publications have a cultural and political significance far beyond their more immediate Northern origin.

These three plays are history plays in every sense of the word. If it has ever been anything other than an editorial convenience to single out ten Shakespeare plays that happen to deal with English history since the Norman Conquest, and invent for them a genre of their own, then this category eminently fits my selection: all three plays set out to probe the recent past for its mental and material impact on the present. This is obvious on the level of plot. Friel uses the Ordnance Survey of the 1830s as his central metaphor for an exploration of the themes of conflict and cooperation in Anglo-Irish relations. Parker projects an imaginative history of modern Irish writing into the events and characters of the 1798 rebellion of the United Irishmen. And McGuinness uses the 'blood sacrifice' of the 36th (Ulster) Division in World War I – all but wiped out on 1 July 1916 in the Battle of the Somme – as a foil for his dramatic anatomy of the Ulster Protestant psyche. Each play thus focuses on a specific historical event, relates that event to issues of current concern in modern Ireland, and hence 're-members' its significance from a contemporary perspective.

But it is not their topical relevance that concerns me most about these plays. What is most significant about them, I want to argue, is that each play employs a different conceptual approach to the staging of history, and that each explores the resources of the stage to offer a different definition of the very nature of the historical. In short, what interests me about these plays is not *what* they remember, but *how* they remember. Showing that this is no mere academic distinction will be the business of this chapter. In the short section that immediately follows I will suggest – by way of a brief digression – a conceptual framework for this discussion, then move on to consider all three plays in turn, and finally assess in a brief conclusion the currency of the historical positions offered in these plays.

The muse of history

In J. M. Coetzee's novel *Waiting for the Barbarians*, published in the same year as the first of my three plays (1980), the unnamed magistrate of an allegorical frontier settlement is confronted with the dark, incomprehensible forces of an equally unnamed Empire, whose representative he is, but whose officers now arrive to accuse him of negligence in his duties. In what appears to be 'a new phase of aggressive imperialism',[11] the magistrate is suspected of conspirational contacts with the enemy, the mysterious, hardly visible 'barbarians' just beyond the borders of the state, in whose culture the magistrate has developed a historical interest. This cross-cultural contact, intensified by his illicit sexual liaison with a 'barbarian' woman, is viewed as transgressive and dangerous; consequently, the magistrate is stripped of his powers, imprisoned, and now awaits – in a Kafkaesque setting – a trial that never comes.

His own view of the events is quite different. To him, the state has been the aggressor, preferring rather to incite conflict with harmless neighbours than to foster peaceful relations. From his perspective, the Empire is dominated by a brainless military machinery. In an interview with Colonel Joll of the ominous 'Fifth Bureau', who have masterminded the take-over of the frontier town, the magistrate's scholarly interest in 'barbarian' culture is made to appear positively prejudicial to the safety of the Empire. Enraged at the discursive and military injustice done to him and his 'barbarian' neighbours, the magistrate exclaims that posterity will eventually come round to his point of view: 'History will bear me out!' The emphatic statement draws a dismissive response from the Colonel: 'Nonsense. There will be no history, the affair is too trivial.'[12]

The basic constellation of cultural agents in *Waiting for the Barbarians* has some bearing on the Irish situation as it is conceived in the three plays under discussion here. The parallels are neither direct nor compelling, but they throw some conceptual light on the issues I want to take up in this chapter: Friel's play depicts advancing English soldiers in confrontation with a native culture that is increasingly seen to retreat into either oblivion or the mysticism of the Celtic twilight; Parker chooses as his protagonist a figure that radiates with the desire to overcome age-old hostilities and a largely self-inflicted sense of cultural antagonism; and McGuinness explores the psychic identity crisis of a community threatened by its own ghosts and myths. All these features run in some form or other through Coetzee's novel which posits two cultures in conflict with each other, installs at the point of physical contact a figure self-conscious of his shortcomings, and vaguely hints at the crisis of imperial self-definition. Given this cultural moment of conflicting loyalties, ruinous self-perception and an overpowering sense of estrangement and loss, the Colonel's dismissal of the magistrate's case as 'trivial' seems all the more shocking.

The authoritative decree that there 'will be no history' sums up in one phrase a dominant critical perspective on history, or better, on historiography: all history-writing is the work of ideology; history is not a disinterested, neutral truth-finding exercise but the production of partial and biased narratives that serve specific interests – most frequently, as in this fictional example, the retrospective interests of the victors. The decisions about *what* to report, and *how*, are theirs. Written history is partial and selective, it bestows the stamp of relevance only on what the rulers choose to have remembered about the past at any given moment, however benign the intention of historians. So that, even when they claim to report the past 'as it really was', their appeal to objective neutrality is seen as pure ideology. Put more crudely, in the words of one of Stewart Parker's characters from *Northern Star*: 'History's a whore. She rides the winners.'[13]

This materialist criticism of historiography is well known; what I want to argue here is that such a view is as true in the abstract as it is stifling in the particular. The response of Coetzee's magistrate is of course a reflex to which a critical tradition that describes itself as dissident or radical can immediately relate. A sense of justice, a knowledge of the power of discourse, an awareness of the materialist forces of history, would all persuade us that the magistrate needs to be defended as much as Walter Benjamin's dispossessed have a right to be redeemed in the annals of a materialist history.[14] This view predominates wherever history is seen first as a matter of brute force, then as a matter of rhetoric.

But things are never that easy. Coetzee's magistrate is an intermediate agent, an exponent of the liberal, humanist approach, caught between an expanding colonial power and a retreating indigenous people. We may ask ourselves for a moment what rhetorical shape *his* version of the events would assume. Given his exculpatory pose throughout the novel, the history that would 'bear him out' may just as well be little more than the apologetic discourse that will wash him free of white colonial guilt, a history that exchanges one colonial perspective – repressive, imperial, convinced of its own superiority – for another – benign, understanding, conscious of its own intrusive stance. Another historian would want to write a different history altogether. A desire to break with the discursive dichotomies that force upon us the perspective of the imperialist agenda might inspire the attempt to look beyond inherited limitations and cross the cultural divide – to write, in short, the barbarians' story.

Dangers loom in this enterprise too. To unearth the hidden histories of the victims of the historical struggle whose voices have been silenced, forgotten or marginalised is, of course, an honourable exercise – all 'history from below' is dedicated to this single, liberating idea – but it is also to remain within the grand narrative of oppressor and victim, of victorious and defeated. Derek Walcott has warned that 'by openly fighting tradition we perpetuate it' and, insisting that 'revolutionary literature is a filial impulse', he advises instead an approach to the past that remains aware of all its shaping powers: '[M]aturity is the assimilation of the features of every ancestor'.[15] The ghostly ancestors of Walcott's native Caribbean are surely not easily assimilated. In making this daring integrative gesture he reaches far beyond his own time and place – and the formula, I would like to suggest, can be exported, suitably adapted, to the Irish scene.

When Walcott, in his remarkable essay 'The muse of history', cuts across ethnic and other divisions to celebrate the poetic 'power of a shared imagination'[16] he is, by implication, criticising all partisan history – politically correct partisan history perhaps, but still partisan – of the persistent reflex to fix people in positions defined by skin colour, class affiliation or religious creed. This is one way of saying that by suggesting – as the passage from Coetzee implicitly does – that all unreconstructed history-writing is one huge story of repression, we seriously limit the range of our critical options.

The liberating potential of history is located instead in the bold act of moving beyond the grounds of human difference altogether. Walcott thanks two of his more sinister ancestral ghosts – slave seller and slave buyer – 'for the monumental groaning and soldering of two great worlds',[17] for the creation of a new present out of past pain and misery. These thanks, 'bitter and strange', are not offered lightly, and the implicit target of this courageous gesture is what strikes me as stifling about the view of the historical as *no more* than the repressive ideology of the victors: the denial of agency even in the search for covert creativity, the disabling reduction of tradition to a few acceptable idols, the pre-emptive narrowing down of historical choice. I am not arguing that the project of rewriting history from below, from the margins or against the grain, has become pointless; on the contrary, this project will remain at the core of a radical critical agenda. But what seems imperative now too is the need to find a tradition that champions the poetic potential of history, a narrative that reaches beyond the recurring patterns of victimisation. This history, to be sure, must not be written as a mindless celebratory pastiche but as the resonant and *inclusive* record of imaginative existence.

Returning to the discursive and geographical terrain of Ireland, I want to suggest that the three plays discussed below can all be read, in their different ways, as experimenting with precisely the idea that history is not only a memory of trauma but also a source of imaginative liberation and affective kinship across the most oppressive social and cultural divide. These texts are, like any formal exposition of 'hard facts', cultural acts of memory, and as aesthetic interventions in an ongoing critical debate they offer approaches to the past that enable us to move beyond the limitations of the present. Their specific historical revisionism is thus less to drag back into visibility what has been 'forgotten, repressed, distorted';[18] rather, it is their claim that even a history of conflict is not all trauma, that past bloodshed need not turn each recourse to history into a re-enactment of suffering and pain. What constitutes the force of the historical in these plays is their power to delineate a space 'where a thought might grow',[19] where there is an impulse to move beyond division and strife, beyond the seemingly perpetual but really ephemeral conflict between 'us' and 'them', to an acceptance of the potential richness and liberating legacy of history.

Brian Friel: translating the past

For Brian Friel, *Translations* was always meant as a play not so much about history but about 'language and only language'.[20] In this Friel has been challenged, amongst others, by Christopher Murray, who writes that 'no play is about *only* language', arguing that '*Translations* is a history play'.[21] I incline to Murray's view on this issue[22] and wonder just how far Friel may have been moved to make this statement by way of pre-empting attacks on his historical distortions. Friel got plenty of facts wrong, as is well known,[23] including the most central: the mapping project of the 1820s and 1830s that his play uses as a metaphor for cultural and linguistic colonialism, the Ordnance Survey, was never intended to crudely rewrite the Irish landscape but rather to preserve, with the assistance of the foremost Gaelic scholars of the time, the customary usage of local place-names.[24]

In fact, it was only through the Ordnance Survey that Irish topography became replete with cultural memory. Joep Leerssen has shown that the Ordnance Survey – rather than being an instrument of colonial oppression and cultural alienation – 'was a major contribution to the cultural nationalism of later decades, in that it equated the very land itself with a Gaelic past and a Gaelic-speaking peasantry, thus canonizing the Gaelic tradition as the very bedrock ... of modern Ireland'.[25] But historical accuracy is hardly the most pressing issue in a work of fiction. As Friel has explained himself, 'the imperatives of fiction are as exacting as the imperatives ... of historiography'.[26] Friel is a trickster of course, a manipulator of sources and spectators, and by sidetracking much of the initial debate about the play into a futile wrangle over historical accuracy,[27] he may have been deliberately obscuring the more fundamental issue of how history is used in this play, and to what purpose.[28]

The play is set in 1833 and deals, in abstract terms, with the conceptual struggles attendant on the transfer of Ireland's cultural and linguistic landscape from one set of referents – classical, Gaelic, mythic – into another – modern, English, rational. The deep time of Irish memory and culture is made to clash in this play with the functional, quantitative space of English modernity. There are two timescales in the play. The first tells the story of the arrival in the Irish village of Ballybeg – literally the archetypal 'small town' of Ireland – of a platoon of surveyors, who come to produce new, up-to-date maps of Donegal. The centre of village life, as represented in the play, is an Irish-speaking hedge school where – if you choose to follow Friel rather than his sources – classical learning comes as naturally to the local peasants as the drinking of poteen to the stage Irishman of another tradition. The prevailing sense in the school is that of a culture locked in its past, unable or unwilling to change. As Friel has put it in a diary written at the time of the play's composition, 'the cultural climate [of Ballybeg] is a dying climate – no longer quickened by its past, about to be plunged almost overnight into an alien future'.[29] In the opening scene of the play, this conceptual insight is translated into a kind of *tableau vivant*, with different local characters suffering from a range of mental and physical disabilities: deficient speech (Sarah), limping (Manus), loss of sense of reality (Jimmy), drunkenness (Hugh).

On to this scene intrude three cartographers who could be seen to represent, respectively, romance (Yolland), collaboration (Owen) and authority (Lancey). Their presence in Ballybeg metonymically evokes the play's second timescale, which chronicles the long-term decline of the peasant community of Friel's Irish model village: a new national school, in which all subjects are taught through English, will replace the Irish-speaking hedge school; the English maps drawn of the area will erase a landscape of custom and memory; the Irish language is under threat; the one character in the play who embraces Gaelic culture unquestioningly (Manus) sets out, at the end of the play, 'on his journey westward' – a journey, as in Joyce, into the realm of the dead – and the most violent and dramatic upheaval of Irish society is announced in several references to a countryside reeking with the 'sweet smell' of rotting crops – a bleak portent of the imminent Famine.

The play is melodramatic in character and admirably old-fashioned in style; Friel himself expressed surprise about its phenomenal success. The central issue of the play is the extent of the cultural loss incurred in the act of translation. There are many translations in the play: cultural, temporal, linguistic, historical. The very title of the play contains the hint that what we are hearing on stage is not the real thing at all but only a translation. This is literally true insofar as the language that we hear the characters speak throughout much of the play is, in the logic of the dramatic illusion, not English but Irish.[30] It is aesthetically true insofar as the history of Ireland in the 1830s is translated for us through the idiom of the stage into an image of contemporary relevance.

The spatial translation that is metaphorically central to the plot is effected by the map of Donegal which the Ordnance Survey officers produce in the course of the play. Maps of Ireland, as I have argued elsewhere,[31] are important historical documents of cultural and political conflict. In Friel's play, maps are most directly identified as harbingers of doom when they are metonymically associated with the potato blight: the sweet smell comes from 'just beyond where the soldiers are making the maps'.[32] Many critics have commented on this complicity of the Ordnance Survey map with colonial erasure; what is less often noted is that this link does not amount to a wholesale condemnation of cartography in the play. Other maps make other statements – such as the map of America which Maire studies in the hedge school, or the verbal map evoked in the play's multilingual love scene, or hedge schoolmaster Hugh's mental map which enables him to find his way through the landscape he knows even after it has been transformed on paper into a colonial script. (Owen's worries – which some critics take at face value[33] – that his father might get lost in this 'geography of disinheritance'[34] are really rather pointless. Locals don't need road signs.)

These maps comment on, even contradict, each other in a variety of ways. Maire's perusal of the map of America, for example, is an instance of colonial appropriation that works as an ironic reversal of the native Irish resistance to having Donegal inscribed with English place-names. The mental map that enables cognitive possession of an area irrespective of its toponymic nomenclature might raise the question to what extent any of the geometric Ordnance Survey maps are really instruments of dispossession, capable of 'no less', Kevin Barry argues – with no apparent sense of irony – 'than the casual annihilation of a culture'.[35] This bold statement is wrong historically because, as noted above, it was only through the Ordnance Survey that Irish topography became replete with cultural memory. It is also wrong aesthetically, because it ignores how the characters in the play respond to maps. They see them as images, not as the violent textual imposition of alien place-names. Despite this, the English map of Donegal that is the centrepiece of the action and that literally forms the ground beneath the characters' feet in the first scene of act two, is most frequently discussed – in Friel criticism – in terms not of its visual force but its toponymic structure: it is seen as a mere stringing together of place-names.

But a visual depiction of space is more than a catalogue of names. Map imagery exerts a magnetic pull, it radiates pathos. We can get a sense of this simply by observing the characters in the play. When Maire – the play's life-force – gazes at the map of America in act one, her interest in it is generated by her desire to emigrate; when Yolland draws a verbal map of Norfolk in act two, which Maire later redraws in the clay, their joint map works as a mutual bond of love.[36] Maps in the play are suffused with spatial or erotic desire, they 'glow with affect'.[37] What is lost in the (critics') reduction of the map from a structure of feeling to a mere register of toponyms parallels what is lost in the (playwright's) reduction of the complex dialectic of history to a lopsided political and cultural power struggle that is always already decided in favour of England.

In the play, history is explained as a clash between two rival, antagonistic forces. There is no common ground between the two cultures, as the metaphor of the constantly rewritten map indicates, and there is no language that both cultures share. The more powerful of these cultures is also the less poetic; the weaker side, by contrast, is made up of saints, scholars, story-tellers, and a few dissenting voices. Little if nothing in the play indicates the centuries of contact and communication that have shaped the common history of Britain and Ireland; there are no in-between spaces, no contact zones. This insistence on cultural purity has led Edna Longley to see the play as constructing a pre-colonial, pre-English society, a therapeutic 'image of possibility', offering 'an alternative history, cultural self-respect, however "doomed" that culture itself is shown to be'.[38]

There are, however, instances of genuine historical insight in the play that surpass this dreamwork. The first of these comes when one of the surveyors, Yolland, articulates a romantic longing for the local language and culture, and even announces his desire to learn Irish. The protagonist, Hugh, responds to this expression of nostalgia with a reflection on the transitory nature of language: '[R]emember that words are signals, counters. They are not immortal. And it can happen – to use an image you'll understand – it can happen that a civilisation can be imprisoned in a linguistic contour which no longer matches the landscape of ... fact' (43). Implied in this metaphorical conflation of language and landscape, I want to suggest, is an understanding of the historical dialectic between forgetting and remembrance.

Friel culled the last sentence almost verbatim from George Steiner's reflections on language and culture in *After Babel*,[39] in which the passage occurs as part of the argument that at certain historical moments any given language may enter a state of paralysis, may cease to provide a sign system that matches the mental and emotional range of experience – when it no longer resonates with life. Friel's own understanding of linguistic decay clearly builds on these arguments, though his use of Steiner's analytic abstraction as the perceptive and self-reflexive comment of an individual character prompts the question of whether the play actually succeeds in keeping topic and medium apart, whether it manages, in other words, to distinguish sufficiently between language as linguistic process and language as living element.[40]

Steiner is the immediate source for the quotation but, in the context of the play's historical concerns, a more resonant source for Hugh's insight into the incongruence between language and 'the landscape of fact', as well as the resulting need to accept historical change, would be Nietzsche. In the piece on history included in his *Untimely Meditations*, already briefly referred to in the introduction, Nietzsche argues that an excess of historical consciousness in an individual or a culture can be as detrimental as its entire lack, hence the ability to forget is as important as the act of memory. Cultural survival and progress – or, in Nietzsche's now rather loaded term, 'health' – are achieved only through the adequate balance of forgetting and remembrance, the historical and the unhistorical; 'oversaturation ... with history', by contrast, 'disrupts the instincts of a people, and hinders the individual no less than the whole in the attainment of maturity'.[41] There is ample evidence that this stasis has befallen Ballybeg: Jimmy, the 'Infant Prodigy', who relates more easily to the classics than to the world around him, functions as a veritable pattern of escapist attitudes in his denial of the present; Manus, the lover of Gaelic culture, is steeped in excessive nostalgia; even Hugh himself revels in drunken moments of mythic recall to alleviate the pressures of the moment. The knowledge that change is one of the imperatives of life and that such change always necessitates a measure of historical amnesia comes late in the play, and even then seems to affect no one else besides Hugh.

Nietzsche further argues that excessive fixation on history 'leads an age into a dangerous mood of irony in respect to itself and subsequently into the even more dangerous mood of cynicism'.[42] For much of the play, Hugh cultivates just such an ironic mood verging on cynicism. Satirising the view that wit and eloquence might compensate for material squalor, he identifies 'the mythologies of fantasy and hope and self-deception' enshrined in the Irish language as a hyperbolic 'response to mud cabins and a diet of potatoes' (42). When he later comes round to a hesitant acceptance of the need for change, this should be viewed not simply as surrender in the face of a more powerful adversary but as the realisation that if the past first needs to be preserved, it also needs to be overcome and defeated. Excess of history requires the antidote of the unhistorical.

Hugh reappears on the stage in the very last scene of the play, drunken as always, bitter about losing the job at the new school to an outsider, nostalgic about his and Jimmy's part in the 1798 rising – the one moment, as he chooses to remember their retreat on the march to Sligo, when they 'were Gods' (67). Yet, despite this relapse into myth-making, he clings to his new-found insight, pointing out that it is Jimmy, who wants to wed Pallas Athene, who has ceased to discriminate between myth and history. And since it is not 'the literal past, the "facts" of history, that shape us, but images of the past embodied in language', Hugh explains, 'we must never cease renewing those images; because once we do, we fossilise'. Hence his urgent appeal to 'learn those new [place-]names. ... We must learn to make them our own. We must make them our new home' (66).

The point of these lines is not that Hugh has now finally grasped what other characters in the play, notably Maire, knew all along: to get on in the modern world, fluency in English will prove the more helpful asset. It is rather the insight that it is more damaging, more destructive for a living culture, simply to shed tears over the lost poetry of the tribe. Audiences across Ireland will know what has been lost simply by listening to an English language play in which half the characters nominally speak Irish. That language, Declan Kiberd reminds us, 'declined only when the Irish people allowed it to decline',[43] and to argue instead that its almost total demise is owed to deliberate English suppression is to engage in nationalist dreamwork. In the play, Friel frequently comes close to this position of sentimental revivalism, despite Kiberd's claims to the contrary. Still, the liberating force of Hugh's break with the past is contained in the gesture of counter-colonial appropriation to make the new names 'our own'.

There is some tendency in Friel criticism to read these last statements on the issue of naming as Hugh's pragmatic decision to make some minor adjustments in his routine in order to escape cultural sclerosis. Naming is indeed a principal issue in a play largely concerned with control over discourse. His own Adamic power as a cartographer initially electrifies Owen: 'We name a thing and – bang! – it leaps into existence' (45). Such reflections make the play eminently political and should warn us that more is at stake in Hugh's embrace of the new names than practical worries about being left behind. Place-names preserve memory, as several characters argue, and to change them is to interfere to some extent in the integrity of a culture. Yet even though place defines a culture as much as history offers a sense of self, the true cultural erosion that Yolland fears he is guilty of by having fiddled with ancient Irish toponyms (43) is to allow the *use* of space – its daily enactment in spatial practice – to degenerate into the repetitive incantation of stale, worn-out names.

The ending of the play forces the characters into the relative sanity of partial oblivion. Memory is vital in the construction of culture but cannot be allowed to dictate its terms at the expense of the living. It is Hugh who realises at the end that the reinvention of Ballybeg as a stronghold of Gaelic culture was not, in the first instance, a self-chosen strategy but a response to the English challenge. Echoing Nietzsche,[44] he advises his son Owen that '[t]o remember everything is a form of madness' (67). What the overload of history implies as its imaginative undersong is more than simply the availability of selective versions of the past as a reservoir to be drawn upon in the shaping of the future.[45] Partial memories, as no one in Northern Ireland needs to be told, can be as oppressive as guns. Hugh's invitation to deliberate forgetfulness reflects rather his decision to reject the notion of cultural and linguistic purity. The place-names of Norfolk that Yolland recites in act two – Little Walsingham, Barton Bendish, Saxingham Nethergate, Winfarthing[46] – are equally hybrid products of a history of invasions. To select no longer to be tyrannised by the myth of origin is the exercise of choice. The insight that this option is as real for the Irish as it is for the English would seem partly to redeem a play in which for much of the plot such historical understanding escapes the characters, and in which the sense of history too often ossifies into the reiteration of false contrasts.

'The play does not so much *examine* myths of dispossession and oppression as repeat them',[47] Edna Longley writes, flying in the face of the play's almost universal popularity.[48] The comment certainly comes closer to the spirit of Friel's historical vision than Kiberd's martial praise that '*Translations* is a tough-minded play about the brutal actualities of cultural power.'[49] There is too much in the play designed to placate an audience in search of facile historical analogies to give this statement much plausibility. The theme of the play is the complex interwining of language and identity, and the relevance of this debate to modern Ireland, but no matter how delicate the issue, the politics of the play should not be mistaken for its poetry.

Stewart Parker: the times of the now

An alternative conceptual approach to the staging of Irish history is given dramatic form in Stewart Parker's 1984 play *Northern Star*. The play is concerned with the spirit of political liberty that spread across Ireland in the wake of the French Revolution and that had its (anti-) climax in the unsuccessful rising of the United Irishmen in 1798. Seen through the eyes of one of the leading figures in the rising, the Presbyterian rebel Henry Joy McCracken, the history of the United Irishmen is transformed on stage into a colourful array of voices, images and songs. McCracken is the master of ceremonies. Hiding in a half-finished cottage outside Belfast on the slopes of Cavehill on the eve of his execution, he turns his memories of the seven-year struggle that culminated in the 1798 rising into a sequence of seven scenes acted out on the stage. Each scene represents an 'age', in the manner of the classical notion of the seven ages of man, and the pageant for each age is written in imitation of a different dramatic style. This device makes for brilliant theatre, for a dramatic tour de force rich in literary allusion, wit, comical double-take and ironic anachronism. As in many of his plays, Parker exploits the full range of theatrical possibilities – dance, music, slapstick, mime – but his use of 'literary pastiche', as he called his own technique,[50] demands a lot from the public and has often proved 'too tricky … to win a popular audience'.[51]

The 'Age of Innocence', written in the stilted mannerisms of the first professional Irish playwright, George Farquhar, shows McCracken and his mates in the 'Mudlers Club', where drinking, whoring and conspiring against the government all converge in a test of youthful, irresponsible and misogynistic manhood. The 'Age of Idealism', written in the melodramatic style which Parker borrows from Dion Boucicault, pits political hope against sectarian reality as old patterns of rural rivalry and religious bigotry prove stronger than the ideals of unconditional solidarity. The 'Age of Cleverness' follows, in which the projects for cultural revitalisation, such as the 1795 Belfast Harp Festival, are satirised in the hilarious witticisms of Oscar Wilde. Act one ends with the 'Age of Dialectics', written in the style of George Bernard Shaw, which forces the Irish–English power struggle into the open, bringing 'acute definition and political theory'.[52]

The 'Age of Heroism' borrows its theatrical idiom from the highly stylised speech of J. M. Synge's plays, and dramatises the disappointments that followed on the heels of the initially liberating call to arms and political action. The 'Age of Compromise' forces the revolutionaries to choose between sectarian alternatives whose validity they had never been willing to accept in the first place – a scene of cowardice and self-deceit written in the style of Sean O'Casey. Finally, the 'Age of Knowledge' brings disillusion, despair and ultimately defeat; the scene opens with an earthy prison dialogue in the style of Brendan Behan and ends in the elusive semantics of a Samuel Beckett monologue. These seven theatrical showpieces are framed by scenes of pressing actuality that feature McCracken on the run, in a self-searching but witty dialogue with his mistress, Mary Bodle, on the last night before his execution.[53]

The play is self-consciously theatrical, both in its dramatic technique of using flashbacks that involve a large set of characters all played by the same actors, and in McCracken's rehearsal throughout the play of his farewell speech to the 'citizens of Belfast' (4 *et passim*),[54] to be delivered next day from the scaffold. Perhaps not its most successful aspect is the didactic thread of cross-religious solidarity that runs through the play. 'Let the people once unite and we would burst open the doors, and they would flood out into the clean sunlight. Heady stuff. Intoxicating' (68). Originally commissioned by the Lyric Theatre in Belfast, the play was seriously 'expected to make a difference in Northern Ireland, "because it would show a time when Catholics and Protestants worked together for reform"'.[55]

Yet the theme of Catholic–Protestant unity never quite manages to avoid the stigma of self-imposed political correctness. The slightly lifeless character of Jimmy Hope, for instance, proclaims that '[w]ithout the Protestants of the North, there'll never be a nation' (58), a sentiment that pays lip-service to political tolerance but hardly sounds like a historical reflection on the goals of the United Irishmen, however correct in essence.[56] Of course, Parker knows about such pitfalls, and the play does not foster any naive belief in a non-sectarian future. 'So much for the great revolution of United Irishmen. It comes out looking just like another Catholic riot' (61). And later: '[A]ll we've done ... is to reinforce the locks, cram the cells fuller than ever of mangled bodies crawling round in their own shite and lunacy, and the cycle just goes on, playing out the same demented comedy of terrors from generation to generation' (69).

Passages like this have led Terence Brown to dismiss the play as yet another exercise in viewing Ireland's history in terms of a tragic inevitability.[57] No matter how ready Ireland is for change, history will only repeat itself. As I aim to show further below, such a reading misses the whole point of a play that specifically defines itself *against* worn-out chronologies, that aims to break history's glacial hold on the present. In full knowledge of sectarian aggression it champions social unity and the celebration of cultural difference. While the date and context of its composition may excuse the occasional instance of wishful thinking about cross-community relations, the play is certainly alive to the reality of social conflict. Each age is shown to be the opposite of its titular promise: the Mudlers' innocence is abused first by an informer and then by their own excessive misogyny; idealism is tricked into partisanship; cleverness exposed as empty rhetoric; dialectics end in murder; heroism in failure; compromise leads to instrumentalisation; and knowledge leads to despair. The motto of the play is announced by McCracken in the very first scene (9) and repeated in the last: 'We never made a nation. ... We botched the birth' (81).

Brown would elevate this late pessimism into the central statement of the whole play. It certainly ends on a bleak note of ultimate despair and frustrated aspiration. McCracken, the failed rebel, stops to conjure up one last time the image of his home town of Belfast: 'we can't love it for what it is, only for what it might have been, if we'd got it right, if we'd made it whole. If. It's a ghost town now and always will be, angry and implacable ghosts' (81). Still, even this acknowledgement of failure does not rule out a second chance, as McCracken had suggested earlier, lost in the Beckettian solitude of the 'Age of Knowledge': 'Unless only to begin anew, there is of course that' (78). Yet irrespective of which position one chooses to adopt with regard to Brown's impression of inevitability and stasis, the true historical relevance of the play, I would argue, is an aspect of form rather than of content.

If *Translations* opposes rather schematically 'Irish' and 'English' modes of knowledge production – the tradition of the hedge school versus the science of cartography – no such facile binaries are employed as a structuring device in *Northern Star*. Gerald Dawe, who revered Parker as a teacher, writes that he 'cannot think offhand of another playwright who, in the space of roughly a decade between the mid-1970s to the late 1980s, offered more light *specifically* on the various historical Irelands which inhabit the country called the [sic] Ireland'.[58] This willingness to embrace multiplicity and difference is an aspect both of Parker's choice of topics and of his perspective on Irish history. Roche writes that Parker brought 'a colourful imagination to bear on a [Northern Protestant] community often characterised as dour and grey, by showing that it had a culture worth celebrating, and by bringing an openness of response to key historical events in the life of that community'[59] – such as, in *Northern Star*, the 1798 rising, which is hardly non-controversial territory in Northern Irish Protestant memory.

The mixed and diverse background of that community occasions an emphatic affirmation by Parker who numbers among his own forbears 'Scots–Irish, Northern English, immigrant Huguenot ... in short, the usual Belfast mongrel crew'.[60] Parker resurrects these ancestral wraiths in McCracken. For his protagonist, the rejection of cultural purity that constitutes Hugh's late insight in *Translations* marks not a final revelation but a point of departure:

> *McCracken*: Look at me. My great-grandfather Joy was a French Huguenot, my great-grandfather McCracken was a Scottish Covenanter, persecuted, the pair of them, driven here from the shores of home, their home but not my home, because I'm Henry Joy McCracken and here to stay, a natural son of Belfast, as Irish a bastard as all the other incomers, blown into this port by the storm of history, Gaelic or Danish or Anglo-Norman, without distinction. (7–8)

Of course, McCracken's imaginary republic of castaways is a libertarian dream, and neither does the unconditional approval of his own genealogical hybridity survive the forces of ethnic purity let loose in the play. At the end of the final act, the stage is swept clean of the wreckage of European history that persistently refuses ethnic categorisation. Still, Elmer Andrews thinks – rightly, in my view – that 'Parker wants to re-orient us away from a controversial focus on origins and toward the horizon of new possibility which play' – a key conceptual term for Parker – 'can open up.'[61]

To invest the past with these contemporary concerns is an audacious act of historical revisionism, judged by Richard Kirkland to be 'resolutely contemporaneous in its historical methodology'.[62] Several commentators have noted that Parker wishes to bridge the temporal gap that divides modern Ireland from its ancestral ghosts, 'translating' the spirit of history into a modern idiom.[63] McCracken is the onstage mediator between past and present, between the history he chooses to tell and the audience he addresses. But while there is an element of deliberate anachronism in this technique, it is correct and at the same time not quite enough to argue, as does Christopher Murray, that 'the imitation breaks down barriers between then and now and involves an audience in seeing the historical and the actual as sharing the same space'.[64] McCracken is both part of the story he tells and outside it, but he is no more and no less part of the 'actual' and the 'now' than any of the characters he summons on stage. His linguistic register in between the historical pageants is that of his audience, Elmer Andrews notes,[65] but that hardly means that past and present are seen in a dramatic constellation that is different in essence from any other historical play – which, after all, needs to be put on by actors in the here and now. More importantly, though, the play asks us not to reduce the matter of history to a pattern of experience which circumscribes and confines the actual. I want to suggest that the attempt here is not to view the past as a moral or political lesson in the tradition of Cicero's formula *historia magistra vitae* but to break the 'continuum of history' in the more radical materialist sense suggested by Walter Benjamin.

The play is set, the stage directions inform us, in 'Ireland, the continuous past'. The toponym first broadly generalises the location of McCracken's hideout but is then almost immediately specified as 'a farm labourer's cottage on the slopes of Cavehill outside Belfast' (3). Similarly, the temporal marker 'the continuous past' – which describes not a specific historical time but a grammatical tense – initially implies a conception of the historical as an on-going, uninterrupted, unbroken background flow, only to have that continuum disrupted by the action of a play in which history is rewritten, rearticulated in every moment of the now. It suggests not living in the past but a past seized by the living, because the present – Parker's present, as constructed through the play – does not merely exhibit ancestors 'in funny clothes'[66] but imagines a 'now' critically encompassed by opposing voices, adversarial dynamics and radical historical options. The central structural device of the play – to have the history of the United Irishmen presented as McCracken's 'night thoughts' (the title of the book by Edward Young which he is given by his mother in the play) on the eve of his execution – is almost to transform into an extended dramatic metaphor Benjamin's dictum that '[t]o articulate the past historically' means 'to seize hold of a memory as it flashes up at a moment of danger'.[67]

For the historical materialist, Benjamin writes, the present is reconceived as a messianic 'time of the now' [Jetztzeit][68] through the yoking together of specific historical moments that may be separated by centuries. This historical technique resists the mere adding together of separate incidents along a linear timescale. It charges up the past with retroactive power because to revitalise the historical is not to measure the distance that separates us from our ancestors, but to recognise in the tradition of the past an index of our own future. This 'time of the now' encompasses 'a temporality shot through, inlaid, layered with other times, with past and future temporalities'[69] – precisely the figuration of historical time operative in Parker's play in which the figures of the past are summoned on stage, not in an attempt at parody but in order to borrow their radical energies for use in the present.[70] This past is no nostalgic slide show but 'a disturbing, critical irruption into the present that even if it fans the spark of hope, also signals the present state of emergency'.[71] Thus, in *Northern Star*, 'the historical and the actual [share] the same space', as Murray writes, only in the sense that the present has entered into a constellation with a prior historical moment that implies not simply a causal link but the possibility of redemption. For the past is not a pile of documents but – in Benjamin's memorable formula – 'a fleeting image' that at each historical juncture needs to be wrested away 'from a conformism that is about to overpower it'.[72]

Parker implies as much when he writes, in a programme note to the Belfast premiere of *Northern Star*, that the Irish past 'refuses to express itself in a linear, orderly narrative, in a convincing tone of voice. Tune into any given moment from it, and the wavelength soon grows crowded with a babble of voices from all the other moments, up to and including the present'.[73] This comment points to the multiplicity of historical perspectives on any particular event as well as to the reappropriation of the past in each generation, but can also be read as a rendering of the kind of secret agreement that Benjamin suspected might exist between the generations. In this model, the voices Parker hears on the 1798 wavelength are neither exclusively those of later historians talking 'down' to their ancestors, nor only those from the past talking 'up' to the present. They are, rather, the voices he reimagines dramatically as his own, charged up with *Jetztzeit* and infusing a diacritical present with past and future temporalities. What this means is that any criticism of *Northern Star* on the principles that have been applied to *Translations* would be utterly misguided. The play wants to achieve historical 'accuracy' neither in fact nor in spirit, and is 'historicist' only insofar as it reads its own temporality radically through the aspirations of the past.

The story McCracken tells in the course of the play is about failure, disappointment and defeat, but it is also about the lure of liberty and the desire for change. He unearths almost casually 'the Presbyterian tradition of libertarian republicanism' even if the dangers of nationalism and the 'sectarian underpinning of all political activity in Ireland'[74] which eventually wrecked the movement never remain very far from view. None of the more radical implications of these ideas have enjoyed much popularity in the mainstream Northern Protestant culture from which Parker emerged and for which he wrote. But by celebrating them on stage, by literally conjuring up their disruptive energy, he brushes history, in Benjamin's much quoted phrase, 'against the grain'.[75]

Northern Star is also, on a more general level, an appeal to a flexible and creative use of the past, a suggestion that entrenched adversarial positions may be overcome and transformed in a distinctly playful approach to history.[76] Parker's notion of 'play' must not be misunderstood as mere frivolity, diversion or escapism. 'Play is how we test the world and register its realities. Play is how we experiment, imagine, invent, and move forward. Play is above all how we enjoy the earth and celebrate our life upon it.'[77] This celebration of *homo ludens* owes much in spirit to Johan Huizinga's book of the same title in which the 'play-element in culture' designates life-force, mental creativity and the civilising impulse.[78] In Parker's drama, '[p]lay is the process by which the given world may be imaginatively transformed'.[79] His creative use of the means of the stage testifies to this as much as the wit and humour of his writing.

History is another theatrical resource to be approached playfully. Though critics do not always remark on it, the play tells not one but two histories. The first is the political history of the United Irishmen, filtered through the reflections and memories of McCracken. The second is the cultural history of Anglo-Irish drama, narrated almost casually through the sequence of seven theatrical imitations.[80] These two histories do not only tell different stories, they also occupy different conceptual ground. Both proceed chronologically but while the first implies inherent causality, the second traces increasing social resonance; while the first examines the impact of material forces, the second champions mental liberty; while the first outlines a seemingly continuous pattern of conflict, the second celebrates the triumph of the creative imagination. It is true that this literary history which the play imaginatively performs deals with a growing sense of dispossession and exile, starting as it does with the 'breezy comedy' of Farquhar and ending with a 'grim Beckettian apocalypse'.[81] But by juxtaposing a history of personal frustration and political defeat with the story of the slow emancipation from cultural oppression – with the finding of a distinct literary voice – Parker challenges most poignantly any readings of the play that would reduce it, as Brown's does, to 'an interpretation of Ireland's past as cyclical nightmare'.[82]

Frank McGuinness: history and the single witness

Frank McGuinness's play *Observe the Sons of Ulster Marching Towards the Somme* deals, if not with a cyclical view of history, certainly with a nightmare. The play explores the psychic disposition and identity crises of eight volunteers from the north of Ireland who, prior to the First World War, signed up for service in the Ulster Volunteer Force (UVF), were then recruited into the 36th (Ulster) Division of the British forces, and ended up fighting alongside other British divisions in the Battle of the Somme on 1 July 1916.

The foray against the German lines on that day, 'the largest engagement fought since the beginnings of civilization',[83] was a disastrous decision in military terms, and over half of the men sent out of the trenches to attack the German positions were killed or wounded in a matter of hours. The whole episode was senseless carnage on a gigantic scale,[84] but elevated into a mythic moment of heroic human sacrifice in support of the union with Britain – a bond now 'sealed in blood' – this battle has always held a special place in Northern Irish Protestant memory,[85] comparable in significance only with that other decisive battle fought to defend a Protestant Ireland from Catholic insurgents – significantly, also on 1 July – the Battle of the Boyne (1690). The link between both battles is made explicit on almost the first page of the play: 'The sons of Ulster will rise and lay their enemy low, as they did at the Boyne, as they did at the Somme, against any invader who will trespass on to their homeland.'[86]

The subject matter of the play is thus the Protestant community of the north and the cultural myths that have helped to sustain that community's very special blend of martial prowess, selective memory and stubborn resistance to compromise and change. First staged in 1985, the play has received accolades from all sides, if not always for the right reasons.[87] The Battle of the Somme and Irish participation in it (both Catholic and Protestant) is surely an integral part of Ireland's twentieth-century history, yet even some of the play's most perceptive critics see it as sympathising with 'an alien point of view'[88] or as an exercise in 'imagining the other'.[89] McGuinness wrote the play in explicit opposition to such views: 'From the foundation of the Irish state there have been systematic efforts to equate the term Irish with one of the tribes, the Catholic majority, in the Republic. To counter such conveniences it is still necessary to assert the validity of the Protestant tradition.'[90] It is my impression that what is 'genuinely difficult'[91] about the play derives not so much from its focus on a historical experience that routinely seems to puzzle critics from south of the border[92] but rather from the formal complexity of this history play and from the conceptual framework it adopts.

The play comes in four parts. Part one is a long and angry soliloquy spoken by Pyper, a veteran of the Somme, who appears as his younger self in the rest of the play (more on this soliloquy below). The other three parts tell the story of the eight volunteers in a continuous series of selected flashbacks. In part two, 'Initiation', the eight men arrive in the training camp; their dialogues are marked by male bravado and tough talk of fighting, always undercut by the younger Pyper's latent homosexuality.

In part three, 'Pairings', five months into the war, the soldiers are on leave in Ulster. The eight men are divided into four couples; in each pair, one of the men is shown in deep personal crisis which only an act of intimate friendship can momentarily heal. The final part, 'Bonding', is set in a trench near the Somme on the eve of the decisive battle,[93] where we see the homosocial alliances between the men broaden into a group identity with a distinct cultural and political profile. At the end of the play, apart from Pyper, the 'sons of Ulster' will all perish on the battlefield.

Images of wasted flesh – flesh that is unclothed, eaten, sexually consumed, killed, exposed – recur throughout the play and link in distinctly religious terms the two prominent themes of sexuality and death. In their search for a personal faith, politics and religion overlap crucially for all the men. One dialogue in part three ends with a rousing speech in imitation of a Grand Master of an Orange Lodge. That speech, the most outspoken statement of loyalist prejudice in the play, is exposed as no more than a defensive and porous lifeline, 'all lies' (59), but it nevertheless appears to be the only route open to the characters in their attempt to fight off the traumatic revelations about themselves that the war experience has initiated. The true sadness of the play, the depressing verdict on the theme of loyalty – personal or political – is that this 'strange thing',[94] as Edward Carson described Ulster's unshaking loyalty to the Union in the House of Lords in 1922, can only be had at the price of utmost self-denial.

Part three is a powerful dramatic exercise in creating an imaginary Ulster homeland. The individual locations visited by the men in their home province together form an 'Ulster of the mind', a mental map of a cultural landscape replete with history and myth. The stage directions specify four individual locations: first, *'Boa Island, Lough Erne, carvings'*; second, *'a Protestant church'*; third, *'a suspended ropebridge'* – presumably the Carrick-a-rede rope bridge which connects the Antrim coast near Ballycastle with an offshore rock formation; and fourth, *'the Field, a lambeg drum'* – probably the Orange field at Edenderry, a 'sacred site' in the loyalist tradition: 'Holiest spot in Ulster' (43). In this cultural landscape the men experience their deepest transformation of character – significantly, not on a foreign battlefield but on their home ground. The dramatically evoked links between the specific and the general (a ropebridge; a church), between the mythic and the historical (the pre-Christian carvings; the orange field), between natural and man-made landscape elements, between profane and sacred sites, together construct an Irish map that differs from Friel's both in shape and in meaning – McGuinness's is a map that functions as a spatial survey of the Protestant historical consciousness etched into Ulster's natural geography. The different locations and the different traditions for which they stand complicate any understanding of the province as a monolithic cultural entity;[95] similarly, the men abandon stereotype in the four separate but interlocked dialogues that shift around themes of self-definition, missed callings, delusions of greatness, the cruelty of the gods, repressed fears and the horrors of war.

In the trenches, as the men are ready to go over the top (part four, 'Bonding'), they first abuse Catholic political myths in a garbled version of the Easter Rising and then attempt to re-enact a Protestant counter myth, the Battle of the Boyne. Sectarian abuse is thus followed by a play-battle within a battle play.[96] But, in the trenches, the Battle of the Boyne ends in a Protestant defeat, since Pyper, carrying one of his mates as King William on his shoulders, trips and falls. Clearly, the two battles (Boyne and Somme) are consciously collapsed into each other by the characters, but as the different results announce, such transhistorical links cannot be sustained in a play which is finally about the impossibility of translating the past into the present in terms of either an inherent congruence or a cyclical repetition. Historical and spatial equations are exposed as facile escape routes, dangerous and demeaning delusions. In the final image, young Pyper reaches across time and history to feed his older self the lines we heard him speak at the beginning: 'The house has grown cold, the province has grown lonely.' 'There would be, and there will be, no surrender' (80). Significantly, the titular 'bonding' turns out to be not so much an emotional handshake between the men in the trenches but a crippling deal between the generations.[97]

What fascinated most critics about this play by a Catholic from the south was its sympathetic and faithful portrayal of the psychic drama of Ulster Protestantism, a specific form of Irishness rarely given fair treatment in either the arts or the media. The repeated address in the play to 'the Protestant gods' – a reference to unionism's political 'founding fathers' such as Carson, but also a play on the inherent contradictions of a deeply Protestant culture celebrating its heroes in pagan rituals – appeared to strike a raw nerve, especially in the south. Grene writes that 'McGuinness seeks an understanding of the psychological, spiritual and political ethos of Protestant Unionism, resisting the crude stereotyping of it which has been all too common among Irish nationalists.'[98] This seems right, but how far the play can be forced into this public profile is a trickier question than the formula implies.

In Murray's useful summary, the play as a whole shows eight men, soldiers, 'as they form friendships which enable their identities to clarify and then coalesce into a collective consciousness of their specific Irishness'.[99] Yet this transition from friendship to Irishness – from private to public – is hardly straightforward in a play in which the dialogues and the activities of the characters, both in France and in Ulster, are so fragmentary and personal that they would appear to defy any attempt to appropriate their experiences in the name of a public agenda. Of course the very title of the play, connecting two deeply historicised toponyms, invites us to do just that, and when Pyper reveals, in a rare moment of frank talk without 'riddles' (57), that the true story behind his tale of the three-legged prostitute, which bewilders the other men in part two, is the suicide of his

French wife (56–7) in which he is somehow guiltily implicated, he also chooses to read a political moral into an intensely personal fate. For the death of his wife coincided with the 'real horror of what [he] found in Paris' (56), the death of his creative powers (he is a sculptor); and his failure as an artist he blames squarely on the legacy of his culture: 'when I saw my hands working they were not mine but the hands of my ancestors, interfering, and I could not be rid of that interference' (56). His own reading is that it was his urge to protest which made it impossible for him to escape the retributive backlash of his forbears, and thus left him no choice but to continue the same old battle cry of 'No surrender!'.

Yet even though the play itself frequently encourages us to translate the personal into the public, the attempt to decant the action of the play into a reliable background narrative is inherently problematic, because the very personal (and frequently contradictory) exchanges between the characters always offer a measure of resistance against their streamlining into a political moral. This is neither a play like Friel's which openly brings philosophical issues to bear on a political moment, nor a play like Parker's which drags political agents from the history books into the limelight of the stage. Both these plays openly assume public voices, in dialogue or argument, but *Observe the Sons* is a play entirely inhabited by common soldiers and their quiet, private voices.[100] It is, of course, a staple of Protestant thought to place the conscience of the individual squarely at the centre of public scrutiny, and among the most successful rhetorical strategies of nationalism has always been the attempt to strictly discipline the self in the interest of a public cause. But the link between the personal and public levels of meaning in this play is less one of symbolism or metonymy than of direct equation. There *is* no distinction between private and public in this play, no space for individual definition. In this sense the opening scene in the training camp is not just a topical choice of setting, but a spatial rendering of the denial of selfhood.

In many ways the play identifies this denial as the central problem of the characters and the culture that they define (and that is in turn defined through them). The subtextual rhythm of recurring themes – of authority and obedience, sexuality and shame, death and deliverance, etc. – verbally echoes the drumbeat that frequently accompanies the action. Huge lambeg drums and their deafening sound epitomise Orange culture. Their beat can physically hammer the self into public shape, as one of the characters discovers; metaphorically, it signifies the ruthless and monotonous self-discipline which forces the intimacy of each individual inner struggle into a public pattern, and thus claims each personal fate as an exemplary illustration of the grand narratives of Ulster Protestantism.

Or does it not? Only one personal fate – that of Pyper – can after all be verified, for the dramatic structure leaves unclear whether we have unmediated access to the history of the eight men – unmediated, that is, within the terms of the dramatic illusion – or whether what we hear on stage is all happening inside the elder Pyper's head.[101] The distinction between personal and public memory is thus blurred from the start. The uncertainty we are faced with when trying to read the personal into the public mirrors the emphasis of the play on the unreliability of all narration, even when what we are hearing are purportedly 'original' voices.

This is not only a problem for the audience but for the characters too. Pyper especially revels in moments of inexplicable antics where the point is precisely the incomprehension he causes in his listeners, both on and off stage. Significantly, the play dramatises not the war effort as such – no officer makes an appearance; we hear nothing about the progress of the campaign – and only indirectly traces the impact of the war on the formation of social identity of the people back home. No authoritative perspective, no discursive background causality, is available (other than what we choose to impose on the play through our knowledge of external circumstances). The title of the play equally involves the audience in an uncertain act of memory. Grammatically, it is an imperative, but who is asking us to observe these men on their way to the battlefield, and why? And what are they marching towards; that is to say, what does the 'Somme' *mean* other than a river in France and the site of a historic battle?

It is only in the last act, when Pyper invites his God to 'observe the sons of Ulster' and when the meaning of the Somme is being defined against the rivers of their home province, that the line is revealed not as a political imperative but as a desperate prayer. The reference to 'sons' may be merely a patriarchal and gender-ignorant shorthand for Northern Protestants; it may also indicate the causal link between their fate and the very genesis of Ulster Protestant identity. There are, significantly, no women in the play, and this absence points to wider issues than the identification of Ulster Protestants as a misogynistic masculine brotherhood. These men are 'lost' in the archetypal sense of having no home, no cradle to return to. What are they marching towards? The opposite of home – death and destruction – only finally to accept 'the constitution of silence'.[102] Their aggression, their self-hatred – and the desire 'to satisfy our blood lust' (12) is what the elder Pyper diagnoses as the real motivation to take up arms in defence of their province – allows no recognition of the other across gender boundaries, no genuine personal growth. This is a dead-end culture with no hope for reproduction.

Gender anxieties are, in any case, displaced on to the men's uncertain masculinities.[103] There are signs of repressed homosexuality in Pyper, who irritates his mates with repeated references to his 'fine skin' (17 *et passim*), and all men are forced, when back home on leave, into corporal intimacies to alleviate the psychic pressures of the war.[104] McGuinness has commented that '[f]or those men to come to a full appreciation of what they were fighting for, they had to learn what is conventionally called the female side of themselves. To know they were fighting for whole human beings, for full human beings.'[105]

These uncertain gender identities of the characters unfold their full meaning only with reference to their political fate, which is equally fragmentary, equally devoid of the reassuring certainty of purpose and structure. The opening speech by Pyper – in many ways the clue to the whole play – reflects this partial blindness after years of hostile repression. Pyper wakes from an uneasy sleep to accuse in rage his initially obscure interlocutors – the readers? the audience? the ghosts of his fallen comrades? all of the above? – of enlisting him against his will in an act of mistaken and enforced public remembrance: 'Again. As always, again. Why does this persist? What more have we to tell each other? I remember nothing today. Absolutely nothing' (9). Pyper's memory, these first lines reveal, has become public property, called upon in the repetitive ritual of daily recollection. In a sense the speech almost reads like a deliberate dramatic effort to prove Marx right who famously wrote that '[t]he tradition of the dead generations weighs like a nightmare on the minds of the living'.[106]

Pyper's refusal to co-operate in the collective search for historical meaning is directed both against the professional keepers of the past – 'I am not your military historian. ... There are sufficient records, consult them' (9) – and against the poets: 'You are the creator, invent such details as suit your purpose best. ... I will not talk, I will not listen to you. Invention gives that slaughter shape' (9). 'Invention' here encompasses the double meaning of rhetorical *inventio* and historical fabrication, and the whole irony behind Pyper's refusal to 'give that slaughter shape' is of course that he is himself one of the prime shape-givers in the play. He is a sculptor, albeit a failed one, and if what we are about to hear on stage is indeed largely his private rather than a public form of remembrance, he is also a story-teller, a narrative shape-giver. He also gave political shape to his country, even if this only came into constitutional existence five years after the Somme: 'I helped organize the workings of this province. A small role. Nothing of import' (10). His limited public role does not let him off the hook, though, for Ulster's ghosts are vindictive, denying Pyper the escape from memory: 'Must I remember? Yes, I remember' (11).

There is a sense in which Pyper's life after the war can be read not only as a form of repentance imposed upon him by his dead comrades (who are revealed as the principal addressees of his words when they start appearing as ghosts on the stage) but also as a direct and necessary continuation of his wartime experience of death and deprivation: 'I at least continued their work in this province. The freedom of faith they fought and died for would be maintained. There would be and there will be no surrender' (10). But this link between the Somme and the rhetoric of loyalism is a deliberate slip into political propaganda, the validity of which both Pyper and the play render deeply questionable.

There is, I believe, a more complex meaning behind the elder Pyper's horror at being turned 'into an example' (9). His insight is not merely that cultural memory has to be constructed in open contradiction to any 'singular version of the past as experienced by all the soldiers'[107] because such narrative singularity denies the very plurality of their wartime experience. Far more depressingly, Pyper sees the historical account – any account, it would seem – of his experience in essential denial of the very understanding gained by the men in their moment of ultimate recognition in the trenches, when the true delusion of repetitive history and the real source of their terrible fate – their destructive death wish – was revealed to them. To ignore *this* truth is not merely to distort the facts, it is to deny history altogether. When the elder Pyper reappears in the very last scene of the play, his passage through time – both the time of history and the time of the play – has followed, much like unionist political thought, the path of contraction and minimalism. One loaded word – 'Ulster' – has now come to stand for a memory of identity so complex that it defies the very attempt to be expressed in rhetoric. Ritual chant has replaced reflection.

Reviewing the change in character Pyper undergoes in the play, it is tempting to conclude that the battle experience led him finally to succumb to the tribal lure that he spent his youth rebelling against. Criticism is almost united on this point[108] and it would be futile to argue that this is not in some form the case. In the opening speech we clearly get a sense of Pyper having spent his postwar life in support of a cause he initially rejected. In fact he blames his comrades for this circular curse: 'You have never forgiven that I started out wrong. I looked on my family, my traditions, my faith, with greatest cynicism. It is your curse upon me. After the war, for you, I had to be different again. To be extreme. The world lay in ruins about my feet. I wanted to rebuild it in the image of my fallen companions. I owed them that much' (10).

But if we see, in the opening scene, a Pyper returned to the tribe, we also detect shades of his former self, a Pyper still in rebellion against the ghosts of his past, even if those ghosts have taken on a different guise after the Somme. Any critical assessment of Pyper's postwar identity as yet another 'Protestant god' needs to take account of these ironies. Pyper's initial 'outburst' (9) demonstrates that he is clearly not convinced, as his own sectarian rhetoric would affirm, that 'we, the Protestant people ... are God's chosen' (10). Rather, he is keenly aware of his own liabilities in the transmission of historical knowledge. For in terms of his relevance for the historical record, Pyper is the figure of the sole survivor. It is through his consciousness alone that we gain knowlegde of the events, of the different personalities involved, of the silent individual shapes implicated in the very public slaughter. His memory affects the telling of the tale but without him there would be no tale at all.

Knowing from the first scene onwards that he will be the only survivor colours our reception of the dialogue. We are focused on the figure of Pyper and alert to what makes him different. Hence the initial shock when he turns out to be a sardonic nihilist entirely unimpressed by wartime propaganda. On its simplest level, the play dramatises the pressures of (personal) memory on the single individual who escaped alive from the massacre, who lived to tell the tale. It is thus a version of a particular historical genre: the narrative based on a single witness.[109] Importantly, the historical responsibility of this speaking position is not recognised in legal thought. Testimony by a single witness, Carlo Ginzburg reminds us, is rejected in both the Jewish and the Latin juridical traditions by the general principle of *testis unus, testis nullus*: one witness, no witness.[110] Clearly, there is danger in all history-writing that would accept the outright rejection of such evidence. For the single witness, doubtful credibility only increases the burden of truth, especially since 'among the Latin words which mean "witness" there is *superstes* – survivor'.[111] Ginzburg comments that '[l]aw and history, it seems, have different rules and different epistemological foundations',[112] but for the survivor Pyper, legal disbelief and historical responsibility are not easily separated.

Rather, they coexist in unresolved tension. What is Pyper's responsibility as the single witness? Is he answerable to himself only, to his lost comrades, or to posterity? Has he in fact, by virtue of his horrific experience, absorbed the voices of his comrades into his own? This perspective opens up the possibility that the characters in the play are really divergent aspects of a single self. Alternatively, in view of the public significance of the dramatic action, the play invites us to read the destructive single-mindedness of Ulster loyalism as the psychic drama of denial and repression. Its monolithic profile is, then, the consequence of historical trauma. The central question that confronts the elder Pyper is how to separate the truth of his own historical experience from the discursive functions it has been forced to serve. It is for his alleged tampering with this truth, preserved only in his memory, that he keeps being haunted by the disturbing voices of the dead.

All too often, of course, political appeals to the dead are really rather shameless strategies of self-admiration: 'In the name of God and the dead generations ... Ireland, through us, summons her children to her flag and strikes for her freedom.'[113] The reference to the Easter Rising has obvious topical relevance in the context of McGuinness's play but there is a more substantial point to be made here. In a play entitled *Gatherers* (unpublished), written alongside *Observe the Sons*, McGuinness decodes nationalist rhetoric in what one critic has called 'a modernist inversion of the Proclamation of the Irish Republic'.[114] The passage in question reads: 'CHORUS: Irishmen and Irishwomen, in the name of *ourselves* and of the *living* generations, from which we have received *no* tradition, *no* nationhood, Ireland through us summons *nobody* to *no* flag and strikes for *nothing*.'[115]

The point of this inversion is less to expose treasured myths about the Rising as false rhetoric than to acknowledge the historical truth that since all narratives have a problematic relationship with reality, any 'document can express only itself ... its immediate context ... its origin ... its purpose'.[116] This statement should not be misread as mindless relativism or unlimited scepticism but as an affirmation of that very reality which is the stuff of all history. It is critical towards, *but does not deny*, the referentiality of all written history.[117] The real incentive to action for the 1916 rebels was not some obscure obligation to the dead but an overriding concern with the present. The testimony they left behind, farcically rewritten here by McGuinness, is – in the first instance – evidence of precisely this commitment.

In the same way, Pyper's remembrance should be less concerned with the past than with its very own temporality. For what remains of this particular war experience, the play shows, is Pyper's testimony, and that testimony is, finally, 'only' what it is: one historical fact among others. It cannot point beyond itself but it defines its own reality. One way of reading the play is, then, to see it as an exercise in the unearthing of what Pyper's 'fact' – the account of his very own reality – *should* include (but clearly has not included in the seventy years that separate the battle and the play): alternative histories, alternative sexualities, the fluidity of gender, male intimacy, weakness and self-doubt, even deviant religions and a deeply personalised and secular faith – in short, all that was blotted out in the battle and in the subsequent rewriting and cultural appropriation of that battle.

The answer to the question above about Pyper's responsibility is, then, that his only obligation must be to the truth of his experience. This truth has not had much recognition in the culture it helped to sustain. For the death of his comrades – Pyper calls it their 'extermination' (12) – happened not only on the battlefield, it happened again in the reception of their histories by posterity. Their true selves – their complicated, contradictory, oppositional selves – were sacrificed on the altar of the public need for positive identification as much as their real bodies perished on the battlefield. It is significant that Pyper, who escaped that latter death, includes himself in the question addressed to his dead comrades: 'Answer me why we did it. Why we let ourselves be led to extermination?' (12) *His* death is both the public kind of ruthless political appropriation and the personal kind of a distorted or unclaimed memory. The play, finally, reaffirms the truth of that memory on the public stage.

Conclusion

In one of the most important critical interventions into the debate about the relation between literature and Irish national identity in the last decade, Declan Kiberd has taken his cue from Brian Friel to argue that the task at the centre of the project of national 'invention' which he envisages for Ireland must be the act of translation.[118] 'Carrying over' – i.e. translating – the past into the present is a historical option that promises reconciliation of all the different cultural traditions in Ireland. What makes Friel's play such a suitable metaphor for this national project is that there is no original which the play could be a translation *of*. Each translation is thus really an invention, a kind of conquest of the past. That conquest, when the object is a formerly colonised culture like Ireland, is not wholly destructive because 'coded into even this imperial gesture [is] the recognition that the plundered culture possessed many a quality worth stealing'.[119] Thus, in each act of translation the elusiveness of the source may license creativity, the mode of transfer honour the colonised culture, and the disruptive impact on the target language subvert imperial hegemony.

This is the helpful dismissal of origins – or, better, the rejection of the tyranny of memory that the discourse of 'pure' origins entails – which Friel's hedge schoolmaster recommends towards the end of *Translations*. But the danger of each translation is, surely, its potential to silently morph into the next original. (That Friel's play is already considered a 'classic' after a stage history of only twenty-five years might be seen to confirm this.) For what any translation aspires towards, Walter Benjamin has noted, 'is undeniably a final, conclusive, decisive stage of all linguistic creation', and although no translation will ever reach that stage, the ideal as such remains its ultimate 'goal'.[120] Hence, even if the source of any translation can be imagined, invented or simply dreamt up, there is still the need to produce a fresh copy for contemporary use, a new story, which will then prompt the next wave of rewritings or inventions. From the perspective of the colonised, this copy, ideally, revamps the past not to faithfully preserve it but to have it disrupted, distorted and creatively misinterpreted. Nevertheless, each new copy or translation needs to be consistent within itself if it is to successfully 'carry over' its historical baggage – even if the 'original' contents of that baggage are latent rather than manifest, and require the creative work of translation to bring them nearer the full expression of that 'pure language' which Benjamin suggested was hidden or 'imprisoned'[121] in the actual linguistic form of a work. Each translation, then, in reimagining the present, is not only bound to the past as a reservoir of ideas, it is also committed to imposing coherence and structure on that past. But perhaps what the 'modern nation' (Kiberd's term) needs is not another image of a past merely transformed and adapted, reconfigured for present purposes, but an acceptance of its own incoherence and hybridity, and of the historical coexistence of many different forms of identity.

McGuinness's play would seem to warn against the idea of translation altogether. To translate the meaning of the Boyne into the Somme is an exercise in deluded tribalism, and in itself dangerous. As in *Mutabilitie*, it is more important to recognise and accept rupture, transformation and change – the kind of change that in order to be fully absorbed into a new national vision may require a critical authority beyond the power of the translator. Parker's technique of letting the energies of the past irrupt into the present also seems less interested in the salvaging aspect of translation than in the ability of the past to shock us into recognition. Ultimately, Friel's play may not advocate translation as a historical therapy either, affirming as it does the need to cut crippling links with the past. There is in all these plays much that is 'carried over' and exchanged, but the term that best describes this interaction between past and present, I want to suggest (drawing on the work of Francis Barker), is not 'translation' but 'parallax': the 'apparent displacement, or difference in the apparent position, of an object, caused by actual change ... of position of the point of observation' (*OED*). For 'object' read 'the past': from such a perspective, neither original nor translation can ever be a stable entity in itself, for both are continuously shifting position and point of view, both are intrinsically linked to each other and are thus always, by necessity, called upon simultaneously rather than in isolation.

The concept of the parallax emphasises our respective distance to the past while unsettling our position in the present, and acknowledges difference as a condition of spatial, temporal and cultural particularity. It enables a historicity that 'moves back and forth between past and present in movements of recognition and of differentiation',[122] elevating into a pattern of historical consciousness the incessant babble of different voices, complicated by a plurality of listening positions, rather than a newly translated and 'updated' version of the past. Kiberd writes that 'modern Irish writing set up shop under the sign of Babel'.[123] To celebrate the plurality of these tongues appears to me more important than to promote a concept of translation which 'allows a people to reach back longingly to a lost universal language', even if that dream is conditional on 'the knowledge that [this universal language] can never be repossessed'.[124]

While Friel's play obviously has paradigmatic status for Kiberd, his book does not mention Stewart Parker once, and accords Frank McGuinness only a passing reference on the very last page. I would suggest that placing *Translations* in the context of these other two plays allows us to get a more nuanced sense of Friel's conceptual approach to the staging of history. It is obvious that he places his hope for the survival of culture in the successful achievement of historical translations, even if, as Jimmy warns Maire, 'you don't cross ... borders casually'[125] – and presumably we are meant to imagine those borders as simultaneously cultural, sexual, spatial and temporal in kind. This emphasis on borders squares with Friel's concept of history as essentially a clash between cultures that allows no intermediate space. But, crucially, the play grounds the very possibility of historical memory in the state of temporary forgetfulness.[126]

In Parker's play, the crossing of borders is the very condition of modern Ireland, almost to the point where the borderline existence erases all culturally demarcated territories. Almost, but not quite, because at the end of the play both English political domination and sectarian bigotry have maintained their sway over Ireland. But in blasting a utopian moment out of the continuum of history (in Benjamin's phrasing) to align it with his own present, and by contrasting the political history of the United Irish rebellion with the literary history of Anglo-Irish drama, Parker imaginatively challenges the very intransigence of history. Mental play becomes a mode of access to a radically revisionist image of the past. McGuinness, finally, operates perhaps most recognisably the idea of the parallax. He offers us, in *Observe the Sons*, two temporally distinct visions of the Battle of the Somme, one of them a spectrum of eight individual perspectives, the other struggling towards its (as yet unrealised) potential of true testimony. The audience is challenged to relate these views to each other in a continuous movement of recognition and differentiation. The play thus forces us at all points to realign the actual experience of the past with its later discursive or mnemonic form.

Is it, then, legitimate to call these texts 'history plays', as I suggested we should at the beginning of this chapter? In 1592 Thomas Nashe saw the figure of 'brave *Talbot* (the terror of the French)' – the last of the old warrior elite in *1 Henry VI* – 'triumphe againe on the Stage' after having 'lyne two hundred yeares in his Tombe', 'his bones newe embalmed with the teares of ten thousand spectators at least ... who, in the Tragedian that represents his person, imagine they behold him fresh bleeding'.[127] If Nashe is to be trusted, then, a history play in the tradition of the Shakespearean prototype would require either the celebration of past heroic action or the creation, in the present, of a sense of *communitas*. That collective experience is generated through the immediacy of the dramatic action, Talbot's 'fresh bleeding'. On this count, probably none of the plays I have discussed would qualify. There are no heroes, at least there is no unqualified concept of a 'hero', and there is little attempt to create a communal theatrical experience that is unambiguously focused on the shared tradition of a common national past (there is a bit of that in Friel).

But all these plays, like Shakespeare's, reflect on the process of history and on the existential disquiet and confinement of the individual in that process. They do not ask questions about the moral quality of the ruler and the attribution of historical blame but they do disturb, perhaps even more profoundly than do Shakespeare's English histories, the sense of a past safely tucked away in the historian's archive. There is, clearly, no immediate concern in any of these plays with the 'accurate' representation of historical events but rather the negotiation of their possible meaning in the present. There is construction rather than imitation, poesis rather than mimesis, but crucially, also, there is the theatrical attempt to uphold against the presumed 'nightmare' of history the life-giving force of a historical consciousness sensitive to all the traditions of the past. Against oppression, bitterness and propaganda, these 'landmarks of modern Irish drama'[128] hold memory, play and the power of true testimony.

In attempting to answer the question of why such historical revisionism should be so prominently articulated in contemporary Irish drama, it would be foolish not to point to the impact of what one Irish critic identified some years ago as the main reason for the ongoing public debate about Ireland's national past, 'the unfinished business of history daily enacted in the bombings and shootings in the North'.[129] But if the 'Troubles' were the reason for many Irish playwrights to turn to history with a heightened sense of urgency, the preliminary and hopefully permanent end of the armed civil conflict in Northern Ireland[130] may allow us to find new answers to old questions. It is quite possible, as Kiberd has suggested in a different context for a different body of writing, that these plays have already moved beyond 'the field of force out of which they came'.[131] If so, there can surely be nothing wrong with a critical practice that seeks to affirm the impact of the changed circumstances of the present on the works of art from the past. And since one might share the dream that the present moment is – if not fully, then at least partially – driven by the desire to reach across cultural and ethnic divides, to acknowledge the fatal errors of an imperial past, and to invest seriously in the reconciliation of divergent cultural traditions, even plays which on the surface deal with nothing but death, loss, estrangement and the brutality of political repression may now be read in a different, far more positive light.

Frank McGuinness would appear to support this cause. 'I want to create a theatre [of?] celebration',[132] he has said about his own stake in the business of creating what he calls 'an Irishman's theatre'. But where, in McGuinness's theatre, is the celebration? 'Loss, despair, failure, violence, damnation, death and fear of suicide,' he helpfully summarises his work, 'these are the themes of the theatre I've tried to create. Where's the celebration?'[133] He gives one answer himself. The celebration is there in what he calls 'the simplest truth': 'We have been, we are, we will be.' Grammatical tense is only camouflage here. What he celebrates is life and survival, but also memory: we will be because we remember who we were. This means that we are, after all, not like Nietzsche's cattle, we are not grazing on the meadows of the present with no sense of time and history. If man and memory may indeed enter into a celebratory rather than a tragic bond on the Irish stage, another part of the answer could quite simply be the enactment (in drama) of a vision of history that imaginatively reaches beyond the repetitive patterns of conflict.

Notes

1 Claire Gleitman, 'Reconstructing history in the Irish history play', in Shaun Richards (ed.), *The Cambridge Companion to Twentieth-Century Irish Drama* (Cambridge: Cambridge University Press, 2004), 218–30: 218.
2 See Chapter 2, note 98.
3 Lynda Henderson, 'A fondness for lament', *Theatre Ireland* 17 (1983), 18. Quoted after Gleitman, 'Reconstructing history', 218.
4 Rüdiger Imhof, 'The past in contemporary Irish drama', in Jürgen Kamm

(ed.), *Twentieth-Century Theatre and Drama in English* (Trier: Wissenschaftlicher Verlag, 1999), 589–610: 590. See also Christopher Murray, 'The history play today', in Brendan Kenneally (ed.), *Cultural Contexts and Literary Idioms in Contemporary Irish Literature* (Gerrards Cross: Colin Smythe, 1988), 269–89.
5 Gleitman, 'Reconstructing history', 219.
6 For a summary of recent trends in contemporary Irish drama, see Chapter 8 in Christopher Morash, *A History of Irish Theatre, 1601–2000* (Cambridge: Cambridge University Press, 2002), 242–71.
7 On Field Day, see Marilynn Richtarik, *Acting Between the Lines: The Field Day Theatre Company and Irish Cultural Politics, 1980–1984* (Oxford: Clarendon, 1994); her chapter 'The Field Day Theatre Company', in Richards (ed.), *The Cambridge Companion to Twentieth-Century Irish Drama*, 191–203; and Richard Kirkland, '"Nothing left but the sense of exhaustion": Field Day and counter-hegemony', in Kirkland, *Literature and Culture in Northern Ireland since 1965: Moments of Danger* (Harlow: Longman, 1996), 121–48.
8 See Morash, *A History of Irish Theatre*, 235–6.
9 See Christopher Morash, 'Irish theatre', in Joe Cleary and Claire Connolly (eds), *The Cambridge Companion to Modern Irish Culture* (Cambridge: Cambridge University Press, 2005), 322–38: 334–5.
10 Ibid., 336.
11 Teresa Dovey, *The Novels of J M Coetzee. Lacanian Allegories* (Cape Town: Donker, 1988), 208. Dovey comments on the allegorical setting: 'Although geographically this remote outpost does not correspond to any actual setting in South Africa, it clearly represents a particular phase of South African colonial history: the phase of bureaucratized control which succeeds the phases of exploration and agrarian settlement ... and which, in the South African context, heralds the phase of militarized totalitarian control' (209).
12 J. M. Coetzee, *Waiting for the Barbarians* [1980] (London: Minerva, 1997), 125.
13 Stewart Parker, *Northern Star*, in: *Plays 2: Northern Star, Heavenly Bodies, Pentecost*, Methuen Contemporary Dramatists (London: Methuen, 2000), 32.
14 The reference is to the seventh section of Walter Benjamin's *Theses on the Philosophy of History* [*Über den Begriff der Geschichte*] to which I shall return below.
15 Derek Walcott, 'The muse of history' [1974], in Walcott, *What the Twilight Says. Essays* (London: Faber, 1998), 36–63: 36.
16 Ibid., 61.
17 Ibid., 63.
18 As Ulrich Schneider thinks in 'Staging history in contemporary Anglo-Irish drama: Brian Friel and Frank McGuinness', in Geert Lernout (ed.), *The Crows Behind the Plough. History and Violence in Anglo-Irish Poetry and Drama* (Amsterdam: Rodopi, 1991), 79–98: 97.
19 Derek Mahon, 'A Disused Shed in Co. Wexford', *Collected Poems* (Oldcastle: Gallery Press, 1999), 89.
20 Brian Friel, 'Extracts from a sporadic diary' [first pub. 1980], in Tim Pat Coogan (ed.), *Ireland and the Arts*, A special issue of literary review (London: Namara, n.d. [1982?]), 56–61: 58.
21 Christopher Murray, *Twentieth-Century Irish Drama: Mirror up to Nation* (Manchester: Manchester University Press, 1998), 216.

22 Fintan O'Toole thinks differently. According to him, Friel does not write history plays 'but plays that mock history'. He sees the plays as set in a mythical temporality where 'the times and reasons, the historical context, matter hardly at all. What matters is the image.' See his 'Marking time: from *Making History* to *Dancing at Lughnasa*', in Alan J. Peacock (ed.), *The Achievement of Brian Friel* (Gerrards Cross: Colin Smythe, 1993), 202–14: 202–3. O'Toole's critique – directed principally at *Making History* and *Dancing at Lughnasa* – is trenchant but he sets himself a straw target when he opposes the notion that Friel's plays amount to a 'composite history of Ireland' (202). This is not the purpose of a history play, and hardly what Friel is aiming for.

23 For a brief summary of Friel's major historical distortions, regarding especially the hedge school and the Ordnance Survey, see Sean Connolly, 'Translating history: Brian Friel and the Irish past', in Peacock (ed.), *The Achievement of Brian Friel*, 149–63: 149–53.

24 On the history of the Ordnance Survey, see J. H. Andrews's definitive study *A Paper Landscape. The Ordnance Survey in Nineteenth Century Ireland* (Oxford: Clarendon Press, 1975) which Friel used in the writing of the play, as he has freely acknowledged. Other books Friel consulted include a volume of local memoirs once intended as part of a series meant to accompany the Ordnance Survey maps, Colonel Thomas Colby's *Memoir of the City and North Western Liberties of Londonderry* (Dublin: n.p., 1837), Patrick John Dowling's classic study, *The Hedge-Schools of Ireland* (Dublin and Cork: Talbot Press, 1935) – a work in which the hedge-school tradition is largely romanticised – and George Steiner's *After Babel. Aspects of Language and Translation* (London: Oxford University Press, 1975). Richard Kearney's chapter on *Translations* in his *Transitions. Narratives in Modern Irish Culture* (Dublin: Wolfhound, 1988) contains a three-page appendix which lists the passages from Steiner which Friel used in the play, sometimes quoting Steiner almost verbatim.

25 Joep Leerssen, *Remembrance and Imagination: Patterns in the Historical and Literary Representation of Ireland in the Nineteenth Century*, Field Day Monographs 4 (Cork: Cork University Press, 1996), 102.

26 John Andrews, Kevin Barry, Brian Friel, 'Translations and A Paper Landscape: between fiction and history', *The Crane Bag* 7, no. 2 (1983), 118–24: 123.

27 In 'Notes for a future edition of Brian Friel's *Translations*', *Irish Review* 13 (winter 1992/3), 93–106, the historian of geography J. H. Andrews attempts to set the record straight on what he considers the 'historical truth' (93) of the Ordnance Survey. Andrews's interventions are valuable but problematic. He is surely correct when attacking 'the credulity shown by serious scholars in swallowing *Translations* as a record of historical truth or at any rate historical probability' (93), but positivist and interpretative approaches to the past simply cannot be piled up in the manner Andrews suggests when he distinguishes between 'mythological' and 'historical' options as two possible ways of reading the play (93).

28 That more is at stake in this debate than merely historical 'facts' has been pointed out by Şean Connolly, who argues that the play 'represents a distortion of the real nature and causes of cultural change in nineteenth-century Ireland so extreme as to go beyond mere factual error' ('Dreaming history: Brian Friel's *Translations*', *Theatre Ireland* 13 (1987), 42–4: 43). For an extensive

discussion of history and fiction in Friel's language plays, see Richard Pine, *Brian Friel and Ireland's Drama* (London: Routledge, 1990), 144–56.
29 Friel, 'Extracts', 59.
30 Nicholas Grene comments on the oddity of this device: '*Translations* translates what is by the play's own terms of definition untranslatable; its subtle and eloquent English speaks the lost and hidden language of Irish. An outside audience is allowed to understand an inside situation which is unintelligible to outsiders' (Grene, *The Politics of Irish Drama: Plays in Context from Boucicault to Friel* (Cambridge: Cambridge University Press, 1999), 45). In addition, Irish is heard on stage only in the form of several place-names, English is heard in full stylistic excellence. There is also, as Grene notes, no sense of difference in the *use* of either Irish or English by the characters (ibid., 44). Hugh, for instance, speaks both Irish and English on stage, depending on who he is talking to, but nowhere in his speech do we get a sense of what separates the two languages conceptually, despite the argument of the play as a whole that this linguistic difference is emblematic of the wider cultural divide between England and Ireland.
31 Bernhard Klein, *Maps and the Writing of Space in Early Modern England and Ireland* (Basingstoke: Palgrave, 2001).
32 Brian Friel, *Translations* (London: Faber, 1981), 21. Further references in the text are to this edition.
33 For instance, Gerald Fitzgibbon thinks that as a result of the new place-names 'Hugh ... is in danger of losing his way in his native landscape' ('Historical obsession in recent Irish drama', in Geert Lernout (ed.), *The Crows Behind the Plough*, 41–60, 52–3); and Richard Pine quotes the exchange between Hugh and Owen over where the priest lives as evidence of the 'collapse of orientation' in the play (*Brian Friel*, 165). This failure on the part of some Friel critics to distinguish between Hugh's mental map and the Ordnance Survey map can be taken as an instance of the lack of critical distance that mars superficial appreciations of the play. George O'Brien's remark in *Brian Friel* (Dublin: Gill and Macmillan, 1989), 105, that '[t]here is no necessary connection between the theodolite and the dictionary' is an important corrective of these positions, as is Declan Kiberd's reading in *Inventing Ireland: The Literature of the Modern Nation* (London: Vintage, 1995), 617–18. What is at issue in this scene is surely not the loss of spatial orientation but, as O'Brien writes, the loss of 'a network of cultural encodings, a tissue of interrelated namings and of cognitive assumptions made on the basis of acquaintance with those names' (George O'Brien, *Brian Friel*, 105–6).
34 Kiberd, *Inventing Ireland*, 617; 618.
35 'Translations and A Paper Landscape', 118.
36 In this I disagree with Declan Kiberd who, in an otherwise perceptive essay on *Translations*, argues that '[t]he hopeless stupidity of the attempt to impose a foreign grid on Irish reality is manifest in the fact that Yolland's model is etched in shifting sands' (*Inventing Ireland*, 619). The allusion to Foucault is tempting but misleading, for to assume that all cartography must be permanent is to ignore its experimental character. Yolland and Maire's map *does* work, both as a romantic code and as a means of communication, even to the point of allowing Maire to reiterate it in another scene.
37 John Gillies, 'The body and geography', *Shakespeare Studies* 29 (2001), 57–62: 58.

38 Edna Longley, '"When did you last see your father?" Perceptions of the past in Northern Irish writing, 1965–1985', in Longley, *The Living Stream: Literature and Revisionism in Ireland* (Newcastle upon Tyne: Bloodaxe, 1994), 150–72: 159.
39 In Steiner, the sentence reads: 'A civilization is imprisoned in a linguistic contour which no longer matches, or matches only at certain ritual, arbitrary points, the changing landscapes of fact' (*After Babel*, 21).
40 I am borrowing these expressions from Derek Walcott who writes that 'the truest writers are those who see language not as linguistic process but as living element' ('The muse of history', 62).
41 Friedrich Nietzsche, 'On the uses and disadvantages of history for life' [1874], in Nietzsche, *Untimely Meditations*, trans. R. J. Hollingdale (Cambridge: Cambridge University Press, 1983), 57–123: 83.
42 Ibid.
43 Kiberd, *Inventing Ireland*, 616.
44 And Steiner: 'To remember everything is a condition of madness' (*After Babel*, 29).
45 See also Elmer Andrews, *The Art of Brian Friel: Neither Reality Nor Dreams* (Basingstoke: Macmillan, 1995), 178.
46 We know that Yolland recites these names because we hear Maire repeat them in act three (60). All these names are Anglo-Saxon or Scandinavian in origin.
47 Edna Longley, *Poetry in the Wars* (Newcastle upon Tyne: Bloodaxe, 1986), 190.
48 For a fairly uncritical view that celebrates the 'immense richness of *Translations*' (187), see Ulf Dantanus, *Brian Friel: A Study* (London: Faber, 1988). Elmer Andrews briefly revisits the most trenchant criticism of *Translations* before giving his own summary of the play in *The Art of Brian Friel*, 166–81. Nicholas Grene, in a very perceptive reading of the play, suggests the 'brilliant balancing-act of the text' and its mediation of various political and cultural positions, as the reason for its popularity: '*Translations* ... offers an interpretation of Ireland to suit a wide variety of interpretees, making of the potential contentiousness of its subject a multi-dimensional asset' (*The Politics of Irish Drama*, 47).
49 Kiberd, *Inventing Ireland*, 618–19.
50 See his 'Foreword', initially written for *Three Plays for Ireland: Northern Star, Heavenly Bodies, Pentecost* (London: Oberon Books, 1989), now reprinted in the Methuen edition (note 13 above).
51 Anthony Roche, *Contemporary Irish Drama: From Beckett to McGuinness* (Dublin: Gill and Macmillan, 1994), 218.
52 Terence Brown, 'History's nightmare: Stewart Parker's *Northern Star*', *Theatre Ireland* 13 (1987), 40–1: 41.
53 Akiko Satake offers a detailed discussion of the historical references contained in these seven scenes in 'The seven ages of Henry Joy McCracken: Stewart Parker's *Northern Star* as a history play of the United Irishmen in 1798', in Eamonn Jordan (ed.), *Theatre Stuff: Critical Essays on Contemporary Irish Theatre* (Dublin: Carysfort Press, 2000), 176–86.
54 Parker, *Northern Star* (Methuen edition). Further references in the text are to this edition.

Staging history in contemporary Irish drama 119

55 Murray, *Twentieth-Century Irish Drama*, 197. Internal quote from Claudia W. Harris, 'From pastness to wholeness: Stewart Parker's reinventing theatre', *Colby Quarterly* 27, no. 4 (1991), 233–41: 237. Reprinted in Eberhard Bort (ed.), *'Standing in Their Shifts Itself ...' Irish Drama from Farquhar to Friel* (Bremen: European Society for Irish Studies, 1993), 281–93. See also Claudia Harris, 'Stewart Parker', in William W. Demastes and Bernice Schrank (eds), *Irish Playwrights, 1880–1995: A Research and Production Handbook* (Westport, CT: Greenwood Press, 1997), 279–99: 286.

56 The idea of 1798 as an all-Ireland rebellion that acknowledged and thus gestured at overcoming internal differences was the overruling theme of the bicentenary celebrations in 1998. Kevin Whelan wrote in the *Irish Times* on 24 March 1998: 'The United Irishmen ... were trying to negotiate a political structure here and with Britain, capable of representing Irish people in all their inherited complexities and allegiances; the peace process today is trying to do the same thing' (quoted after Roy Foster, 'Remembering 1798', in Ian McBride (ed.), *History and Memory in Modern Ireland* (Cambridge: Cambridge University Press, 2001), 67–94: 85). Foster points out that this repackaging of 1798 '[prioritised] the intentions of the principal actors ... above the actual outcome of events' (85).

57 See Terence Brown, 'Awakening from the nightmare: history and contemporary literature', in Brown, *Ireland's Literature: Selected Essays* (Mullingar: Lilliput Press, 1988), 243–56: 246–9. In 'Let's go to Graceland: the drama of Stewart Parker', in Jacqueline Genet and Elisabeth Hellegouarc'h (eds), *Studies on the Contemporary Irish Theatre* (Caen: Presse Universitaire de Caen, 1991), 21–33, Brown focuses on Parker's use of music and argues again that *Northern Star* and the other two plays of his 'triptych' of plays about Ireland, *Heavenly Bodies* and *Pentecost*, 'share a sense of Irish history in its local, regional and national manifestations as fated, doomed' (25).

58 Gerald Dawe, *The Rest Is History* (Newry: Abbey Press, 1998), 68.

59 Roche, *Contemporary Irish Drama*, 220.

60 Parker, 'Foreword', *Plays: 2* (Methuen edition), xiii.

61 Elmer Andrews, 'The will to freedom: politics and play in the theatre of Stewart Parker', in Okifumi Komesu and Masaru Sekine (eds), *Irish Writers and Politics* (Gerrards Cross: Colin Smythe, 1990), 237–69: 241.

62 Kirkland, *Literature and Culture in Northern Ireland*, 36.

63 See Murray, *Twentieth-Century Irish Drama*, 198; and Elmer Andrews, 'Stewart Parker', in Jochen Achilles and Rüdiger Imhof (eds), *Irische Dramatiker der Gegenwart* (Darmstadt: Wissenschaftliche Buchgesellschaft, 1996), 113–29: 120.

64 Murray, *Twentieth-Century Irish Drama*, 198.

65 Andrews, 'Stewart Parker', 117.

66 I adopt this phrase from Greg Dening's imaginative and powerful critique of historical re-enactments. See his 'Deep times, deep spaces: civilizing the sea', in Bernhard Klein and Gesa Mackenthun (eds), *Sea Changes. Historicizing the Ocean* (New York and London: Routledge, 2004), 13–35: 16.

67 Walter Benjamin, 'Theses on the philosophy of history', in Benjamin, *Illuminations*, trans. Harry Zohn, ed. Hannah Arendt (London: Jonathan Cape, 1970), 255–66: 257. Though this is the standard English translation of Benjamin's *'Über den Begriff der Geschichte'*, the text is not always faithful to the original and should be treated with care (the original text is available in *Illuminationen*.

Ausgewählte Schriften 1 (Frankfurt am Main: Suhrkamp, 1995 [first edn 1974]), 251–61). The English title is especially misleading. Benjamin offers no academic 'theses' and no 'philosophy of history' but fragments, ideas, speculations on the very term *'history'* (term: 'Begriff' [n], from 'begreifen' [vb] – to comprehend; literally, to grasp).

68 Ibid., 265.
69 Francis Barker, *The Culture of Violence. Essays on Tragedy and History* (Manchester: Manchester University Press, 1993), 108.
70 See Karl Marx, 'The eighteenth brumaire of Louis Bonaparte', in Marx, *Political Writings, Volume 2: Surveys from Exile*, ed. David Fernbach (Harmondsworth: Penguin, 1973), 143–249: 148.
71 Barker, *The Culture of Violence*, 108.
72 Benjamin, 'Theses', 257.
73 Stewart Parker, programme note on *Northern Star*, 1984 production for the Lyric Players, Belfast. Quoted in Andrews, 'The will to freedom', 259.
74 Roy Foster, *Modern Ireland, 1600–1972* (Harmondsworth: Penguin, 1988), 265; 268.
75 Benjamin, 'Theses', 259.
76 See Andrews, 'The will to freedom', 237–43. Andrews emphasises especially the concept of 'play' in Parker's drama.
77 Stewart Parker, *Dramatis Personae* (1986). John Malone Memorial Lecture, Belfast, Queen's University. Quoted in Harris, 'Stewart Parker', in Demastes and Schrank (eds), *Irish Playwrights, 1880–1995*, 292.
78 Johan Huizinga, *Homo Ludens. A Study of the Play-Element in Culture* [1938], trans. R. F. C. Hull (London: Routledge and Kegan Paul, 1949).
79 Andrews, 'The will to freedom', 238.
80 How Parker's 'literary pastiche' works on the stage is another matter. Terence Brown, who has seen the play in production, comments that 'the stratagem seems a slightly too well-worked means of avoiding the theatrical banality of the historical costume drama. Parker may have succeeded in writing a kind of theatrical quiz show. Spot the dramatist is fun, but that game tends to distract the audience from the sombre statement the work is making' (Brown, 'Awakening from the nightmare', 248). Elmer Andrews is equally critical: 'Parker's technique runs the risk of distracting the audience into a literary guessing-game in which the point of his citational mode is missed' ('The will to freedom', 260). Not having seen the play on the stage, I can only speculate, but it may be worth pointing out that both Brown and Andrews criticise Parker not for deliberate obfuscation but for luring them into literary detective work. That may be more of an academic problem, though, for the play should convince on the strength of its rhetorical diversity alone. The historical point behind the constant changes of dramatic style are clear enough, even if one is unable at each moment to correctly 'spot the dramatist'.
81 Grene, *Politics of Irish Drama*, 167.
82 Brown, 'Awakening from the nightmare', 247.
83 Paul Fussell, *The Great War and Modern Memory* (New York and London: Oxford University Press, 1975), 12.
84 Paul Fussell comments that the 'Somme affair' was 'destined to be known among the troops as the Great Fuck-Up' (ibid.).
85 For a thoroughly demythologising account of this battle and the fortunes of

the Ulster Division, see Philip Orr, *The Road to the Somme: Men of the Ulster Division Tell Their Story* (Belfast: Blackstaff Press, 1987).
86 Frank McGuinness, *Observe the Sons of Ulster Marching Towards the Somme* (London: Faber, 1986), 10. Further references in the text are to this edition.
87 See Helen Lojek, 'Frank McGuinness', in Schrank and Demastes (eds), *Irish Playwrights, 1880–1995*, 218–30.
88 Murray, *Twentieth-Century Irish Drama*, 206.
89 See Grene, *The Politics of Irish Drama*, 242. Grene's discussion of the play appears in a chapter entitled 'Imagining the other'.
90 Frank McGuinness, 'An Irishman's theatre', in Genet and Hellegouarc'h (eds), *Studies on the Contemporary Irish Theatre*, 57–66: 58.
91 Grene writes with reference to *Observe the Sons* that 'in a society [ie, the Republic of Ireland] where nationalist belief, active or inert, is so widely accepted, so little challenged ... the imagination of anything other than being Catholic and nationalist becomes genuinely difficult' (*The Politics of Irish Drama*, 242).
92 Fitzgibbon writes that 'McGuinness forces into light the parallel history of Northern Loyalism, a history and mythology which Easter 1916 routinely obscures in nationalist perceptions' ('Historical obsession', 48). The well-known story of Ulster loyalism and the significance of the Somme in Northern Protestant memory hardly needed to be 'forced into light' in 1985. The argument that nationalist perceptions obscure this history may be correct, but such historical amnesia should not be allowed to colour a reading of the play. Edna Longley, a Dublin-born critic writing from north of the border, knows what she is talking about when she observes of the double heritage of 1916: 'when the Rising and the Somme came to be processed by state ideologies [respectively, in the Free State and in Northern Ireland], the manner of their commemoration was shaped by sectarian idioms' ('The rising, the Somme and Irish memory', in Longley, *The Living Stream*, 69–86: 69).
93 This is wrong historically, as the Somme was several miles away from the position of the Ulster Division (near Thiepval) on the British front line. The nearest river would have been the Ancre, but this hardly matters. For a critical account of the facts behind the play, always alive to the tension between historical truth and personal memory, see Orr, *The Road to the Somme*. Orr's study, based largely on the oral testimony of Somme veterans, is a differently focused attempt at historical revisionism. In the preface, Orr reminds his readers that 'it is not always possible or even desirable to alter a veteran's collection of a long-ago battle in the interests of strict historical fact. ... [T]he fascination of the oral testimony in history is its subjectivity, revealing how things were, or seemed to be, for the participant in or witness to historic events' (viii).
94 Famously, these are Edward Carson's words from his speech on the Anglo-Irish Treaty in the House of Lords on 14 December 1922: 'Loyalty is a strange thing. It is something which you cannot get by merely sitting around a table and trying to find a formula for an Oath of Allegiance which means nothing. It is something born and bred in you.' Quoted from the excerpt included in Seamus Deane (ed.), *The Field Day Anthology of Irish Writing*, 3 vols (Derry: Field Day Publications, 1991), vol. 3, 353–62: 362.
95 McGuinness quite consciously thought of his eight volunteers as forming a

topographical and social map of Northern Ireland: 'Collectively [the eight] Ulstermen are drawn from the four quarters of what is now called the Six Counties; Derry and Coleraine in the north, Tyrone in the west, Fermanagh and Armagh in the south, and Belfast in the east. Their trades include blacksmith, weaver, baker, sportsman, preacher, shipbuilders, and sculptor' ('An Irishman's theatre', 61).

96 The wordplay is Edna Longley's, who has described the mock battle of Scarva as 'a play-battle within a play-battle' ('"When did you last see your father?"', 150).

97 For three differently nuanced accounts of the play, sometimes at variance with the reading offered here, see Eamonn Jordan, *The Feast of Famine. The Plays of Frank McGuinness* (Bern: Peter Lang, 1997), 25–45; Helen Lojek, 'Myth and bonding in Frank McGuinness's *Observe the Sons of Ulster Marching Towards the Somme*', *Canadian Journal of Irish Studies* 14, no. 1 (1988), 45–53; and Gleitman, 'Reconstructing history', 219–24. See also the perceptive comments on the play in Michael Etherton, *Contemporary Irish Dramatists* (London: Macmillan, 1989).

98 Grene, *The Politics of Irish Drama*, 247.

99 Murray, *Twentieth-Century Irish Drama*, 204.

100 Pyper may be an exception here because he comes from a 'respectable family whose greatest boast is that in their house Sir Edward Carson, saviour of their tribe, danced in the finest gathering Armagh has ever seen' (McGuinness, *Observe the Sons*, 56). But like another character, Roulston, who may share Pyper's social standing, he appears in the play in defiance of his socially privileged background.

101 Brown writes that '[t]he play is structured as three scenes imagined through the memories of a Somme survivor' ('Awakening from the nightmare', 250). I find no textual evidence to support this claim, nor for Brown's later statement 'that the events we witness [in part three, 'Pairings'] are images in the elder Pyper's memory' (ibid., 251–2). If the latter were true, Pyper must have extraordinary powers of divination, since the descriptions of the three pairs in which Pyper is not involved can hardly be 'memories' but, at the most, retrospective constructions. The same strictures apply to Eamonn Jordan's recent observation that 'we [the audience, the readers] are trapped within Pyper's gaze' (*The Feast of Famine*, 29).

102 T. S. Eliot, 'Four Quartets: Little Gidding' [1942], *Collected Poems* (London: Faber, 1963), 220.

103 For some thoughts on the issue of masculinity in the play see Grene, *The Politics of Irish Drama*, 250–1.

104 Roche comments that 'the questioning of the norms and stereotypes of sexual identity is a crucially recurrent feature [in the play], and in the criticism of the play so far written a consistently overlooked one' (*Contemporary Irish Drama*, 271). In response to Roche's call, the theme of sexuality in the play has since been taken up at more length by Jordan, *The Feast of Famine*, 25–45.

105 Quoted in Lojek, 'Frank McGuinness', 226.

106 Marx, 'Eighteenth brumaire', 146.

107 Jordan, *The Feast of Famine*, 29.

108 Jordan, for instance, writes that the play shows Pyper's 'slow and final submission to the will and imperatives of the tribe' (*The Feast of Famine*, 31). The

position is representative. McGuinness explains Pyper's change in different terms: in the play, '[Pyper's] death wish is thwarted, he learns to love, and he lives' ('An Irishman's theatre', 61).

109 Irrespective of whether the play *is* the narrative of that witness or not – that affects neither Pyper's role nor his memory. I would argue that the play is one possible version of such a narrative.

110 Carlo Ginzburg, 'Just one witness', in Saul Friedlander (ed.), *Probing the Limits of Representation: Nazism and the 'Final Solution'* (Cambridge, MA: Harvard University Press, 1992), 82–96: 84–5.

111 Ibid., 96.

112 Ibid., 85.

113 From the *Proclamation of the Irish Republic (Poblacht na hÉireann)* (1916), reprinted in Deane (ed.), *Field Day Anthology*, vol. 3: 733–4: 733.

114 Fitzgibbon, 'Historical obsession', 48. The farcical version of the Easter Rising told by the character McIlwaine in the play (64–5) similarly proceeds on a logic of inversion of nationalist myths. See Roche, *Contemporary Irish Drama*, 275.

115 Quoted in Fitzgibbon, 'Historical obsession', 48. I have italicised the bits where McGuinness departs from the original text. I have not seen the script of *Gatherers* which is described by Fitzgibbon as 'an unpublished theatre-in-education script, originally commissioned by TEAM Theatre Company and performed by them in Spring 1986' (ibid., 48, n. 6).

116 Renato Serra in 1912, quoted by Ginzburg, 'Just one witness', 95.

117 My unnamed target here is Hayden White who more than any other critic has theorised the discursive debt of historiography to literary models. See his *Metahistory. The Historical Imagination in Nineteenth-Century Europe* (Baltimore, MD and London: Johns Hopkins University Press, 1973); *Tropics of Discourse. Essays in Cultural Criticism* (Baltimore, MD: Johns Hopkins University Press, 1978); and *The Content of the Form* (Baltimore, MD: Johns Hopkins University Press, 1987). Ginzburg's essay 'Just one witness' is principally concerned with the intellectual development of White.

118 Cf. Kiberd, *Inventing Ireland*, chapter 34: 'Translating tradition', 624–37.

119 Ibid., 625.

120 Walter Benjamin, 'The task of the translator', in Benjamin, *Illuminations*, ed. Arendt, 69–82: 75.

121 Ibid., 74 *et passim*; 80.

122 Francis Barker, 'Nietzsche's cattle', in Barker, *The Culture of Violence*, 107.

123 Kiberd, *Inventing Ireland*, 636.

124 Ibid., 637.

125 Friel, *Translations*, 68.

126 Kiberd points out the important parallel with Marcel Proust's notion of associative 'mémoire involuntaire' (*Inventing Ireland*, 629).

127 These comments by Nashe in *Pierce Penniless his Supplication to the Divell* (1592) are among the few contemporary references to Shakespeare's plays. Quoted here from the excerpt in Stephen Greenblatt et al. (eds), *The Norton Shakespeare* (New York and London: Norton, 1997), 3322.

128 Eberhard Bort, 'Staging the Troubles: civil conflict and drama in Northern Ireland', *Journal for the Study of British Cultures* 2, no. 2 (1995), 141–60: 154.

129 Fitzgibbon, 'Historical obsession', 41.

130 Caution prompts me to report that this sentence was last revised in November 2005.
131 Kiberd, *Inventing Ireland*, 4.
132 McGuinness, 'An Irishman's theatre', 60.
133 Ibid., 65.

4

HISTORICISING THE TROUBLES IN NORTHERN IRISH POETRY

This final chapter will be concerned with poetic historicisations of the 'Troubles', meaning by that term both a set of historical events related to the civil conflict in Northern Ireland since 1968 – with all the attendant consequences of a constitutional, collective and emotional crisis – and a discourse produced by those events that branches off into several strands: political, military, cultural, moral, ethical. Both the crisis and its discursive expression have together spawned a rich and varied imaginative literature that is as stunningly excellent at its best as it can be frustratingly self-absorbed at its worst. Both have also given rise to discussions about the dynamics of community relations and the writing of history whose relevance and complexity point far beyond the province of Northern Ireland. Poetry is only one of the arenas in which such discussions have been staged, and though it is perhaps not the most influential, it is certainly one of the most visible. The principal authors I shall be discussing in this chapter are all prolific and critically acclaimed poets, with an impressive array of literary awards to their names: Seamus Heaney, Derek Mahon, and Tom Paulin.

As in the last chapter, my approach here is selective rather than comprehensive – my main focus is on poetic work from the 1970s and 1980s, and within that date range, on specific volumes: Heaney's *North* (1975), Mahon's *The Snow Party* (1975), and Paulin's *Liberty Tree* (1983). John Goodby's recent comprehensive survey of Irish poetry since 1950 rightly warns against a 'simplification of the corpus' of postwar poetry in Ireland,[1] but I make no claim that the work of the three writers I discuss here is representative of Irish poetry in that period as a whole. My aim is, again, to offer not an inclusive comparative analysis but an assessment of the formal possibilities of encompassing history in poetic writing – in this instance, at the particularly crucial historical juncture of the 1970s and 1980s, the most intensely violent phase of the 'Troubles'. Heaney, Mahon and Paulin have, of course, not fallen silent in recent years, but it is their early work that is most directly in dialogue with alternative forms of historical thinking. My reason for choosing to focus specifically on these three poets is that between them, they map out a set of characteristic strategies to come to terms with the *historical* dynamics of the political crisis which can be labelled myth, denial, and radicalism. Such shorthand contractions contain many risks, and much of what follows will be an attempt to explain my use of those terms in the detail they require.

Here I want to make just two points about my selection. First, Heaney, Mahon and Paulin are of course not the only Irish poets who in their work have turned to the 'Troubles', (and in order not to hide behind what are ultimately gratuitous markers of distance, I shall be shedding the inverted commas from here on). The section below will briefly cite some other poetic reponses to the crisis, but the genre of the 'Troubles poem' (again, no more quotation marks after this) is so diverse and heterogeneous that I cannot claim to have done justice to its vast frame of reference (nor have I been intending to do so). If there is the hint of a narrative underlying the poetic uses of history explored here, then it affirms John Goodby's sense of the redirection of poetic sensibilities attendant on generational change. For poets such as Heaney and Mahon, who started writing and were first appearing in print in the 1960s (i.e. before the Troubles), the response to the crisis is more persistently in search of an adequate ethical stance, couched in terms of a necessary moral commitment, than is the case with Paulin or, say, Ciaran Carson, both about a decade younger, for whom the Troubles are clearly 'more insistently part of their mental furniture', 'more constitutive of the self than in that of their predecessors'.[2] This does not mean that this generation of Northern poets was in any way more 'accepting of violence'[3] but it does imply a change of perspective and attitude that is reflected, for instance, in the shift from a relative formal conservatism (Heaney and Mahon) to increasing stylistic experiments (especially Carson).

Second, poetry is not the only literary genre which has served as a forum for the textual negotiation of the effects and meanings of the Troubles. Northern Irish prose and drama especially have been alert to the task of responding to the contextual situation in which they operate as imaginative discourses, yet it is poetry 'which, since the end of the 1960s, has attracted the lion's share of praise from readers and critics and which has been most influential on poetic practice beyond the island'.[4] This public attention seems justified, for it is in poetry that the reality of social and political disintegration has received its most exciting – and, arguably, its creatively most daring – literary treatment.

Anybody praising the achievement of recent Ulster poets as 'exciting' risks being accused of implicitly suggesting that it is *because* of the civil conflict that good poetry came to be written in the north. I want to make no such claim. For one, a generation of poets – Heaney, Mahon, Longley,

Simmons, etc. – were writing long before the first bombs exploded in Belfast, and would have continued to do so even without the Troubles forcing them into the poetic response to an experience neither of them desired to live through. If it is nevertheless true that a shared sense of their public role made many poets in Northern Ireland turn to the Troubles as a topic they could not ignore,[5] it is also worth recalling Michael Longley's angry retort to the mere suggestion that the political violence in Ulster may have quickened his poetic instinct: 'I find offensive the notion that what we inadequately call "the Troubles" might provide inspiration for artists; and that in some weird *quid pro quo* the arts might provide solace for grief and anguish.'[6]

In the early 1970s, Longley had already complained that '[t]oo many critics seem to expect a harvest of paintings, poems, plays and novels to drop from the twisted branches of civil discord'.[7] Yet it was not only foreign academics and the international media in search of sensational 'war poetry' who fuelled that expectation in their writings. Seamus Deane pronounced in 1986, discussing Heaney's 1975 volume *North*, that 'the roots of poetry and of violence grow in the same soil'.[8] If it is hard to see how such a statement can avoid being guilty of precisely the position Longley rejects, it is even harder to see how Deane's metaphor is meant to be read. Does the sharing of 'the same soil' (a specific type of soil or the same stretch of ground?) imply conceptual affinity rather than the accident of spatial and/or temporal co-existence? Or does a poet need to have any direct experience of violence (as agent or victim?) to be able to write poetry? Or is poetry verbal violence of a kind that can usefully be compared to the political violence Northern Ireland had been experiencing for almost two decades when the sentence was being written? Deane's comment raises more thorny questions than it could ever hope to answer.

The terms of the critical debate have shifted since the 1980s, and the issue of poetry and violence is now being discussed with considerable insight, even though the theorising of this link remains deeply problematic.[9] My aim in this chapter is not to continue a discussion over the relative merits of an individual poet's moral or political stance. I start from the premise that the poetry of all three of my authors makes a serious point, and that it is a genuine response to a particular experience, however culturally or ideologically conditioned. My question is more narrowly framed. It is focused, as it has been throughout this study, on the concept of history that constitutes the literary court of appeal in these poems: how has the crisis been historicised in poetry; how has the Troubles poem imagined and processed the encounter with history; what purpose has history served in its poetic representation?

To ask about the operation of poetic historiography rather than about visions of community or conceptions of cultural identity makes sense (to me) because the poetry itself flags this dialogue with an idea of history far more prominently than with what currently constitutes a more fashionable critical concern, the politics of identity. In what follows I shall first attempt to outline some of the historical concerns of the 'classic' Troubles poem as it has been anthologised by Frank Ormsby, and then look in turn at my three main writers, before offering some tentative conclusions.

Anthologising the Troubles poem

Frank Ormsby's 1992 anthology *A Rage for Order* marks a culmination of 'the poetry of the Northern Ireland Troubles' (subtitle) in more senses than one.[10] The first is the surely not very accidental timing of its publication, which coincided almost exactly with the twenty-fifth year of the modern phase of the Troubles – hardly an 'anniversary' but certainly a significant date on which to pause and look back over the literary response to a crisis that had by then lasted a whole generation. It was also the same year in which the Opsahl Report took stock of Northern Irish society and produced what I consider to be still one of the best (if not flawless) analyses of how a divided community has come to terms (or not) with the effects of long-lasting civil disruption.[11] Soon after publication of both the anthology and the Opsahl Report, the peace process would yield its first results, leading to the exhilarating moment of the first – sadly only provisional – IRA ceasefire declared on 31 August 1994.

A different sense in which the anthology marks a culmination is a more narrowly literary one. No anthology can quite escape the danger of solidifying into a canon what until then has been a free-floating body of disparate works by a disparate group of authors. The danger inherent in this act of anthologising is a version of Owl of Minerva syndrome – that what can be recognised as a pattern is no longer a pressing concern – complete with the implication that the evidence of the poetic response has exhausted the imaginative possibilities. Ormsby's title adds another twist to this argument. 'A rage for order' may have indeed been a preoccupation of many poets – Heaney's fear of his potential failure '[t]o lure the tribals shoals to epigram / And order'[12] comes immediately to mind, as does Mahon's definition of poetry in the war zone as 'An eddy of semantic scruple / In an unstructurable sea' (lines that can be found in the very poem from which Ormsby pinches his title).[13] But this urgent poetic quest for (political, social and mental) order is in danger of being trivialised in the arrangement of categories and chapters which the anthologiser must set up, which might be taken to imply that some form of aesthetic order has indeed been found, making the conflict appear manageable, despite the tangible evidence of continuing *dis*order.

The set-up of the anthology could also invite the accusation of being anti-historical in intent, because it leaves the poems hanging suspended in a kind of temporal no man's land stretching from the creation of Northern Ireland as a constitutional entity (1921) to the year of the anthology's publication (1992). As readers of the collection, we are given no information when these poems were written, since no dates are supplied, and there is no indication whether the sequence in which they appear in the book translates into a chronology of publication (it does not). The only exceptions are those poems in which dates are part of the poem itself. This is all the more peculiar as historical themes, and hence fixed moments in time, inform many of these texts. Leaving the reader at a loss regarding the date of the poetic response thus results in an odd blurring of the specific temporalities of the Troubles. This enforced timelessness ignores both the history of the crisis itself – its different phases, their very different dynamics, and the changing nature of the emotional response – and what constitutes, in a sense, their 'prehistory'.

Just as we cannot date the poems in the book, we also have no means of reconstructing the location of a particular poem in the larger oeuvre of the writer. This is not irrelevant because many of the poems which Ormsby anthologises are actually culled from collections with a particular aesthetic design, an overall framework and purpose, in which writers do not merely string together individual poems but construct the sequence as a coherent entity, setting up patterns of mutually illuminating cross-references, all of which are lost in the anthology. The historicising impulse of the poems is thus blurred both by being inserted into the shadowy timeframe of the anthology within which all these poetic interventions somehow occur simultaneously, and by decontextualising them through their subsumption under Ormsby's own thematic categories.

I dwell on these formal points in some detail because I think that the poems themselves are explicitly written to counter the gravitational pull of such dehistoricising tendencies. Many poems, for instance, address specific atrocities of the Troubles or refer to precise historical moments. The elegies in Ormsby's third section (of six) are often written for a specific victim, killed on a specific date in a specific place. Throughout the poems, the prominent themes of suspicion and mistrust, of decayed relations among neighbours, of tribal behaviour patterns, of 'the slickness of the media',[14] etc., are always historically informed. The same holds true for the recurring imagery specific to Troubles poetry, 'of drums, bombs, banners, sectarian graffiti',[15] explosions, corrugated iron, splintered glass, 'Saracen, Kremlin–2 mesh. Makrolon face-shields. Walkie-Talkies',[16] and all the different bombs: car bombs, booby-trap devices, petrol or acid bombs, nail bombs, etc. Inscribed in such poetic catalogues are traces of a material history of the Troubles.

How does history figure in these poems more broadly? One of the principal strategies is to evoke episodes from the past with immediate relevance to contemporary Northern Ireland, setting them into suggestive contrast or parallel with the present. Michael Longley's 'Wounds' is a good example of the contrastive technique. In this poem, Longley – or the speaker in the poem (I doubt there is much difference) – first recovers two images stored in his father's memory, the first of the men of Ulster Division at the Somme (whom we met in the last chapter), and the second of an Anglo-Scottish padre, long-time companion of his father, who finally dies of his war injuries fifty years after the Somme with these last words on his lips: '"I am dying for King and Country, slowly"'.[17] The speaker sees this groundswell of misguided but genuinely felt patriotism repeated in more current death scenes as he buries beside his father 'Three teenage soldiers, bellies full of / Bullets and Irish beer, their flies undone'.

All the dead soldiers in this poem are defenders of the Union but the purpose and sense of urgency that prompted the Ulster Volunteers to die on the battlefields at the Somme has yielded to the pathetic display of dying teenagers, shot in a moment of human need, 'their flies undone'. The bathos of this line, reinforced by the alliterative zeugma 'Bullets and ... beer', is repeated in the final image of the poem which juxtaposes in deliberately incongruous terms the intersection of domestic trivia with the extremity of sectarian killing. Another victim, a bus conductor, who died not in his boots but in his slippers, was shot through the head by a frightened youth, with the TV still running, and the dishes on the table: 'To the children, to a bewildered wife, / I think "Sorry Missus" was what he said'. The public show of heroism of the Ulster Division is reduced to the cowardice of a 'shivering boy' clumsily abusing the privacy of the home.[18]

The same impulse – to read the present as a perverse repetition of an already misguided past – farcically underwrites James Simmons's 'Ulster Says Yes': 'we frightened you Catholics, we gerrymandered, ... // However, we weren't Nazis or Yanks, / so measure your fuss / who never suffered like Jews or Blacks'.[19] Such laboured sarcasm strikes a note of anxiety that runs through many of the more self-deprecating poetic accounts from a Protestant perspective: Gerald Dawe's satire of Protestant self-righteousness in 'Little Palaces', for instance, or John Hewitt's self-accusation of having been a 'coaster'.[20]

A variation of this technique – seeing the past recur in distorted form in the present – is the hallmark of some poems which turn to Ireland's mythic prehistory. Ciaran Carson's 'Bloody Hand' sees the story behind one of the central images of Ulster Protestant identity – the Red Hand of Ulster – re-enacted daily in the shootings and bombings, just as the hand throwing a shadow on the wall might mimic the hand grasping a gun, or the hand of a victim cut off by a bomb might reappear again elsewhere: 'Was it the left hand / Hacked off at the wrist and thrown to the shores of Ulster? Did Ulster / Exist? Or the Right Hand of God, saying *Stop* to this and *No* to that?'[21]

These lines are taken from Carson's 1989 landmark volume *Belfast Confetti* (represented with several poems in Ormsby's anthology), in which he evokes the beaten, war-torn capital of Northern Ireland itself as a paradigm of historical consciousness. He does so in a manner that is no less committed to history for being principally concerned with the modern space of the city. In this collection, points of historical reference at first seem to offer little more than the occasion for numerological wordplay or self-reflective speculation, feeding the endlessly repetitive talk of what might have been, 'Making 69 – the year – look like quotations marks ... there's any God's amount / Of Nines and Sixes: 1916, 1690, The Nine Hundred Years' war, whatever'.[22] Such lines appear to dismiss history altogether, denouncing even just the attempt to *think* historically as a semantic dead end or a route to 'oblivion'. History is presented as a verbal wrangle over dates or a postmodernist *non sequitur* rather than as the recovery of stable, coherent form: the digits 6 and 9 do not add up to the beginning of a historical crisis but are merely scare quotes holding the present at bay.

But from this base the volume develops a sense of history that reads an uncertain past into an uncertain present, falling into a thousand pieces and possibilities – the titular confetti – once it is exposed to the obsessively cross-referencing mind of the poet. In doing so, history – viewed mainly through a sequence of maps whose referentiality to the sensual world is fragmented and fractured – presents itself as happening in the nod of the head, the twinkling of an eye, in the shadow visible around the street corner – and although all of these moments are charged up with sinister energies in the context of a sectarian society where armed gunmen communicate by such signs (and where the material state of the map signals the explosive politics of the situation: on an old map of Belfast, 'the Falls Road hangs by a thread'[23]), this is a scaled-down form of history, lowered from the level of the oppressive grand narrative to the human measure of the everyday and domestic: history as sense and feeling, occurring in the shape of the quotidian.

Carson's acute awareness of the textuality of all historical reference is not a generally shared feature among the more mainstream Troubles poetry anthologised by Ormsby, in which the continuous cycle of repetition and inevitability is frequently offered as the blueprint underlying events in Ulster: 'These are the martyrs / Who die for a future buried in the past'.[24] A similarly static view of the past informs John Hewitt's sense of himself as 'maimed by history',[25] or Thomas McCarthy's notion of bourgeois ignorance where 'History' is not a living process but a pile of books, '[resting] on the brown hall table / beside the bird-guides and seed catalogues'.[26] Such views, for all their commitment to an increased historical awareness, implicitly foster an understanding of history that conceives of the past as a monolithic entity with the near-demonic power to shape and mould contemporaries, in spite of contrary convictions and inclinations.

Other poets articulate a view of history more alive to the constant rewriting and refashioning of the past by the present. For Louis MacNeice, a central influence on a whole generation of Ulster poets, 'history' is the curse of a long memory which 'never dies, / At any rate, in Ireland',[27] maintaining its hold on contemporaries through its ubiquitous presence in the public arena. For 'Wystan' (ie, Auden), one of the speakers in Paul Muldoon's '7, Middagh Street' (where he appears alongside MacNeice, Dali, Chester Kallman and others), this pushes art and poetry into a secondary, subaltern position, '[f]or history's a twisted root / with art its small, translucent fruit // and never the other way round'.[28] Spoken 'with a kind of finality on the subject',[29] these lines appear to disempower any creative writer grappling with the forces of history.

Elsewhere, Paul Wilkins holds a related view in his poem 'A Graveyard in Ulster'[30] in which each burial of a Troubles victim implies that the present is given to amnesia – to the burying of people in earth, thus straightening out, flattening, the twisted knots of existence – in a way that simply leaves no room for engagement with the complexities of the past. Amnesia becomes wish-fulfilment of a different sort in Robert Johnstone's dream that the weight of the past will be lifted off our shoulders by some kind of mnemonic tsunami when 'the wave of history' will eventually 'drown grave, field and thoroughfare / from the Garden of Eden to Edenderry'.[31] In an interesting mental reversal, history is here imagined as a force not of conservation but of obliteration, as the tidal wave that leaves behind *no* memory of the past.

Taken together, these examples might suffice to show that history, in most of the historically oriented Troubles poetry collected by Ormsby, either tends to be equated with the mystical demon that needs to be excised from the here and now, or takes the form of a backward glance at an earlier phase in the existence of Northern Ireland (or in the historic state formations which preceded it), to read the present as some form of inevitable or unfortunate consequence of this past. Conceptions of history that are, in my view, significantly more complex than these positions allow will be discussed in the sections that follow, starting with the work of Seamus Heaney whose contributions to *A Rage for Order* outscore (in numbers) those of any other single contributor.

Seamus Heaney: bodies and bogs

As we have already seen in the brief reference to 'Belderg' in Chapter 1, in Heaney's early poetry – that is, up to and including the landmark volume *North* (1975) – his rewriting or rethinking of history has crystallised around the recurring image of a specific landscape feature: the wet, soggy bogland, 'common ground', mysterious and sexualised, a space apostrophised as hoarder of myth, tradition and folklore. Since the bog poems are probably the most famous in the Heaney canon, I should say at the outset that my return to them in this chapter is not motivated by any mistaken assumption that they alone are representative of his poetic concerns.[32] In the volumes published since at least *The Haw Lantern* (1987), Heaney has left far behind the digging metaphor that was programmatically announced in the opening poem of his first book, *Death of a Naturalist* (1966), as a poetic equivalent of the agricultural vocation of his forbears, and that found such a thrilling imaginative extension in the bog poems. But, despite the move away from the tropes of earth, bog and soil towards a poetry of air, light and spirit, the bog remains a central idea in terms of Heaney's historical concerns. In what follows I shall first consider the local conditions that allow Heaney to elevate such an amorphous, uninhabitable space as a peat bog into a figure of history; second, I will look at the poetic function of this space and discuss more specifically the historical counter-vision it enables; and finally, I shall ask how this project of poetic historiography, developed in the 1970s, comes to terms not only with the legacy of the past but also with the imperatives of the future.

In the ten volumes published to date, Heaney addresses history in many forms, most frequently through quotation and intertextual allusion, often through the adaptation of archaic poetic styles, sometimes through a process of imaginative empathy: for instance, when he assumes historically or mythically defined speaking positions, such as the voice of Joyce and other Irish writers, or when he slips into the identity of the mythical Gaelic bird-king Sweeney (whom we have already met in Frank McGuinness's *Mutabilitie*) in the *Station Island* poems.[33] Such historical gestures, while never free of a sense of imperial injustice, are generally motivated by the search for an inclusive reading of the past that would reconcile or negotiate between opposing cultural traditions. Surprisingly, perhaps, for a poet so centrally aware of history as Heaney, his writing has been more interested in space than in time, and his poetic topographies are suffused with a sense of place that is, on the one hand, literate, learned and conscious and, on the other, lived, illiterate and wholly unconscious.[34] An early poem such as 'Anahorish',[35] for instance, dwells on the learned aspects of etymology as much as on the spiritual kinship with a known and lived location. The reading of his imaginative and actual home, Ireland, as *bogland* serves a historical purpose at once more comprehensive and more politically committed than any direct biographical or topical reference.

Describing the bog as a kind of natural hard disk from which no data will ever be erased, Heaney 'began to get an idea of the bog as the memory of the landscape, or as a landscape that remembered everything that happened in and to it'.[36] The obvious political point behind this image was Heaney's 'tentative unrealized need', as he put it, 'to make a congruence between memory and bogland and, for want of a better word, our national consciousness'.[37] Perhaps *un*conscious (political or otherwise) would have been the better word, for in this poetic bog memory generally lies submerged to be interrupted only by sudden, involuntary recall. For as a historical reservoir, the bog is as untapped as it is infinite: 'The wet centre', Heaney writes in the programmatic poem 'Bogland', 'is bottomless'.[38] This poem exploits the image of the bog as both a cultural archive and a national myth: 'We have no prairies', it opens, 'to slice a big sun at evening' – and elsewhere Heaney has added what the poem only implies: 'but we have bogs'.[39]

To metaphorically equate the bog with historical memory is justified on a material level by the many historical and archaeological artefacts actually discovered in bogs, now frequently on display in another kind of storeroom of historical consciousness, the museum.[40] But the value of the bog as 'an answering Irish myth'[41] to the quintessentially American myth of the free, open space – the prairie – indicates that more is at stake than merely the digging for lost or discarded objects of an earlier civilisation. The bog, for Heaney, defines a territorial numen, a *genius loci*, spirit of place; it is through the bog and its attendant mysteries – literally mysteries in the sense of both skills and secrets – that Ireland as a spiritual as much as a geographical home can claim the status of a tangible truth and a source of *communitas*. The bog, then, signals home and 'belonging' for Heaney, both as a figure of rootedness and of deep, illiterate loyalty. The six-part poem 'Kinship', in which the bog acts as both preserver and saviour of history, as archive and hiding-place, is probably the most sustained attempt in *North* to transform the bog into a kind of historical consciousness: 'enbalmer [sic] / of votive goods ... Sword-swallower ... casket, midden, / floe of history'.[42] The inflationary use of archaic kennings in this poem, a legacy of old Norse poetry, gives some sense that its loyalty lies ultimately with an ancient spiritual presence inscribed in, or rather absorbed by, the receiving earth: indiscriminate sponge, not carefully edited manuscript, would be the approriate metaphor to describe the function of the bog as a historical archive – extended and spatialised here into a mental state, 'outback of my mind'.

The deeper irony about this imaginative use of landscape is that it is ultimately owed not to Irish but to English intervention. For to claim, as one critic has done, that 'Heaney's imaginative sympathies have long been directed toward the preserving landscape, the landscape that magically provides contemporary Ireland with the physical evidence of its cultural tradition'[43] is to walk into a large trap. There is nothing magical about this landscape; to put it bluntly, it was invented (or 'translated', which – as we saw in the last chapter – is much the same thing) by the Ordnance Survey. In the late 1820s the Ordnance Survey, much maligned nowadays owing to its negative depiction in Friel's *Translations*, 'expanded ... into a huge synopsis of the Irish physical and cultural landscape' which 'salvag[ed] the original placenames from neglect or corruption by painstaking inventorization of manuscripts, giving them English transliterations rather than translations' – witness Heaney's 'Anahorish' – 'and capturing a great deal of local lore and learning from communities which would fifteen years later be swept away by the Famine'.[44] This landscape works a bit like the myth of the nation: at its inception, it has already been there forever, 'time out of mind'.[45] There is, of course, a Gaelic tradition of placename poetry that Heaney also imaginatively draws on, but this was less an attempt to infuse landscape with a territorial numen than a form of ordering and classifying topographical knowledge in an effort of mythological cartography. The *dinseannchas* are inventories, catalogues, etymological footnotes, not poetic quests for cultural identity, as Heaney has noted himself.[46] All this does not make the bog poems a lesser poetic achievement but it reminds us that they owe their existence to the craft and skill of the poet, not to some mysterious, 'mould-hugging' Irishness.

Heaney exploits the bog as a historical myth in a sequence of about ten poems, most of them included in the 1975 volume *North*. John Hildebidle has written that '*North* is a book especially concerned with history; or rather, with histories',[47] and he moves on to identify four different historical narratives in the book: there is 'political history' – meaning by that the successive invasions of Danes, Normans and English, all of which get a mention in some form or other; there is 'mythic cultural history' – focused on the bog, and contained in the allusions to the classical world in the two 'Antaeus' poems; there is 'literary history' – evident in numerous references to Baudelaire, Yeats, Wordsworth, and several contemporary writers; and there is Heaney's 'personal history' – prominent especially in the second, more 'journalistic' part of the book. Hildebidle's groupings provide a helpful taxonomy, yet no mere enumeration of the different historical narratives in *North* will illuminate the complex intertwining of poetry and history mediated through the metaphor of the bog. What purpose does this poetic bog serve? Is it an anti-historical figure of stillness and calm, as Heaney's reference to the bog's 'strange assuaging effect'[48] might be seen to imply, or is it the imaginative source of a historical counter-narrative that should principally be read as a comment on another thematic strand running through the book, the colonial nature of the English–Irish encounter?

This question calls first for two lightweight answers. The first is etymological. 'Bog' is one of the few words in the English language with a Gaelic root, hence the mere word reinstates both a language different from the one the word now serves and the cultural memory enshrined in that language. Heaney has made that point himself – '"Bog" is one of the few borrowings of English from the Irish language: the Irish word means "soft"'[49] – and he exploits that sense in 'Kinship', in which the words 'quagmire', 'swampland' and 'morass' are all held up as synonyms for 'bog', while their real significance in the context of the poem is that they all have Germanic roots, in contrast to the Gaelic 'bog': 'But *bog* / meaning soft, / the fall of windless rain, / pupil of amber'.[50] The second answer is geological. Bogs and the slow-burning fuel recovered from them – turf, peat – mark one 'real' difference from Britain – the absence of coal in Ireland: 'They'll never dig coal here, // Only the waterlogged trunks / Of great firs, soft as pulp'.[51] By metaphorical extension, this points to industrialisation as a more hard-nosed, economic difference between Britain and Ireland.

On these two counts, then, what the bog metaphor establishes is less a counter-narrative than a sense of self and particularity. But we only have to take a brief look at the explosive semantics of the word in Tudor times to uncover a different strand of meaning. Edmund Spenser, himself a planter in Ireland (and frequently quoted by Heaney), routinely associates the word with the demonised Irish rebel, the monstrous wood-kerne, 'a flyinge enemye hidinge him self in woodes and bogges'.[52] And Shakespeare, in the *Comedy of Errors,* uses the word with reference to Ireland in a context both misogynistic and scatological. The kitchen maid Nell, a character in the play comments, 'is spherical, like a globe. I could find out countries in her.' 'In what part of her body stands Ireland?' 'Marry, sir, in her buttocks. I found it out by the bogs.'[53] These frames of reference locate the image of the Irish bog squarely in colonial rhetoric, casting Ireland either as a discursive rebel zone or a territorial cesspit. Heaney's poetic appropriation of this focus of English anxieties thus complicates any reading of the bog image as merely a self-conscious response to local conditions. To write about the bog as a symbol of Irishness, to capitalise on its creative powers as a spatialised form of historical memory, always already implies a counter-discourse to English colonial rhetoric.

The most immediate reason for reinventing the Irish bog as a cultural and historical myth, however, was the necessity (as Heaney thought) of finding a set of poetic images which could articulate the experience of a society torn apart by civil conflict: 'symbols adequate to our predicament'.[54] He found these symbols in photographs of 'bog people', human bodies preserved in the ground for over two thousand years by the acidic fluids peculiar to peat bogs. According to the Danish archaeologist Glob, in whose popular book on the topic Heaney first saw these photographs, the 'bog people' were victims of a violence that was visited upon them in the name of either a pagan fertility rite or a form of ancient tribal justice.[55] What Heaney thought he had found in these photographs were, in a phrase he borrowed from Yeats, 'befitting emblems of adversity' (a phrase to which I shall return). In a society whose very survival was threatened by the divisive legacy of a colonial past, the bog – once a prime trope of English colonial discourse about Irish 'savagery' – was enlisted as an imaginative space that might recover some of that society's lost common ground in poetry.

That preservation rather than transformation is the central impetus behind this specific imagery is suggested by Heaney's own reference to the bog as a kind of cultural archive or museum. But the metaphor is in fact more risky than this analogy implies, for the bog brings to light not only what is safely tucked away in the past but also resurrects the original energies invested in the material object: 'Butter sunk under / More than a hundred years / Was recovered salty and white'.[56] Fresh butter, a century old, may be little more than evidence of the surprising work of preservation effected by the acidic fluids in the bog. Its value as a historical artefact is limited to a recognition of continuity in human farming skills, the handing-down of knowledge through the generations. Next to the archaeologically significant 'Great Irish Elk', also recovered from the bog in the same poem, and which is invaluable as a document of Ireland's prehistoric landscape, the butter stands as a figure of the everyday, the domestic, which the bog also absorbs. For as a historical memory, the bog is not selective; rather, it is impartial and 'insatiable',[57] a 'consuming ground that indiscriminately swallows all that comes to it and preserves it intact'.[58] The reactive force of the bog only fully unfolds when what emerge from its dark resting place are not the material objects of a past culture but the human victims of the historical struggle.

The poems 'The Tollund Man', 'The Grauballe Man' and 'Punishment' are all based on specific pictorial references in Glob's book, and all pursue slightly different poetic 'healing' strategies. The benign expression of the Tollund Man, for instance, triggers off a religious response in the poet or speaker, who immediately announces a penitential pilgrimage to the site where the Tollund Man's body now rests. In a deliberate act of spatio-temporal translations the 'man-killing parishes'[59] of Ulster are then aligned with the pagan culture of the Tollund Man and seen as caught up in a similar kind of continuous cycle of death and rebirth. Art replaces religion in 'The Grauballe Man', a poem that is self-consciously a response to the aesthetic artefact of a photograph, rather than to the actual body itself. In its final lines we are asked – with considerable insistence and intensity – to view the Grauballe Man's body as an aesthetic product that has come to life in the speaker's imagination much as it came to life again after centuries of resting in the bog.[60] It is this aesthetic image, 'hung in the scales / with beauty and atrocity',[61] that the poem suggests might be weighed against the actuality of violence and political murder. 'Punishment' finally describes a direct confrontation with the reality of sectarian cruelty. The picture of the bog body that gave rise to this poem – a blindfolded woman with her head shaven as a punishment for her presumed crime, adultery – conjures up images much closer to the experience of the speaker: photographs of women in twentieth-century Northern Ireland, their heads shaven and tarred as a 'punishment' for going out with English soldiers. Such photographs, it is important to remember, record no Iron Age ritual but street scenes in Belfast and Derry in the 1970s. The cruelty, inhumanity and misogyny of such acts prompt an ambivalent response in the speakers who is torn between the 'civilized outrage' that would force him to condemn such acts, and his instinctive understanding of the community's need to protect itself – of the need, as he puts it, for 'tribal, intimate revenge'.[62]

For what are now very well-known reasons (certainly well-known enough to need no detailed repeating here), these final two stanzas of the poem have probably caused more comment than any other lines in this volume. What emerges rather clearly is that the bog uncovers a memory difficult to accommodate. More precisely perhaps, it uncovers analogies between the ritual killings of past and present that strain the loyalties of the speaker to breaking point. What is recovered from Heaney's poetic bog irrupts into, and potentially interferes with, the present. It cannot simply be contained by it. Also, the bog does not merely lie dormant but actively works to make cultural memory return. Among the many words and metaphors Heaney finds for his myth are these: 'Ruminant ground / digestion of mollusc / and seed-pod, / deep pollen bin'.[63] This is no river in which history calmly floats by; this bog is constantly in motion, ruminating, digesting, recycling history. Transcending its function as a natural sponge that absorbs the lived experience of history, the bog here literally comes alive as a generative principle of cultural memory. Heaney's poetic bog is less a distant and non-controversial reservoir of images at the disposal of posterity; it is an independent historical agent, throwing up its contents at its own pace, rhythm and logic.

But are the bog poems 'effective'; that is, do they live up to the poet's expectation of 'pressing back against the pressures of reality'?[64] With a gesture to Auden's (in)famous pronouncement, in his memorial tribute to Yeats, that 'poetry makes nothing happen', John Wilson Foster has answered no, describing the poems in part one of *North* as a form of 'cultural analogizing away from political turmoil into vatic poetry which digs deep but makes nothing happen'.[65] Nor, apparently, does the poet 'make anything happen', for the poetic function of bogland feeds back into a passive authorial posture, and hence into a similarly stagnant historical perspective. Heaney's bog image is the result of a double inward movement: he digs, almost literally, in his native soil, perceived as a form of spatialised history, and he turns inward to face the ruptures within – not outside or across – his own community. This inward turn might imply the loss of a wider perspective that could keep in balance the exterior forces responsible for the civil conflict in Northern Ireland. For Heaney, Foster writes, 'up until and including *North* and *Preoccupations*, poetry and Ireland share an origin and essence in secrecy, mystery, triumphant receptivity, wise passiveness, darkness, earth, primal femininity; their identity is their aboriginality, not their subsequent reformations'.[66] His bog operates on a diachronic not a synchronic level; it stands as a signifier of an unchangeable cycle of death, revenge and deliverance. Despite the historical agency invested in it, there is thus a retractive, conservative force at work in this image; it is designed to appease, explain and assuage, not to confront, challenge and accuse. It inaugurates a cult of near sacred stillness. Heaney's stance is that of an observer who claims not to interfere; his figure of the poet is the 'wise spectator'.[67] There is voyeurism in this pose, as the speaker in 'Punishment' knows ('I am the artful voyeur'), and potential complicity with the agents of violence ('[I] would have cast, I know, / the stones of silence').

But then criticism of this kind is anticipated by Heaney himself. More challenging has been the feminist critique which has pointed to the inherent misogyny of casting the bog as a quintessentially female space: wet, passive, bottomless.[68] In the dualisms of Heaney's early poetry, the male–female dichotomy invariably corresponds to the English–Irish antagonism. Just as problematic as these gender stereotypes is the very conception of history implicit in this image: the resistance to change, the stagnation, the lack of progress, and a linear sequence of events that effortlessly translates into the geological layers of a peat bog. The most striking deficiency of Heaney's bog is the inability to invite a creative use of the past: there is preservation, no end of preservation, only no change.

The implications of Heaney's myth of the bog have been hotly debated in criticism, and the politically committed arguments against it are well known: it sanitises the politics of violence; it lends the killings a historical respectability which they do not deserve; it condones rather than condemns the terror.[69] To this political critique we might add a conceptual critique directed at a view of history that privileges preservation over change. This is especially striking when compared with a writer such as Derek Walcott, whose poetic historiography takes the sea as its paradigmatic figure of history – in poems such as 'The Sea Is History'[70] – thus championing a space in which memory sinks to the ground and is forgotten (and thus unable to haunt the living), which erases the traces of a traumatic past (such as the deep fissures of slave ships on the ocean), and which privileges the fluidity of change over the historian's demand for preservation.[71] For Heaney, one way out of this aporia is the appeal to poetry as imaginative liberation, as a field of force that may act as a counterweight to the real thing – what he has called the 'redress of poetry'.

I want here to suggest another imaginative exit, one that responds to Heaney's spatial concerns. The bog, it has been abundantly clear throughout, is an uninhabitable space, a realm of the dead not of the living. The poetry it has generated is filled with a morbid fascination for the victims killed in the course of history. In some of Heaney's later poems, the dead he gazed at in wonder in bogs or elsewhere return to accuse him of aesthetic escapism. In 'Station Island VIII', for instance, one such victim – Heaney's second cousin – complains to the poet that he has 'confused evasion and artistic tact': 'you whitewashed ugliness and drew / the lovely blinds of the *Purgatorio* / and saccharined my death with morning dew'.[72] The insight that poetry might work to deny as much as redress reality is one reason, I think, why, after the bog poems, Heaney more or less renounced his poetic desire to stare at the dead in awe and fascination in favour of the much more difficult task of dialogue. This Dantesque dialogue with the dead – which dominates collections such as *Field Work* (1979) and *Station Island* (1984) – is frequently set in a self-consciously liminal, intermediary or transitional location, far away from the bog: the beach, strand or coast.

One example of such a poem is 'The Strand at Lough Beg' (from *Field Work*) in which Heaney ministers to his murdered cousin in a ritualised setting taken straight from Dante's *Purgatorio* (in fact the accusatory lines above from 'Station Island VIII' are spoken precisely by this victim of the Troubles). When another Irish coastline – that of Inishowen in Donegal, near the (then) heavily guarded border with Northern Ireland – enters Heaney's work, it is in the first instance a spot where the imagination is held in check by politics. A poet on the beach picks up a stone and imagines it is a message from Hades, or the heart of Guy de Montfort. This romanticising does not impress the border patrol: 'Anyhow, there I was with the wet red stone / in my hand, staring across at the watch towers / from my free state of image and allusion, / swooped on, then dropped, by trained binoculars: // a silhouette not worth bothering about, / ... not about to set times wrong or right'.[73] On the textual surface, the beach appears here only as an inconsequential, creatively inspiring but historically irrelevant place under tight military surveillance. But in the study of travel writing, the coast has recently been much theorised as a contact zone, a liminal space of free encounters, of improvisation, interaction and life,[74] giving a wholly different meaning to Heaney's 'free state of image and allusion'.

When the bog returns in Heaney's more recent collection, *The Spirit Level* (1996), it has absorbed precisely these qualities. The very bog in which the Tollund Man was found is now a realm that enables not the definition of the present in terms of the past but a seizure of the future. The poem in question, 'Tollund', is dated 'September 1994' – the month after the first IRA cease-fire. The bog, formerly the grave of the Tollund Man, is now a space 'hallucinatory and familiar'; it opens up expectantly, allowing the speaker 'to make a new beginning / And make a go of it, alive and sinning, / Ourselves again, free-willed again, not bad'.[75] Twenty years on, the bog no longer stands outside history; it has itself aged along with the times that have 'moved on' and has turned into a self-reflective figure for the future which has defeated the ghosts of the past.

These ghosts (or bog people) Heaney encountered first as images – photographs – and he has never claimed any different in his writings. Now the poems in *North*, when first published by Faber in 1975, did not come with photographs attached,[76] yet the connection has been so frequently insisted upon (and taken seriously) by both the author and his critics that it hardly violates the integrity of the volume to argue for their interdependence. In particular, I want to suggest that the photographs should be set in contrast with the line from Yeats which Heaney has quoted as his point of departure in writing poems about the Troubles, that the task of the poet in times of war is to offer 'befitting emblems of adversity'.[77]

Irrespective of what might make them 'befitting', emblems are no straightforward comments on a reality happening outside the poem. An emblem is first of all an aesthetic image that offers some kind of moral or meditative comment, and that needs to be contemplated in conjunction with a textual address. Meaning is constructed through the interaction of image and text, and since the reading of an emblem is generally theorised 'in terms of a temporal sequence rather than a spatial design'[78] – meaning that the image first needs to be recognised as an enigma or a puzzle before the text can be accepted as offering some form of resolution – the inversion which Heaney practises when he refers to his *texts* as emblems is particularly important, for this implies that the construction of meaning is inherent in the movement from text (poem) to image (photograph) rather than in the other, more conventional route from image to text, favoured in emblem theory.

This means that in the trajectory from the purely abstract fabrication of the poem to the mimetic image of the dead body, the poems take us first on an imaginative flight before releasing us into history. Rather than offering facile escape routes from the realities of the Troubles, the poems use their emblematic quality to force us back into a confrontation with actuality. Put differently, the photographs (though of course they are themselves mediated through the aesthetic lens of the camera) are on offer as a corrective to what we encountered first: the fine verbal art of the poem. The reception of the poem thus reverses its production process (where image preceded text).

Important also in this context is the notion of 'adversity' that Yeats specifically emphasised: opposition, a state of 'contrariness', a deliberate contrast. Poetry has to offer an imaginative alternative to experience, not simply propaganda or a versified repetition of the everyday. It does so in the bog poems, I suggest, not by advertising the link between poetry and politics in a propagandist fashion but by the subtle (and perhaps slightly oblique) technique of offering poetic templates as a moulding device for a thoroughly historicised consciousness of the present. This does not mean that relief from current pressures can be found in the realisation that the Troubles are simply a new instalment of a worn-out historical pattern.[79] Rather, in contrast to the assumption of such a one-to-one relationship between poetic meaning and political statement, the poems attempt to open up the limitations of political thought precisely through an imaginative appeal to history. For history, as the poetry insists, is not a repetitive cycle of the inevitable; it is an imaginative 'outback' full of hidden alternatives, untapped resources, forgotten voices. This is what the bog metaphor, despite its conceptual limitations, might remind us of.

Derek Mahon: lives and afterlives

Derek Mahon's poetry is also much given to the visual, to the point where individual poems enact a veritable ekphrasis. One famous instance is the poem 'Courtyards in Delft', based on a series of paintings by the Dutch genre painter Pieter de Hooch. (Its most direct point of reference is usually assumed to be the 1658 de Hooch painting of a Delft courtyard now in the

National Gallery in London.[80]) The poem, which ostensibly takes us far away from present-day Ulster into the fledgling Dutch Republic of the mid-seventeenth century, is in fact a sustained interrogation of the ethos of Ulster Protestantism. The opening stanza describes the scene captured in the painting, an open courtyard in the Dutch town of Delft: 'Oblique light on the trite, on brick and tile – / Immaculate masonry, and everywhere that / Water tap, that broom and wooden pail / To keep it so'.[81] The domestic order is reflected in the stillness of the air, the unruffled trees. The pride taken in the proper and well-kept yard by 'House-proud … wives' is generated by the combination of business acumen, 'thrift', and the keeping up of façades, achieved in the obsessive cleanliness of 'scrubbed yards'.

Stanza two describes absences, negatives, prohibitions, in this scene of bourgeois bliss. Missing from the painting, the poet suggests, are iconographic pointers to hidden passions or flaws in the outward display of order and godliness common to so many examples of seventeenth-century Dutch genre painting (by Vermeer, Terborch and others). On de Hooch's canvas (of the National Gallery painting) nothing disturbs the carefully arranged scene; everything is in its place. No cracks appear in the façade of this private, quiet world. The women in the painting, especially the girl on the left who turns her back to us in anticipation of a visitor, would not budge from their 'proper' place, steadfast even if the paint should 'disintegrate' or the 'ruined dykes admit the esurient sea'.

Yet, underneath the calm veneer, this world is in uproar, for the ruthless imposition of order and strict discipline will produce its own measure of violent resistance. Such local knowledge is imported into the canvas by a poet who imagines himself as an inhabitant of the world of the painting, 'A strange child with a taste for verse', set apart from more aggressive companions and their games of war, played out on 'parched veldt and fields of rain-swept gorse'. The violence alluded to here, result of the bourgeois repression and false morality of which the painting is the visual instance, and the reference to 'gorse', ubiquitous in the north of Ireland, are the first hints that the poem might be engaged in the act of spatio-temporal translation between seventeenth-century Holland and twentieth-century Ulster.[82] The final stanza continues both threads before ending in a disturbing vision of forceful liberation: 'If only, now, the Maenads, as of right, / Came smashing crockery, with fire and sword, / We could sleep easier in our beds at night.' The word 'Linen' in the third line of this stanza is another regional pointer to Ulster, while the release imagined here through the act of violent destruction is a devastating comment on the repressive nature of Ulster Protestantism, which has, of course, generated its own fair share of politically motivated violence. To emphasise the threat that hangs over the blissful domestic scene is not an extraneous imposition of the poet; the sense of imminent danger is already present in a painting where all doors and windows stand open, exposing the safe inner haven to potential menace from outside.

That Mahon is aligning his own community with the Protestant Dutch culture of the 'Golden Age' has been noted by many critics. My principal interest in this poem is the nature of Mahon's historical reference. Why Delft? The choice is deeply apposite, as a brief historical excursion shows. In the seventeenth century, Delft – once a lively centre of national importance – was beginning to turn more and more conservative.[83] It remained wealthy and would continue to support international ventures – such as the Dutch East and West India Companies – but its economic base was shrinking and local business was in decline, contrary to the development in the Low Countries at large, where trade and industry were expanding. Importantly, given the context here, the city also began to differ from other, more liberal Dutch towns by allowing religious intolerance to be practised: Calvinists dominated the civic administration and were openly hostile to Catholics and non-Calvinist sects, barring them from public office. The town's conservatism was even reflected in the layout of the city. Regularity and order characterised the buildings and the road network, in contrast to the maze of narrow streets and alleys typical of many other Dutch towns of medieval origin: 'The town's neat and orderly appearance, so suited to the mentality of its inhabitants, found its clearest expression in the work of De Hooch and his colleagues'.[84]

Clearly, Mahon did not select the de Hooch paintings at random from the many examples he could have chosen. The similarities he finds with the modern-day Protestant community in Ulster are not confined to the obsessive concern with external appearance and the belief that order, discipline and 'scrubbed yards' translate into an inherent godliness. Nor do the historical analogies, which are compelling, exhaust the conceptual parallels. There is also Mahon's understanding of how space – especially architectural, civic and domestic space – defines the outlook of a culture and its potential for change, while his analogy also emphasises the isolation of both Delft and Ulster within, and their self-inflicted difference from, the larger political networks of which they form a part.

The invisible 'outside' of the painting, hinted at on the 1658 National Gallery canvas only by the woman in the archway, who is staring through this archway at something beyond our field of vision, encompasses two exterior frameworks: the wider 'national' network which gives political meaning to this non-aristocratic, burgher household, and the public world of men and historical action absent from the female space of the painting. Both these 'outsides' are signified by the painting's inward turn: Dutch national identity, in the seventeenth century, defined itself precisely through the celebration of domestic order, and genre painting was the most prominent medium to advertise the allegorical connection. (No wonder that as a sign of their contact with the outside world, many of these paintings show national or world maps on the walls of their domestic interiors, a habit Mahon notes in passing with his reference to the 'linen / Map of the world'.)

In this poem, what differentiates Mahon's address to the past from Heaney's and the other examples discussed above is both his poetic engagement with the problems of representing history and the nature of his attempted, but failed, solution. Mahon responds not only to a specific historical moment which his poem sets into suggestive contrast with the present. He also, crucially, comments on the representational metadiscourse that makes possible de Hooch's self-image of a culture: a highly stylised form of realism that, by its own internal logic, is forced to ignore all input of the creative imagination. The outlook provided by the open door to the left of the painting, down the short archway into some back yard or garden, is striking in its narrowness. This technique of concealment endemic to linear perspective – which hides from us both what the figures in the painting can see and also what might be 'seen' on a plane of consciousness other than that of external perception – is what the poem exhibits as the stifling existential condition to which the present – or one *version* of the present – is still enthralled.

The violence in the final stanza, I suggest, is imagined on at least one level of meaning as the drastic solution that would give access to other forms of 'truth' – the 'dreams of fire', for instance, which the boy-speaker imagines for himself – by cutting through the restrictions imposed on it by representational realism. In the context of the poem's historical concerns, the violence suggests other meanings too, of course. For instance, it can be seen as an attack – born out of frustration – against the implication of necessary continuity that underwrites the patterns of all such historical explanations. What the furious Maenads, conjured up from Greek myth, are called in to destroy, is not a particular society as such, or its own chosen form of cultural expression. It is rather, I would suggest, a reaction against a view of the past that denies historical alternatives or radical options, that disallows the shape-shifting and side-tracking, the dead ends and inconsistencies, the errors and new beginnings – in short, the whole irrational stuff of human *lives* – in favour of the belief in a linear and orderly progression of the individual fates that make up 'history'.

Appropriately enough, this can best be demonstrated in a poem called 'Lives', first published in Mahon's 1972 volume of the same title, *Lives*, and later – presumably because of its highly apt subject matter – dedicated to Heaney, on whose bog poems (then largely unpublished) it is a kind of proleptic comment. The poem recounts the farcical life-journey of what could be a bog body, 'buried ... in the / Earth for two thousand years', tracing its absurd metamorphoses: 'First time out / I was a torc of gold', 'Once I was an oar', 'I was a bump of clay // In a Navaho rug'.[85] These minimal selves are fragile identities soon 'unceremoniously subverted':[86] the torc is dug up and sold on the market, '[f]or tea and sugar'; the oar marked only a grave and then 'soon decayed'; the owner of the rug was 'struck down ... by an electric shock'.[87] Yet the proliferation of selves finds continuation in what the speaker in the poem calls her different lives: 'So many lives, / So many things to remember! / I was a stone in Tibet, // A tongue of bark / At the heart of Africa'.[88] The speaker's expansive migrations through continents – Europe, Asia, America, Africa – and materials – gold, wood, clay, stone, bark – finally come to an end in her current identity as an 'anthropologist' – that is, a professional researcher into past human 'lives' – now armed '[w]ith my own / Credit card, dictaphone, // Army-surplus boots / And a whole boatload / Of photographic equipment'.[89] The bitter punchline of the poem is that this overload of equipment and knowledge puts an end to these preposterous travels: obsessive concern with the past first fixes identity in time and place and then threatens to erase it altogether.

> I know too much
> To be anything any more –
> And if in the distant
>
> Future someone
> Thinks he has once been me
> As I am today,
>
> Let him revise
> His insolent ontology
> Or teach himself to pray.[90]

One could read this final twist as an expression of despair, as a procedure 'of reduction, of stripping down, peeling away until there is nothing left'.[91] Alternatively, it may signal the dangers inherent in the playful juggling of identities without the security of an assured selfhood: 'The self has been lost or abandoned or diffused into all the roles it plays',[92] only to deny to posterity that theatrical option of the performative self. I prefer to read it as a rejection of the impulse – whether anthropological or historical – to see the present as the result of a linear evolutionary process that can be traced back rationally and coherently through layers of time and experience. The poem, to me, is a hesitant, if ironic, celebration of the many imaginable 'lives' of history; lives we risk losing sight of if we accept unquestioningly the implied historical equations of 'Courtyards in Delft'.

In many of Mahon's poems there is, as in these two examples, a persistent concern with forms of historical thinking that edge towards a sense of the past strikingly at odds with the figure of history defined by Heaney's relocation of historical memory in a landscape of peat bogs. In terms of its historical address, however, no myth corresponding to Heaney's sustained poetic elaboration of a single motif is available in Mahon's poetry. The comparison is not merely gratuitous. Peter McDonald has warned that although Heaney's poetic meeting with the past 'has been seen widely as ... paradigmatic' for the Northern Irish experience, this is to ignore that 'Heaney's uses for history are not the same as those of other poets from the same place and generation; nor are they necessarily the most advanced and challenging of poetic dealings with history'.[93]

McDonald argues further that 'Derek Mahon's poety [sic] seems at first to have escaped the pressures of history altogether, insofar as these are seen as particular and pressing contingencies of events upon the individual life. The poems have always gravitated towards a cold and unpeopled area, one that exists before, or after, what we recognise as history.'[94] This more or less reiterates the earlier position of Seamus Deane who thinks that 'Derek Mahon's poetry expresses a longing to be free from history.'[95] Defenders of this argument can solicit support from lines scattered throughout Mahon's poems, such as these in 'The Last of the Fire Kings': 'Either way, I am / Through with history – / Who lives by the sword // Dies by the sword',[96] or these in 'Rathlin': 'Bombs doze in the housing estates / But here they are through with history'.[97] What I want to argue is to some extent the opposite view: Mahon's poetry aims not to escape but rather to embrace history in all its diversity and unrealised potential – only ultimately to deny the very possibility of this liberating vision of a multidimensional, protean past.

The 1975 volume *The Snow Party* is generally considered to be Mahon's most sustained poetic engagement with the Northern Irish Troubles. The link is tentative at best, though the opening poem 'Afterlives' invites a reading along those lines. The poem comes in two parts. The first is a four-stanza, early-morning meditation from a window overlooking London, where the sparkle of the 'morning light', the 'white / Roofs' of the city, and the '[r]ain-fresh' brilliance of the atmosphere define the 'bright / Reason' that might put an end to sectarian strife and kindle instead the hope for a world '[a]blaze with love and poetry', revitalised by 'the power of good'. In the final stanza of part one, the speaker comments on these naive musings in no uncertain terms: 'What middle-class cunts we are / To imagine for one second / That our privileged ideals / Are divine wisdom, and the dim / Forms that kneel at noon / In the city not ourselves'.[98] The 'dim forms' are suggestive here; they indicate a general blurring of perception, shattering the earlier confidence in a clearly recognisable, ultimately rational world, 'bright', 'white' and 'fresh'. They also evoke kneeling gunmen taking aim, an allusion explored further in the second part of the poem, in which the speaker finds himself 'going home' to Belfast, '[f]or the first time in years'.

The return trip is clearly fraught with anxieties, and as the speaker steps ashore he finds 'a city so changed / By five years of war' that vision fails him, allowing him to discern, again, only 'dim forms': 'I scarcely recognize the places I grew up in, / The faces that try to explain'. The concluding stanza offers a complex reflection on the link between history and experience: 'But the hills are still the same / Grey-blue above Belfast. / Perhaps if I'd stayed behind / And lived it bomb by bomb / I might have grown up at last / And learnt what is meant by home'.[99] This is ostensibly an expression of regret, a comment about the speaker's growing sense of alienation from his native community. Change has occurred within a setting of permanence, the hills surrounding the city. The suggestion is clearly that other decisions might have been taken, that other lives might have been possible, *if only* 'I'd lived it bomb by bomb'. Elmer Andrews reads these lines as an elegiac reflection on 'lost possibility',[100] but I wonder whether this is quite the right term. It is, after all, neither very desirable nor very safe to live through a political crisis 'bomb by bomb', and the experience of armed struggle hardly constitutes the object of the speaker's longing. But he clearly registers that there is something to be gained even from bombs: both maturity and a sense of home. Enough people have, of course, done just that – lived through the crisis 'bomb by bomb' – and it is these other experiences, other lives, that are vindicated by the speaker.

If 'Afterlives' can be said to follow the earlier 'Lives' in more than an intertextual sense, it does not merely express regret over a lost life (the speaker's notion of what might have been, had he 'stayed behind') but acknowledges the multiplicity of lives that have been not only possible, but quite real. In Belfast, lives have certainly been lost – many through bombs – but a multitude of lives can be gained by imagining history not as it unfolds from the fixed viewpoint of a single life but as the collective and diverse experience of multiple lives (and of their afterlives in memory). The next poem, 'Leaves' (the title, I think, a play on both 'lives' and 'leaving') offers an afterthought on the afterlife: 'Somewhere there is an afterlife Of dead leaves, / A stadium filled with an infinite / Rustling and sighing. // Somewhere in the heaven / Of lost futures / The lives we might have led / Have found their own fulfilment'.[101] The 'lost futures' evoke both the very real losses that the Troubles have brought and also the imaginative losses incurred by making specific choices that rule out alternatives; the poem starts, significantly, with an ironic glance at the 'prisoners of infinite choice'. What lurks behind all these poetic reflections about life and its proliferation in others' lives and in unlived lives is, I suggest, a sense of history that does not accept the reduction of the past to the mere one-dimensionality of a single perspective.

Writing about the links between poetry and politics, Mahon has explained that '[t]he war I mean' – that the Northern Irish poet takes sides in – 'is not, of course, between Protestant and Catholic but between the fluidity of a possible life ... and the *rigor mortis* of archaic postures, political and cultural'.[102] We could see this war being waged in 'Courtyards in Delft' where the archaic posture was less the mental intransigence of Ulster Protestantism than the mistaken assumption that history can *only* be thought of in terms of equations and continuities, that the world of the poem *necessarily* corresponds to a conflated 'Ulster/Dutch interior'.[103] Mahon's poetry longs for access to the 'possible lives' that invigorate the past with the fluidity of the imagination, yet the ultimate denial of this hope gives his poetry a note of bleakness and despair that is all the more effective for its stunning formal excellence and measured control.[104]

Possibly the most exciting, certainly the most celebrated, poetic instance of this comes in the closing poem of *The Snow Party*, 'A Disused Shed in Co. Wexford'. The banality of the title is part of the poetic programme. This daring revisionist poem recuperates lost lives, 'lost people', in the margins of time and space. Insignificance is raised to semantic prominence, remoteness redefined as centrality. There is, to some extent at least, a historiographical agenda behind this tactic, a kind of poetic history from below, an attention to the quotidian rather than the exceptional. Whatever material objects or 'lost lives' Mahon's poetic beam of light singles out in this poem, its shadowy fringe existence yields to a luminous place in the spotlight.

Light metaphors are appropriate when discussing a poem in which the central imagery is structured around a thousand mushrooms growing towards a single source of light. The imaginative scenario unfolded in the two opening stanzas of this poem works by a combination of expansive space and deep, emotional longing, generating a particular 'feeling tone' in the wide geographic sweep that first races through continents, passing abandoned places of human endeavour – 'Peruvian mines', 'Indian compounds' – and then zooms in from the general to the particular, from the geographic to the chorographic, to come to rest in a seemingly incongruous, disused Irish shed: 'And in a disused shed in Co. Wexford, // Deep in the grounds of a burnt-out hotel, / Among the bathtubs and the washbasins / A thousand mushrooms crowd to a keyhole'.[105]

The foregrounding of spatial issues has been a notable concern in all of Mahon's poems discussed so far;[106] in 'A Disused Shed' Mahon rides possibly his most daring attack on imaginative and territorial 'limits'. The emotional resonances recorded in these opening stanzas – 'diminished confidence', 'desire', 'patience and silence' – mark the shed out as a terrain of human endurance, humiliation and suffering, a space – like the abandoned mine in Peru or the deserted compound in India – on which the attention of men once focused, before they moved on. But the sites of historical action fallen out of use, the forgotten 'places where a thought might grow', left behind and abandoned once they had served their purpose, linger on in memory in a kind of 'afterlife'.

Unanimous admiration for Mahon's depth of vision has disguised the extent to which this poem is actually a satire, a long, rambling poem about rotten fungi. The pitiful mushrooms have been in the shed 'since civil war days' of 1922/3 (the whole scenario was suggested by J. G. Farrell's novel *Troubles* (1970), set during the civil war), and little has prepared them for the sudden 'cracking lock / And creak of hinges' that announces the first visitor in 'half [a] century'. In an anthropomorphic and hyperbolic tour de force, the speaker risks tripping over his own metaphors by describing the mushrooms as 'magi, moonmen, / Powdery prisoners of the old regime, / Web throated, stalked like triffids, racked by drought / And insomnia', and after several more stanzas revelling in their plight, the poem reaches its dramatic conclusion:

> They are begging us, you see, in their wordless way,
> To do something, to speak on their behalf
> Or at least not to close the door again.
> Lost people of Treblinka and Pompeii!
> 'Save us, save us,' they seem to say,
> 'Let not the God abandon us
> Who have come so far in darkness and in pain.
> We too had our lives to live.
> You with your light meter and relaxed itinerary,
> Let not our naive labours have been in vain!'[107]

To compare the thousands of dead at Treblinka and Pompeii to a bunch of mushrooms '[crowding] to a keyhole' in a decaying shed is an audacious gesture of discursive appropriation, redeemed only (if at all) by the intensity of Mahon's own historical longing. Edna Longley has noted the 'religious view of history'[108] in his poetry, and the passionate concern for the 'weak souls among the asphodels'[109] is informed by Walter Benjamin's project to fuse, in his 'Theses' (written in another historical moment of extreme danger), 'materialism and Jewish mysticism by discovering in the latter enough messianic drive to sustain the flawed spirit of the former'.[110]

The mushrooms – whose 'feverish forms' remind us of the increasingly squalid historical ground that has been covered in *The Snow Party* since the 'dim forms' of the opening poem – can be variously read, I suppose, as symbols for the 'defenseless people struggling for the luminosity of redemption',[111] as 'emblematic of lives lived under duress, of the imprisoned, the decaying and the forgotten',[112] as the victims of historical progress, or as any other image that foregrounds human loss and the struggle of the individual for historical recognition. The shed has even been read as 'the self-isolated ... statelet of Northern Ireland', an 'allegory of sectarianism', with the mushrooms close to the keyhole representing 'assertive' Protestants and those further away from the door 'abject' Catholics.[113] Whichever reading is preferred, their utter incongruity as images is surely more significant than the exact nature of their symbolic referents. For one thing, mushrooms need no light, since fungus is 'characterized by the absence of chlorophyll, [and derives] sustenance from dead or living organic matter' (*OED*, sense 1a), and second, their propensity for sudden growth surely minimalises the traumatic impact on their ranks of the 'deaths' and 'nightmares' which Mahon laments. (Their toxic effect on the human brain is perhaps a more appropriate association in a poem that could be read as a hallucinatory sequence of dream images.)

'Part of the point' behind the symbol, Edna Longley thinks, 'is the ironic swivel to molehill rather than mountain',[114] but even this hardly answers the question of how these withered mushrooms avoid being crushed by the heavy pathos they are made to bear. In essence, I would argue, the mushrooms capture the overwhelming sadness of the unhistorical existence, for, as a form of vegetable life, history is denied them. Yet the poem's anthropomorphic gesture aims precisely to confirm that in the human world there is no such thing as an unhistorical condition; history is the existential moment of contingency that from the start defines all sensory and material phenomena. From this perspective it would be wrong to argue that the mushrooms are 'outside history',[115] or that they have yet to be released 'into ... history',[116] for their struggle has been deeply historical all along. Their pathos is not only engendered by the historical tragedies which they are made to stand for in the poem but also by the evident ease that allows their plight to be dismissed as irrelevant and unhistorical. Their pathetic insignificance is the inverse measure of the vastness, the inclusivity, of the idea of history that Mahon's poetry asks us to adopt.

Reading Mahon's poetry as deeply engaged in such an intense dialogue with history still means to fly in the face of a certain branch of critical opinion,[117] although the consensus seems to be shifting somewhat towards an appreciation of the historical concerns of his poetry.[118] In this section I have been reading Mahon's repeated references to 'lost lives' not as an expression of metaphysical loneliness but as the serious projection, in poetic terms, of an alternative historiographical thinking. There is, of course, a completely different Mahon: the cleared-eyed visionary of human despair, the poet of outcasts, exiles and barren wastelands, a dweller in Arctic zones of sub-zero humanity, 'perfecting [his] cold dream / Of a place out of time, / A palace of porcelain',[119] who 'celebrates ... the perfection of art, an intense *quidditas* which exists outside history'.[120]

I remain unconvinced by the image of Mahon as a poet of either an atemporal aestheticism or 'a usually unemphatic, but convinced historical apocalypticism',[121] but then this eternal shape-shifter is always already one step ahead of his readers – metaphorically in his poetry, which always adds an unexpected twist to put these readers off their guard, and literally in the countless rewritings and revisions his poems have undergone over the years, which only adds to the frustration of the critics.[122] I myself have preferred the second version (of at least three that have been published) of 'Courtyards in Delft' because it suited my argument, and maybe this simply goes to show that with poetry there is, as with history, always another angle from which to look, always another life to be lived.

Tom Paulin: poetry and politics

No doubts about a deep interest in the dynamics of history and its impact on the present have, to my knowledge, ever been raised about the poetry of Tom Paulin. It would indeed be odd to deny a passion for history in a writer who has repeatedly included the very word history in the titles of his poems. In Paulin's first two volumes, *A State of Justice* (1977) and *The Strange Museum* (1980), this engagement with the past still takes a form that is far more directly interested in straightforward political history than in any imaginative redefining of what the historical in a fuller sense might signify in poetry. Thus, in 'Settlers', Paulin evokes the Ulster Crisis and the 1912 Larne gunrunning in the context of unionist protests against the Home Rule Bill. An institutional network of 'Iceworks', 'Kirk' and 'Army' is projected on to a 'black' urban landscape of 'gantries, mills and steeples',[123] locus of theology and industry (in both senses of the word). History is imagined as the slow process of community formation, of 'begin[ning] to belong'. Knowledge of imminent historical action is transmitted through side glances and taciturn secrecy ('The men watch and say nothing'), and moments of touch and feel ('He touches the bonnet', 'a warm knowledge on his palm' – the 'warm knowledge' a deliberate contrast to the earlier 'Iceworks'). The isolated settler community thus sworn together finds its most potent visual expression in the image of guns hidden under floorboards across the Presbyterian landscape of Antrim.

Paulin has repeatedly referred to the year 1912 as the nadir in the history of the Ulster Protestant community, selectively and fatally linked to 1690 (Battle of the Boyne) in the memory of most unionists who 'cling desperately to a raft constructed from two dates – 1690 and 1912. The result is an unusually fragmented culture and a snarl of superficial or negative attitudes. A provincialism of the most disabling kind.'[124] According to Paulin, this distorted form of historical consciousness is peculiar to a community that 'possesses very little in the way of an indigenous cultural tradition of its own',[125] and his solution to this collective mental crisis, which he puts to poetic effect in *Liberty Tree* (1983), is to usurp that same structure of historical thinking and place the year 1798 squarely in its midst – the year in which a radical dissenting tradition that originated in the north found political expression in the rebellion of the United Irishmen. There is something hurtful and vicious about Paulin's scathing attacks on the Ulster Protestant community (in which he grew up), and perhaps McDonald is right in applying the terms of the criticism to the form of the critique itself.[126] Nevertheless, Paulin's polemics are driven by genuine passion, and throughout his writings it is that community's social and political future which is the overriding concern of his poetry. The point of attack, in Paulin's poetry and prose, is their sense of history.

Before stepping into the historical syntax of Ulster Protestant consciousness, armed with the date 1798 and focused on a radical reordering of that syntax, Paulin's poetic historiography was constructed in slightly different terms. In 'Before History', historical action is imagined as rising out of the spiritual hunger for form, visualised as the moment of early awakening in the silent darkness, when the 'tyranny of memories'[127] is felt to its full potential. A similar idea informs the poem 'A Partial State', in which '[s]tillness, without history' characterises the brief lull before 'leviathan spouts, / bursting through manhole covers' to wreak havoc on a province that is beyond salvation because, as the final words of the poem proclaim in apocalyptic certainty, '*What the wrong Gods established / No army can ever save*'.[128] This is in effect a reversal of the dictum of Stephen Dedalus, whose moment of awakening was figured as an escape from, not a confrontation with, the nightmare of history. Yet, despite this reversal, both formulae imagine an existential moment unaffected by the dynamics of history (either 'before' or 'after'), as if it was indeed possible, let alone desirable, to be '[p]lunging', like Paulin's Trotsky, 'from stillness into history'.[129]

For the fictional Trotsky, this initiation to history signifies the beginning of his engagement with the revolution; similarly, in 'The Idea in History' a grasp of history occurs in tandem with a process of individual formation, like a poetic *Bildungsroman*: 'Out of a soft starfish / The first eye opened / To a pure shrill light. // When the mind grew formal, / Caught in the nets of class, / History became carpets, chairs'.[130] This notion of history as a force that exists, or might exist, independent of human concerns, only to confiscate authority over human destiny at certain historical junctures – by being fully embodied, for instance, in a specific individual (such as Trotsky) – gives way in Paulin's later poetry to a more purposeful and political appropriation of the past.[131] Thus, in *Liberty Tree* (1983), Paulin's third volume, the poetic intervention in the historical moment of 1912, 'where the *Fanny* sleaks up the Elbe / for a yarn wi'the Kaiser', no longer even allows, as 'Settlers' still did, for moments of human contact. The scene has hardened into an accusation of emotional minimalism and imaginative scarcity:

> Boot polish and the Bible,
> the Boy's Brigade is arming.
> This is the album you found
> in your grandmother's sideboard,
> the deedbox with her burial papers,
> a humped ledger and a lock
> of that dead uncle's hair.
> There is so little history
> we must remember who we are.[132]

The alliterative forcefield of 'Boot-polish', 'Bible' and 'Boy's Brigade' first claims an almost natural extension in 'ledger and … lock', only to then allow the single remnant of body memory to enter the poem, by using the enjambment of lines 5 and 6 to change the meaning of 'lock' from security device (recall the guns under the floorboards) to a tress of hair. The transmission of biographical knowledge through the generations is constructed as a closed-off, always already scripted handing-down of selected, personalised, but strangely cold objects – 'album', 'deedbox' – while biblical historiography fuses with 'humped ledger' and 'burial papers' into the defining letters of authority.

The final two lines attempt, in effect, to usurp just that authority. The 'little history' that is almost forgotten, to the point of erasing identity so completely that no one remembers who they are, is conjured up in a bid to suppress that history even further and rewrite it from a perspective that brings a different tradition into view. In so doing, these lines are reminiscent of Mahon's furious Maenads who perform a similar act of verbal violence on the structure of a historical memory that is perceived as lacking and faulty. Elsewhere in *Liberty Tree* Paulin describes the barren landscape of Ulster Protestantism in similarly bleak terms: 'in the dead centre of a faith, / Between Draperstown and Magherafelt, / ... the Word has withered to a few / Parched certainties, and the charred stubble / Tightens like a black belt, a crop of Bibles'.[133] Paulin has been taken to task for the 'breathtaking arrogance' of such stanzas which describe – with an assurance rivalling the 'parched certainties' he condemns – a debased 'culture of twigs and bird-shit' and thus hardly avoid 'servicing the dominant stereotypes of Northern Irish Protestants'.[134] If there is an attempt here to 'lay bare [the] arcane symbolic complexities'[135] of Ulster Protestant identity, this poetic excavation is carried out in terms distinctly unsympathetic to the community it aims to expose.

But the larger point made in these lines, when viewed in the context of the whole collection, is to probe the quality of the terrain in which the titular 'liberty tree' is to be planted. The Northern Irish version of this symbol of the French Revolution Paulin imagines as an evergreen plant common to the northern hemisphere, 'juniper, / green juniper': 'On this coast / it is the only / tree of freedom / to be found'.[136] Change in Ulster depends on this tree taking root in the 'charred stubble' of the Bible Belt, transferred here from the American Midwest to the fundamentalist ground of Protestant Ulster. In keeping with the organic metaphor, warring ideologies – Presbyterian faith against republican ideals – are served up as mutually exclusive plants: 'a crop of Bibles' versus the libertarian juniper tree. The conflict is hostile to compromise: there is no space in Paulin's poetry for peaceful coexistence; the 'little history' must be filled with a fuller concept of a collective past – which Paulin, in effect, aims to provide in *Liberty Tree*.

'[F]or Tom Paulin', McDonald has argued, 'poetry has been infected by the emergencies of the time, and is unapologetically a part of the discourse by which it is surrounded and threatened.'[137] The whole structure and purpose of a volume like *Liberty Tree* confirms the accuracy of that claim. In marked contrast to Derek Mahon, Paulin wishes to engage, via poetry, in the political struggles of the present. His attempt in *Liberty Tree* to elevate a specific historical moment into a defining mark of a culture has led Clair Wills to argue that his work is 'determined by an awareness that, for modern political structures to have force and authority, they must be capable of a flexible appropriation of tradition'.[138] This is accurate, though poetry, in order to appropriate a specific tradition, must first clear a discursive space for it and uproot the historical traditions that currently occupy the strategic position from which history dominates memory.

'[F]or the republican', Paulin has written, history 'is a developing process which aims at the establishment of a full cultural identity.'[139] He sets about this task, shamelessly and boldly, by partially appropriating the very structure of unionist historical thought itself. We get a first idea of this in the organic metaphor that he uses throughout *Liberty Tree*: the 'planting' of a new tradition. This is ironic to start with, as it renews an early modern political metaphor for colonisation ('plantation') that brought the ancestors of today's Ulster Protestants to Ireland in the first place. The tradition of radical republicanism within that community – essentially the tradition Paulin wants Ulster Protestants to adopt – is claimed to be not created anew but simply revived as a 'tradition [that] went underground after the Act of Union',[140] but this is about as convincing as the claim of fringe loyalist thinkers that the true ancestors of Ulster Protestants are the Cruthin, an ancient British people that lived in Ulster long before the arrival of the Gaels.

By 'planting' a new tradition, Paulin relegates historical debate to botanic realms where the 'green / springy resistance' of the juniper tree might outgrow 'the warped polities of other trees / bent in the Atlantic wind': 'For no one knows / if nature allowed it / to grow tall / what proud grace / the juniper tree might show / that flared, once, like fire / along the hills'.[141] Of course it is not 'nature' that will allow the juniper tree to grow tall and recapture the image of forgotten radicals roaring across the hills (the origin of such an image in the romantic tradition alone should raise our eyebrows), but political action backed by a historiographical practice of deliberate appropriation. The naturalising metaphor returns in other poems, for instance in 'Presbyterian Study', in which we are told to 'wait on nature' until the eighteenth-century Presbyterian freethinkers who are explicity named elsewhere (and whom we have already met in Parker's *Northern Star*: 'Munro, Hope, Porter and McCracken'[142]) are fully restored to memory: 'for they live, / Those linen saints, lithe radicals, / In the bottled light / Of this limewashed shrine'.[143]

What differentiates this form of historical appropriation from the unionist parading of specific dates to the exclusion of others is, first of all, the self-consciousness of the partisan gesture to create this 'aesthetic republicanism'[144] and, second, a radical awareness of the textuality of history (absent from unionist thought), seen in terms of an empty slate, a mental vacuum, to be filled – or first emptied and then refilled – with a *political* history of choice. Unlike unionist thought, it is squarely focused on a politics of change: 'Making history into freedom, and not bondage, is an imaginative as well as a political project.'[145] Accusations of polemics or complaints that Paulin is 'historically selective'[146] are misguided because such a view of history is enabled by nothing else.

Paulin's essay 'Paisley's progress' (1982), published shortly before *Liberty Tree*, offers an illuminating contrast at this point. The Presbyterian preacher and unionist politician is a figure that haunts Paulin's poetry and prose. For instance, a character in one poem claims that '"Paisley's plain tongue, his cult / of Bunyan and blood / in blind dumps like Doagh and Boardmills – / that's the enemy"',[147] and in the decayed chronology of 'Desertmartin' he rises from the mists of time as the pied piper after the 'free strenuous spirit' of Presbyterian radicalism has given way to 'servile defiance': he is 'the Big Man' who will 'lead his wee people / To a clean white prison, their scorched tomorrow'.[148] The essay similarly capitalises, ironically, on the strangely magnetic, backward-oriented dynamism in the politics of Paisley, '[who] more than any other Unionist politician appears to belong to a dreamtime of Presbyterian aborigines – giant preachers who strode the Antrim coast long before the birth of Christ'.[149] The essay certainly does not take the phenomenon of 'Paisleyism' lightly. Paulin's analysis of 'unofficial' unionist thought, as embodied by Paisley, in fact aims to lay bare its entirely unexpected but nevertheless compelling structural parallels with the politics of militant republicanism (of the IRA variety): class politics, the advocacy of the popular voice, defiance of human law, the religious intensity of the struggle, the refusal to compromise, a fierce (theological or ideological) zealotry, etc., are common to both rhetorical traditions, as is – crucially – the idea of martyrdom for a superior cause. Both traditions occupy different ends of the Irish political spectrum but from the perspective explored here, 'Irish culture is really unified at its extremes.'[150] The insight can be seen to inspire the whole poetic strategy of historical appropriation pursued in *Liberty Tree*.

Paulin, Sean O'Brien notes, 'believes in making, and his work *depends* on making, value judgements of a kind about whose legitimacy many theorists have necessarily been sceptical'.[151] This fuels an uncompromising, at times vicious, rejection of the 'liberal' or 'balanced' judgements of literary theorists, and aligns Paulin – in spirit, not in politics – with those Presbyterian orators for whom 'ideas are a form of high explosive' and who 'express a constantly challenging or polemical mind-set' which 'is one result of a belief in the right of private judgement'.[152] Paulin's partisan defence of radical republicanism is his version of a near chiliastic rhetoric, alive to the moment, intense, sharp and visionary, exciting and excitable, always prepared to judge and condemn. The whole project of a revised history of Presbyterian aspiration, the poetic 'dream / of that sweet / equal republic',[153] is, of course, doubtful in the extreme when the exercise is considered in material, not purely historical terms: '[Paulin's] myth of the United Irishmen ... has little in common with orthodox Republican politics, and his attempt to associate Republican Socialism with Protestantism has no relation whatever to contemporary reality'.[154] The fatal course of the Troubles was hardly to be affected by this poetic revisionism, and although this is a general argument against all the poets I have looked at in this chapter, it is of particular relevance to Paulin who has always claimed that his work owes nothing to the dreamy landscapes of the ivory tower vista but is grounded in concrete, physical experience.

Neil Corcoran has pointed a way out of this impasse by emphasising how Paulin's utopian vision encompasses 'a place possible at present only in the poem, not the *polis*: not the historically identified and constructed "Ireland" but the imaginary, renewable potential of a still unconstructed "someplace"'.[155] Paulin himself would perhaps defend his utopian stance with the argument that concludes, 'Paisley's progress': 'History, by its very nature, has no answers.'[156] Such a statement might fly in the face of a historiography nourished on the theological tradition of typology and exemplum but it confirms Paulin's conviction that if stoicist non-activity is the chosen method of political involvement, the day will simply be seized by the enemy. To come to terms with the Troubles, even to change their course, it is imperative to take sides and not shy away from political intervention.

Conclusion

For the purposes of this chapter, Paulin's willingness to rewrite history, 'to adapt its ingredients to the most exacting and inventive of purposes',[157] offers an important contrast to the literary engagement with history as represented by Heaney and Mahon: while Heaney resorts to the myth of the bog as a catalyst for his vision of healing, offering it as a historical reservoir of images and counter-images, 'befitting emblems of adversity', and while Mahon invites imaginative play with the unlived or unrealised 'lives' and 'afterlives' of history, only ultimately to deny the liberating potential of this process of 'self'-proliferation, Paulin operates with a strong sense of historical urgency, radically reinscribing the past with contemporary meaning. For all three writers, the present cannot be confronted without the knowledge and experience of history, and all three have developed refined poetic forms to historicise the devastating reality of the Troubles rather than escape into an aesthetic no man's land, '[t]hat kitsch lumber-room ... stacked / with a parnassian dialect'.[158] This makes the creative use of the past in the the context of Troubles poetry another instance of the fruitful dialectical relationship between literature and history in contemporary Irish writing which I have been exploring throughout this study.

In Northern Irish poetry, Patricia Craig concludes her 1992 essay on Paulin and others, 'history in general ... no longer suggests itself as a nightmare' – as it did to Stephen Dedalus – 'or, for that matter, a dream, an oppressing or a justifying force, but acts instead as a catalyst, a measure for present anxieties, or a source of imaginative nourishment'.[159] Leaving aside the odd phrase 'history in general' – opposed to 'local history' by Craig – which signifies nothing if not an entirely false dichotomy between public and private, this conclusion acknowledges the willingness on the part of Ulster poets to confront, rather than to ignore or circumvent, a range of diverse historical traditions and experiences. Poets, Craig argues, recuperate the past before it disappears in the rubble left behind after decades of sectarian warfare. My attempt in this chapter has been to take this argument further: for all three writers (though the implication of a *unified* poetic effort on their part would be entirely wrong), 'history' is not only set in some form of poetic juxtaposition with the present, not simply 'retrieved' for the purposes of imaginative conservation in poetry; rather, its energies are salvaged in a poetic attempt to shape a future released from the suffocating grip of a traumatic memory. History, to put it in epigrammatic form, becomes a form of survival, not a tool of colonial oppression or narrative confinement.

Notes

1 John Goodby, *Irish Poetry since 1950: From Stillness into History* (Manchester: Manchester University Press, 2000), 3.
2 Ibid., 9.
3 Ibid.
4 Ibid., 1.
5 For a recent reassessment of the 'interpretative expectation' (143) placed on the shoulders of Irish poets in the first years of the Troubles, see Goodby's account in ibid., 143–51.
6 Michael Longley, *Tuppenny Stung: Autobiographical Chapters* (Belfast: Lagan Press, 1994), 73.
7 Ibid. Longley is quoting from one of his own contributions to *Causeway* in the early 1970s.
8 Seamus Deane, 'Seamus Heaney: the timorous and the bold', in Deane, *Celtic Revivals* (London: Faber, 1986), 174–86: 180.
9 On poetry and violence, see Peter McDonald, 'Poetry, narrative, and violence', in McDonald, *Mistaken Identities: Poetry and Northern Ireland* (Oxford: Clarendon Press, 1997), 41–80; Jonathan Hufstader, *Tongue of Water, Teeth of Stones: Northern Irish Poetry and Social Violence* (Lexington, KY: University Press of Kentucky, 1999); and Patrick Grant, *Literature, Rhetoric and Violence in Northern Ireland, 1968–98. Hardened to Death* (Basingstoke: Palgrave, 2001).
10 Frank Ormsby (ed.), *A Rage for Order: Poetry of the Northern Ireland Troubles* (Belfast: Blackstaff Press, 1992).
11 See Andy Pollak (ed.), *A Citizens' Inquiry: The Opsahl Report on Northern Ireland* (Dublin: Lilliput Press for Initiative '92, 1993).
12 Seamus Heaney, 'Whatever You Say Say Nothing', *North* (London: Faber, 1975), 59.
13 Derek Mahon, 'Rage for Order', *Collected Poems* (Oldcastle: Gallery Press, 1999), 47.
14 James Simmons, 'Lament for a Dead Policeman', *Poems 1956–1986* (Oldcastle: Gallery Press, 1986), 181.
15 Ormsby, 'Preface', *A Rage for Order*, xvi.
16 Ciaran Carson, 'Belfast Confetti', *The Irish for No* (Oldcastle: Gallery Press, 1987), 31.

17 Michael Longley, 'Wounds', *Poems 1963–1983* (London: Secker & Warburg, 1991), 86.
18 I am reading these connections into a poem which, as Peter McDonald has rightly pointed out, 'provides little in the way of coherent relation between the incidents remembered and described' (*Mistaken Identities*, 64). Nevertheless, despite the poem's '[resistance to] narrative resolution' (ibid., 65), the thematic analogies, and especially the repetition of the word 'bewilderment' (in the form of its cognate 'bewildered') in section two of the poem, invite us to make such connections.
19 James Simmons, 'Ulster Says Yes', *Poems 1956–1986*, 197.
20 See Ormsby, *A Rage for Order*, 53; 49–51.
21 Ciaran Carson, 'Bloody Hand', *Belfast Confetti* (Oldcastle: Gallery Press, 1989), 51.
22 Ciaran Carson, 'Queen's Gambit', *Belfast Confetti*, 35.
23 Ciaran Carson, 'Turn Again', *Belfast Confetti*, 11.
24 Richard Murphy, 'Amazement', *The Price of Stone* (London: Faber, 1985), 39.
25 John Hewitt, 'The Dilemma', *Collected Poems*, ed. Frank Ormsby (Belfast: Blackstaff Press, 1991), 132.
26 Thomas McCarthy, 'Counting the Dead on the Radio, 1972', *The Non-Aligned Storyteller* (London: Anvil Press Poetry, 1984), 28.
27 Louis MacNeice, 'Valediction', *Collected Poems* (London: Faber, 1966), 52.
28 Paul Muldoon, '7, Middagh Street', *Meeting the British* (London: Faber, 1987), 39.
29 McDonald, *Mistaken Identities*, 213.
30 See Paul Wilkins, 'A Graveyard in Ulster', in Ormsby (ed.), *A Rage for Order*, 277.
31 Robert Johnstone, 'The Fruit of Knowledge', *Eden to Edenderry* (Belfast: Blackstaff Press, 1989), 77.
32 The bog poems have been extensively discussed elsewhere. I have found most helpful the discussions in Thomas C. Foster, *Seamus Heaney* (Dublin: O'Brien Press, 1989); in Neil Corcoran, *The Poetry of Seamus Heaney: A Critical Study* (London: Faber, 1998 (revised and extended edition of an earlier 1986 study on Heaney)); and in Andrew Murphy, *Seamus Heaney*, Writers and Their Work (Plymouth: Northcote House, in association with the British Council, rev. edn, 2000). Most discussions of the bog poems, while identifying the bog as a historical myth in Heaney's poetry, do not analyse the implications of that statement for a conception of history, as I attempt to do here.
33 See Seamus Heaney, *Station Island* (London: Faber, 1984).
34 These are the terms he spells out in his essay 'The sense of place' (1977), included in *Preoccupations: Selected Prose, 1968–78* (London: Faber, 1980), 131–49.
35 See Seamus Heaney, *Wintering Out* (London: Faber, 1972), 6.
36 Seamus Heaney, 'Feeling into words', *Preoccupations*, 41–60: 54.
37 Ibid., 54–5.
38 Seamus Heaney, 'Bogland', *Door into the Dark* (London: Faber, 1969), 41–2: 42.
39 Heaney, 'Feeling into words', *Preoccupations*, 55.
40 A point Heaney makes himself in ibid., 54.
41 Ibid., 55.

42 Seamus Heaney, 'Kinship', *North*, 40–5.
43 Sidney Burris, *The Poetry of Resistance: Seamus Heaney and the Pastoral Tradition* (Athens, OH: Ohio University Press, 1990), 77.
44 Joep Leerssen, *Remembrance and Imagination: Patterns in the Historical and Literary Representation of Ireland in the Nineteenth Century*, Field Day Monographs 4 (Cork: Cork University Press, 1996), 101–2.
45 Cf. Benedict Anderson, *Imagined Communities: Reflections on the Origin and Spread of Nationalism* (London: Verso, 1983).
46 He calls the *dinnseanchas* 'a form of mythological etymology' in 'The sense of place', 131.
47 John Hildebidle, 'A decade of Seamus Heaney's poetry', in Robert F. Garrat (ed.), *Critical Essays on Seamus Heaney* (New York: G. K. Hall, 1995), 39–55: 39.
48 Heaney, 'Feeling into words', *Preoccupations*, 54.
49 Seamus Heaney, *Bog Poems*, illustrated by Barrie Cooke (London: The Rainbow Press, 1975), 5.
50 Heaney, 'Kinship', *North*, 34.
51 Heaney, 'Bogland', *Door into the Dark*, 41.
52 Edmund Spenser, *A View of the Present State of Ireland*, ed. R. F. Gottfried, *The Works of Edmund Spenser: A Variorum Edition*, ed. Edwin Greenlaw et al., 10 vols (Baltimore, MD: Johns Hopkins University Press, 1949), vol. 10: 'The Prose Works', 40–231, ll. 3061–2.
53 *The Comedy of Errors*, 3.2.113–17. Quoted from *The Norton Shakespeare*, ed. Stephen Greenblatt et al. (New York and London: Norton, 1997).
54 Heaney, 'Feeling into words', *Preoccupations*, 56.
55 See P. V. Glob, *The Bog People* (London: Faber, 1969). The book is still in print.
56 Heaney, 'Bogland', *Door into the Dark*, 41.
57 Heaney, 'Kinship', *North*, 34.
58 Murphy, *Seamus Heaney*, 35.
59 Seamus Heaney, 'The Tollund Man', *Wintering Out*, 37.
60 The birth metaphor, Neil Corcoran notes, is in fact suggested by the sequence of images in Glob's book. Corcoran, *The Poetry of Seamus Heaney*, 71.
61 Seamus Heaney, 'The Grauballe Man', *North*, 35–6.
62 Seamus Heaney, 'Punishment', *North*, 37–8.
63 Heaney, 'Kinship', *North*, 34.
64 A phrase Heaney adapts from Wallace Stevens. See the title lecture in Heaney, *The Redress of Poetry. Oxford Lectures* (London: Faber, 1995), 1–16.
65 John Wilson Foster, *The Achievement of Seamus Heaney* (Dublin: Lilliput Press, 1995), 30.
66 Ibid., 33.
67 McDonald, *Mistaken Identities*, 52.
68 For a pioneering essay, see Patricia Coughlan, '"Bog Queens": the representation of women in the poetry of John Montague and Seamus Heaney' [1991], recently republished in Claire Connolly (ed.), *Theorizing Ireland* (Basingstoke: Palgrave, 2003), 41–60.
69 See the early review of *North* by Ciaran Carson, 'Escaped from the massacre?', *The Honest Ulsterman* 50 (winter 1975), 183–6.
70 Derek Walcott, *Collected Poems, 1948–84* (London: Faber, 1984), 364–7.
71 See Tobias Döring and Bernhard Klein, 'Of bogs and oceans: alternative histories in Seamus Heaney and Derek Walcott', in Bernhard Klein and Jürgen

Kramer (eds), *Common Ground? Crossovers Between Postcolonial and Cultural Studies* (Trier: Wissenschaftlicher Verlag, 2001), 113–36.

72 Seamus Heaney, 'Station Island VIII', *Station Island*, 81–3.
73 Seamus Heaney, 'Sandstone Keepsake', *Station Island*, 20.
74 See, for instance, Greg Dening, *Islands and Beaches. Discourse on a Silent Land, Marquesas 1774–1880* (Honolulu: University of Hawaii Press, 1980), 3.
75 Seamus Heaney, 'Tollund', *The Spirit Level* (London: Faber, 1996), 69.
76 Though an earlier limited edition of just the eight bog poems in *North* did come with illustrations by Barrie Cooke – but these were artistic impressions of bones and bog bodies, not the photographs from Glob's book. See Heaney, *Bog Poems*.
77 The line appears in 'Meditations in Time of Civil War' [1928], *Yeats's Poems*, ed. A. Norman Jeffares (Dublin: Gill and Macmillan, 1989), 308–14: 310, and is quoted by Heaney in 'Feeling into words', *Preoccupations*, 57.
78 Michael Bath, *Speaking Pictures. English Emblem Books and Renaissance Culture* (London and New York: Longman, 1994), 4.
79 As Ciaran Carson thinks, 'it is as if [Heaney] is saying, suffering like this is natural; these things have always happened; they happened then, they happen now, and this is sufficient ground for understanding and absolution' ('Escaped from the massacre?', 184; quoted in Thomas C. Foster, *Seamus Heaney*, 55).
80 Pieter de Hooch, *The Courtyard of a House in Delft* (1658), National Gallery, London, NG835. That this is the painting in question is indeed more an assumption than a certainty, since Mahon never specified which of the de Hooch paintings he had in mind. The National Gallery painting can be viewed online at http://www.nationalgallery.org.uk/cgi-bin/WebObjects.dll/CollectionPublisher.woa/wa/work?workNumber=NG835 (accessed 17 December 2005).
81 Derek Mahon, 'Courtyards in Delft', *Collected Poems* (Oldcastle: Gallery Press, 1999), 105. All Mahon quotes are taken from this edition, except for the final stanza of 'Courtyards in Delft', which is quoted from *The Hunt by Night* (Oxford: Oxford University Press, 1982), 10. This final stanza in which 'Maenads [come] smashing crockery, with fire and sword' is retained in the versions of the poem included in *The Faber Book of Irish Poetry* (1986) and *The Penguin Book of Contemporary Irish Poetry* (1990) but not in the three collections of Mahon's own verse which contain the poem: *Courtyards in Delft* (Dublin: Gallery Books, 1981), *Selected Poems* (Harmondsworth: Penguin, 2000), and *Collected Poems* (1999). In each of these cases Mahon cut the final stanza, fearing perhaps that it might be mistaken as an incitement to violence, or that the additional stanza 'makes too explicit and self-punishing what was guiltily suggestive' in the previous lines (Goodby, *Irish Poetry since 1950*, 220).
82 And the word 'veldt' adds another comparative twist, aligning Northern Ireland with South Africa, and situating both in a wider history of British imperialism.
83 See Peter C. Sutton, *Pieter de Hooch* (Oxford: Phaidon, 1980). I largely follow Sutton in this paragraph.
84 Ibid., 16.
85 Mahon, 'Lives', *Collected Poems*, 44–6: 44.
86 Elmer Andrews, 'The poetry of Derek Mahon: "places where a thought might grow"', Elmer Andrews (ed.), *Contemporary Irish Poetry: A Collection of Critical*

Essays (Basingstoke: Macmillan, 1992), 235–63: 243.
87 Mahon, 'Lives', *Collected Poems*, 44–5.
88 Ibid., 45.
89 Ibid.
90 Ibid., 45–6.
91 Seamus Deane, 'Derek Mahon: freedom from history', in Deane, *Celtic Revivals*, 156–65: 158.
92 Andrews, 'The poetry of Derek Mahon', 244.
93 Peter McDonald, 'History and poetry: Derek Mahon and Tom Paulin', in Gerald Dawe and John Wilson Foster (eds), *The Poet's Place: Ulster Literature and Society. Essays in Honour of John Hewitt, 1907–87* (Belfast: Institute of Irish Studies, 1991), 193–208: 193. The same essay is included in Andrews (ed.), *Contemporary Irish Poetry*, 86–106, and in expanded form in McDonald's *Mistaken Identities*, 81–109.
94 McDonald, 'History and poetry', 194.
95 Deane, 'Derek Mahon', 156.
96 Derek Mahon, 'The Last of the Fire Kings', *Collected Poems*, 64.
97 Derek Mahon, 'Rathlin', *Collected Poems*, 107.
98 Derek Mahon, 'Afterlives', *Collected Poems*, 58–9: 58.
99 Ibid., 59.
100 Andrews, 'The poetry of Derek Mahon', 247.
101 Derek Mahon, 'Leaves', *Collected Poems*, 60.
102 Derek Mahon, 'Poetry in Northern Ireland', *Twentieth Century Studies* 4 (1970), 93; quoted in Elmer Andrews, 'Introduction', in Andrews (ed.), *Contemporary Irish Poetry*, 1–24: 17.
103 As Edna Longley thinks. See her 'Derek Mahon: extreme religion of art', in Michael Kenneally (ed.), *Poetry in Contemporary Irish Literature* (Gerrards Cross: Colin Smythe, 1995), 280–303: 289.
104 On formal aspects of Mahon's poetry, see Edna Longley, 'The singing line: form in Derek Mahon's poetry', in Longley, *Poetry in the Wars* (Newcastle upon Tyne: Bloodaxe, 1986), 170–84.
105 Mahon, 'A Disused Shed in Co. Wexford', *Collected Poems*, 89–90: 89.
106 For some thoughts on 'the chemistry between place and psyche' (290) in Mahon's poetry, see Longley, 'Derek Mahon: extreme religion of art', 290–5.
107 Mahon, 'A Disused Shed', 90.
108 Longley, 'Derek Mahon: extreme religion of art', 296.
109 A phrase from the epigraph of the poem, a quotation from Seferis, *Mythistorema*.
110 Joris Duytschaever, 'History in the poetry of Derek Mahon', in Duytschaever and Geert Lernout (eds), *History and Violence in Anglo-Irish Literature* (Amsterdam: Rodopi, 1988), 97–110: 100. Duytschaever's essay is a sustained attack on Stan Smith who sees in Mahon's poetry a 'refusal of the concept of history', arguing that 'Mahon steadfastly refuses Benjamin's perception' (Stan Smith, *Inviolable Voices. History and Twentieth-Century Poetry* (Dublin: Gill and Macmillan, 1982), 191; 193). As should be clear from my own discussion, I find myself in disagreement with Smith's position.
111 Duytschaever, 'History in the poetry of Derek Mahon', 106.
112 Neil Corcoran, *English Poetry since 1940* (London and New York: Longman, 1993), 190–1.

113 Goodby, *Irish Poetry since 1950*, 171.
114 Edna Longley, 'Poetry and politics in Northern Ireland', in Longley, *Poetry in the Wars*, 185–210: 205.
115 Richard Kirkland, *Literature and Culture in Northern Ireland since 1965: Moments of Danger* (London: Longman, 1996), 17.
116 Deane, 'Derek Mahon', 163.
117 See in particular Smith, *Inviolable Voices*; and Deane, 'Derek Mahon'.
118 See Duytschaever, 'History in the poetry of Derek Mahon'; Longley, 'Derek Mahon: extreme religion of art'; McDonald, *Mistaken Identities*, 81–109; and Jerzy Jarniewicz, 'Derek Mahon: history, mute phenomena and beyond', in Elmer Kennedy-Andrews (ed.), *The Poetry of Derek Mahon* (Gerrards Cross: Colin Smythe, 2002), 83–95.
119 Mahon, 'The Last of the Fire Kings', *Collected Poems*, 64.
120 Tom Paulin, 'A terminal ironist: Derek Mahon', in Paulin, *Writing to the Moment: Selected Critical Essays, 1980–1996* (London: Faber, 1996), 80–4: 81.
121 Corcoran, *English Poetry*, 187.
122 On Mahon's revisions, see Peter Denman, 'Know the one? Insolent ontology and Mahon's revisions', *Irish University Review* 24, no. 1 (1994), 27–37.
123 Tom Paulin, 'Settlers', *A State of Justice* (London: Faber, 1977), 8.
124 Tom Paulin, 'Introduction', in Paulin, *Ireland and the English Crisis* (Newcastle upon Tyne: Bloodaxe, 1984), 9–22: 17.
125 Ibid.
126 See McDonald, *Mistaken Identities*, 104.
127 Tom Paulin, 'Before History', *The Strange Museum* (London: Faber, 1980), 1.
128 Tom Paulin, 'A Partial State', *The Strange Museum*, 18.
129 Tom Paulin, 'Trotsky in Finland', *The Strange Museum*, 30.
130 Tom Paulin, 'The Idea in History', *The Strange Museum*, 25.
131 This change is to some extent reflected in Paulin's editorial introduction to *The Faber Book of Political Verse* (1986) in which he writes that 'in some societies – particularly totalitarian ones – history is a more or less inescapable condition' (quoted after the reprint of the introduction in Paulin, *Writing to the Moment*, 101–39: 103).
132 Tom Paulin, 'After the Summit', *Liberty Tree* (London: Faber, 1983), 29.
133 Tom Paulin, 'Desertmartin', *Liberty Tree*, 16.
134 McDonald, *Mistaken Identities*, 86; 85.
135 Ibid., 96.
136 Tom Paulin, 'The Book of Juniper', *Liberty Tree*, 24; 27.
137 McDonald, 'History and poetry', 194.
138 Clair Wills, 'Tom Paulin: enlightening the tribe', in Wills, *Improprieties. Politics and Sexuality in Northern Irish Poetry* (Oxford: Clarendon Press, 1993), 121–57: 122.
139 Tom Paulin, 'Britishmen', *Ireland and the English Crisis*, 137–42: 141.
140 Tom Paulin, 'Introduction', *Ireland and the English Crisis*, 17.
141 Paulin, 'The Book of Juniper', *Liberty Tree*, 26–7.
142 Tom Paulin, 'Father of History', *Liberty Tree*, 32.
143 Tom Paulin, 'Presbyterian Study', *Liberty Tree*, 49–50.
144 Kirkland, *Literature and Culture in Northern Ireland*, 107.
145 Elmer Andrews, 'Tom Paulin: underground resistance fighter', in Michael Kenneally (ed.), *Poetry in Contemporary Irish Literature* (Gerrards Cross: Colin

Smythe, 1995), 329–43: 332.
146 Edna Longley, *Poetry in the Wars*, 198.
147 Tom Paulin, 'And Where Do You Stand on the National Question?', *Liberty Tree*, 67. The reference to Bunyan is repeated in the allusion to Bunyan's Puritan prose biography, *A Pilgrim's Progress* (1685), in the title of the Paisley essay.
148 Paulin, 'Desertmartin', *Liberty Tree*, 16.
149 Tom Paulin, 'Paisley's progress', *Writing to the Moment*, 28–47: 30.
150 Ibid., 46.
151 Sean O'Brien, 'Tom Paulin: the critic who is truly a critic', in O'Brien, *The Deregulated Muse* (Newcastle upon Tyne: Bloodaxe, 1998), 181–8: 181.
152 Tom Paulin, 'The fuse and the fire: northern Protestant oratory and writing', originally the introduction to 'Northern protestant oratory and writing, 1791–1985', *The Field Day Anthology of Irish Writing*, ed. Seamus Deane, 3 vols (Derry: Field Day Publications, 1991), vol. 3, 314–18; quoted from the reprint in *Writing to the Moment*, 85–94: 87.
153 Paulin, 'The Book of Juniper', *Liberty Tree*, 27.
154 Andrews, 'Tom Paulin', 337.
155 Corcoran, *English Poetry*, 215.
156 Paulin, 'Paisley's progress', *Writing to the Moment*, 47.
157 Patricia Craig, 'History and its retrieval in contemporary Northern Irish poetry: Paulin, Montague and others', in Andrews (ed.), *Contemporary Irish Poetry*, 107–23: 108.
158 Tom Paulin, 'A Nation, Yet Again', *Liberty Tree*, 45.
159 Craig, 'History and its retrieval', 122.

CONCLUSION

Much of the literature I have discussed in this study might be said to be focused on rebuilding, reassembling – and thus newly creating – what before has been scattered, fragmented, displaced. The sense of history as a mode of imaginative survival is stronger in some examples than it is in others; but many of the authors discussed here use the past as a resource that invites a constructive, forward-looking approach rather than the repetitive stance of inevitability and self-evident failure.

If the culture of public commemoration in Ireland (both north and south) can often be partisan and divisive,[1] literature as one alternative mode of collective memory has more to offer than an eloquent (and rarely heeded) appeal to reconciliation. To conjure up, in literature, a time when 'hope and history rhyme'[2] (even though they plainly do not) means not simply to add poetic flourish to the peace process. By offering alternative models of historical causality, by suggesting new affective alliances and forms of emotional kinship, by constructing (to use Bakhtin's coinage) a 'creatively effective past'[3] rather than a past already prefigured as the constant recurrence of defeat and destruction, literature can achieve what will always be beyond the reach of those historical discourses that press themselves far more prominently – more monumentally, in Nietzsche's sense – on our consciousness than the quiet literary voices I have assembled in this book.

The present study can, of course, be no more than the beginning of a reassessment of the uses of history in contemporary Irish writing. The issue as such has been central to debates in Irish studies for some time, and will remain one of its vital concerns. My specific readings and conclusions, based as they are on a limited selection of texts, might not be generally applicable to a wider corpus of writing, but there are some notable affinities with other critical projects. For instance, Linden Peach has recently placed the contemporary Irish novel of the 1980s and 1990s in a forcefield defined by the opposite pull of 'continuity and disruption',[4] seeing it as centrally concerned with the recovery of silenced or marginalised voices – a critical framework that relates directly to my discussion of Famine fiction in Chapter 2. Other critics see the uses of the past in contemporary Irish drama and film in terms that imply, like my readings in Chapter 3, not simply a rejection of the past but its creative revision and reinterpretation, even though their conclusions are frequently bleaker than my own.[5] And my final chapter on the differently nuanced *imago* of the past in Troubles poetry will hopefully be seen in the context of John Goodby's recent call not to force Irish poetic practice into a unitary tradition or schematic narrative but to acknowledge its broad 'variety'[6] – even though I explore that variety, owing to the limitations of a multi-genre study, with reference to only three Northern poets. If Irish studies, as a field, remains motivated by a desire 'to reconnect Irish culture to the many and multifarious stories that make up its past',[7] then the analysis of the many different ways in which such connections are forged in literature should make a meaningful contribution to this critical agenda.

Since this book is based on a division into genre, the usefulness of this division deserves a final reflection. The sequence in which I have arranged the chapters – moving from prose to drama to poetry – could perhaps be seen to reiterate a position that Yeats advanced long ago in his 1893 lecture on 'Nationality and literature'. Yeats proposed that a national literature falls into an early, a middle and a late phase, a sequence he saw as exactly corresponding to the triad of epic, dramatic and lyric modes. His core image for that development was that of a tree growing from a single trunk into ever more finely structured patterns of twigs and leaves, thus describing a movement from 'unity to multiplicity, from simplicity to complexity'.[8] In this model of literary evolution the epic took as its proper subject matter the foundational myths and binding norms of the 'race' or national community at large, while drama focused on individuals (or characters) and their deeds in historical time, and the lyric – as the 'highest' style – transcended time and the individual by giving expression to a culture's finest moods, emotions and sensibilities.

The model served one obvious political function by placing English literature in a period of decline after the flowering of Romantic poetry (the lyric phase), while showing Ireland in the ascendant (just entering its dramatic phase, and on course for lyric excellence). Given this ingenious appropriations it is perhaps helpful to remember that Goethe, who discussed his conception of the influential triad epic–dramatic–lyric in the *West–East Divan* [1829], did not think of the literary styles (or 'natural poetic forms') as ranked in any kind of hierarchy. He imagined them as forming not a tree but a circle. Their respective strengths or corresponding human actions – narrative clarity (epic), personal agency (drama) and the excited, enthusiastic address (lyric) – are present in each individual literary work, shaping it to different degrees; it is by arranging these individual works in a pattern according to the respective dominance of one of their three 'main elements' that the poetic forms ultimately 'unite' in a complete circle.[9]

The two models are not, of course, in competition with each other: they are different examples of structural thought. For my purposes, two of their key points – correspondence between genre and cultural self-expression, and equality among generic forms – usefully supplement a third, made long ago by Bakhtin and Medvedev, who argue that 'every genre has its methods and means of seeing and conceptualizing reality, which are accessible to it alone'.[10] Bakhtin and Medvedev offered this observation in the context of an explicitly anti-formalist exposition of a sociological approach to the study of literature; their argument, in essence, is that genre is not only deeply rooted in the world – that it is part of a specific social environment, that its 'phonetic temporal body occupies a definite place in life'[11] – but that its various forms and subgenres literally enable cognition: 'the genres of literature enrich our inner speech with new devices for the awareness and conceptualization of reality'.[12] Genre, in other words, is not merely a means of embellishing a specific subject matter that could be expressed in any other form; it is, rather, a way of shaping the world, of making us see. Historical consciousness, the argument could be extended, is equally a product of the possibilities and limitations of generic representation. Genre creates meaning: the rich social texture of life in the novel, the antagonistic structure of drama, the psychic or visionary force of the lyric, all enable certain forms of historical thought while restricting others. The triad implies a mutually beneficial alliance but no necessary hierarchy: each element complements the other two in rethinking, reimagining a range of possible Irish 'pasts'.

In sharing a sense of history as an important cultural investment in the future, most of the writing discussed in this study is creatively and imaginatively engaged in just this work of cultural memory. Certainly the literary turn to the national past seems almost compulsive in Irish writing: what this does not indicate, at least not exclusively, is an understanding of history as a static, repetitive litany of suffering and pain. The dialogue between literature and history can be exceptionally fruitful – often taking the form of a celebration of diversity, of multiplicity, of possibility – which has its roots not in a negative fixation on the past but in a concern with historical and cultural change in the present, and in a desire to abandon explanatory models no longer suited to current needs. Pearse saw 1916 as the culmination of a history of rebellions defined in terms of prefiguration and anticipation, as a clearly visible dateline along which Irish history could be sequentially arranged into a meaningful teleology. But such chronologies can be as oppressive as the imperialism they are constructed against. Literature disputes that dates necessarily form a line, or that all history is defined through such linearity: it views the past through a looking-glass, as a constantly changing pattern of many shapes, forms and colours: a history populated by the living not the dead, a past that sustains the present.

Notes

1. For some incisive reflections on commemorative practices in Northern Ireland, and the role of the 'Troubles elegy' within them, see Edna Longley, 'Northern Ireland: commemoration, elegy, forgetting', in Ian McBride (ed.), *History and Memory in Modern Ireland* (Cambridge: Cambridge University Press, 2001), 223–53.
2. Seamus Heaney, 'The Cure at Troy', quoted from Frank Ormsby (ed.), *A Rage for Order. Poetry of the Northern Ireland Troubles* (Belfast: Blackstaff Press, 1992), 319.
3. M. M. Bakhtin, 'The *Bildungsroman* and its significance in the history of realism (toward a historical typology of the novel)', in Bakhtin, *Speech Genres and Other Late Essays*, trans. Vern W. McGee, ed. Caryl Emerson and Michael Holquist (Austin: University of Texas Press, 1986), 10–59: 34.
4. Linden Peach, *The Contemporary Irish Novel: Critical Readings* (Basingstoke: Palgrave Macmillan, 2004), 1.
5. See, for instance, Joe Cleary, 'Modernization and aesthetic ideology in contemporary Irish culture', in Ray Ryan (ed.), *Writing in the Irish Republic: Literature, Culture, Politics, 1949–1999* (Basingstoke: Macmillan, 2000), 105–29.
6. John Goodby, *Irish Poetry since 1950: From Stillness into History* (Manchester: Manchester University Press, 2000), 10.
7. Claire Connolly, 'Introduction: Ireland in theory', in Connolly (ed.), *Theorizing Ireland* (Basingstoke: Palgrave, 2003), 1–13: 13.
8. William Butler Yeats, 'Nationality and literature', in *Uncollected Prose by W. B. Yeats*, 2 vols, ed. John P. Frayne (London: Macmillan, 1970), vol. 1, 266–75: 268.
9. See Johann Wolfgang Goethe, *West-östlicher Divan* [1829], *Gedenkausgabe der Werke, Briefe und Gespräche*, ed. Ernst Beutler (Zurich: Artemis, 1948), 480–1.
10. M. M. Bakhtin and P. N. Medvedev, *The Formal Method in Literary Scholarship: A Critical Introduction to Sociological Poetics* [1928], trans. Albert J. Wehrle (Baltimore, MD and London: Johns Hopkins University Press, 1978), 133.
11. Ibid., 131.
12. Ibid., 135.

SELECT BIBLIOGRAPHY

Achilles, Jochen, and Rüdiger Imhof (eds), *Irische Dramatiker der Gegenwart* (Darmstadt: Wissenschaftliche Buchgesellschaft, 1996).
Allen, Michael (ed.), *Seamus Heaney*, New Casebooks (Basingstoke: Macmillan, 1997).
Andrews, Elmer (ed.), *Contemporary Irish Poetry: A Collection of Critical Essays* (Basingstoke: Macmillan, 1992).
Andrews, Elmer (ed.), *Seamus Heaney: A Collection of Critical Essays* (Basingstoke: Macmillan, 1992).
Andrews, Elmer, *The Art of Brian Friel: Neither Reality Nor Dreams* (Basingstoke: Macmillan, 1995).
Annwn, David, *Inhabited Voices: Myth and History in the Poetry of Geoffrey Hill, Seamus Heaney and George Mackay Brown* (Frome, Somerset: Bran's Head Books, 1984).
Assmann, Jan, and Tonio Hölscher (eds), *Kultur und Gedächtnis* (Frankfurt: Suhrkamp, 1988).
Bakhtin, M. M., and P. N. Medvedev, *The Formal Method in Literary Scholarship: A Critical Introduction to Sociological Poetics* [1928], trans. Albert J. Wehrle (Baltimore, MD and London: Johns Hopkins University Press, 1978).
Barker, Francis, *The Culture of Violence. Essays on Tragedy and History* (Manchester: Manchester University Press, 1993).
Beckett, J. C., *The Making of Modern Ireland, 1603–1923* (London: Faber, 1969).
Benjamin, Walter, *Illuminations*, trans. Harry Zohn, ed. Hannah Arendt (London: Jonathan Cape, 1973).
Bolger, Dermot (ed.), *Druids, Dudes and Beauty Queens. The Changing Face of Irish Theatre* (Dublin: New Islands, 2001).
Bort, Eberhard (ed.), *'Standing in Their Shifts Itself ...' Irish Drama from Farquhar to Friel* (Bremen: European Society for Irish Studies, 1993).
Bourke, Angela, et al. (eds), *The Field Day Anthology of Irish Writing, Vols 4 and 5: Irish Women's Writing and Traditions* (Cork: Cork University Press, 2003).
Boyce, D. George, and Alan O'Day (eds), *The Making of Modern Irish History. Revisionism and the Revisionist Controversy* (London: Routledge, 1996).
Brady, Ciaran (ed.), *Interpreting Irish History. The Debate on Historical Revisionism, 1938–1994* (Dublin: Irish Academic Press, 1994).
Brewster, Scott, et al. (eds), *Ireland in Proximity: History, Gender, Space* (London: Routledge, 1999).

Select bibliography

Brown, Terence, *Ireland's Literature. Selected Essays* (Mullingar: Lilliput Press, 1988).
Burke, Peter (ed.), *New Perspectives on Historical Writing* (University Park, PA: Pennsylvania State University Press, sec. edn 2001).
Burris, Sidney, *The Poetry of Resistance. Seamus Heaney and the Pastoral Tradition* (Athens, OH: Ohio University Press, 1990).
Cairns, David, and Shaun Richards, *Writing Ireland: Colonialism, Nationalism and Culture* (Manchester: Manchester University Press, 1988).
Campbell, Matthew (ed.), *The Cambridge Companion to Contemporary Irish Poetry* (Cambridge: Cambridge University Press, 2003).
Campbell, Stephen J., *The Great Irish Famine: Words and Images from the Famine Museum, Strokestown Park, County Roscommon* (Strokestown, Ireland: Famine Museum, 1994).
Cleary, Joe, and Claire Connolly (eds), *The Cambridge Companion to Modern Irish Culture* (Cambridge: Cambridge University Press, 2005).
Connolly, Claire (ed.), *Theorizing Ireland* (Basingstoke: Palgrave, 2003).
Coogan, Tim Pat (ed.), *Ireland and the Arts*, A Special Issue of Literary Review (London: Namara, n.d [1982?]).
Corcoran, Neil (ed.), *The Chosen Ground: Essays on the Contemporary Poetry of Northern Ireland* (Bridgend, Glamorgan: Seren Books, 1992).
Corcoran, Neil, *English Poetry since 1940* (London and New York: Longman, 1993).
Corcoran, Neil, *After Yeats and Joyce. Reading Modern Irish Literature* (Oxford: Oxford University Press, 1997).
Corcoran, Neil, *The Poetry of Seamus Heaney. A Critical Study* (London: Faber, rev. edn 1998).
Curtis, Tony (ed.), *The Art of Seamus Heaney* (Dublin: Wolfhound Press, rev. edn 1994).
Dantanus, Ulf, *Brian Friel. A Study* (London: Faber, 1988).
Dawe, Gerald, *The Rest Is History* (Newry: Abbey Press, 1998).
Dawe, Gerald, and John Wilson Foster (eds), *The Poet's Place: Ulster Literature and Society. Essays in Honour of John Hewitt, 1907–87* (Belfast: Institute of Irish Studies, 1991).
Deane, Seamus, *Celtic Revivals* (London: Faber, 1986).
Deane, Seamus (ed.), *The Field Day Anthology of Irish Writing*, 3 vols (Derry: Field Day Publications, 1991).
Demastes, William W., and Bernice Schrank (eds), *Irish Playwrights, 1880–1995. A Research and Production Handbook* (Westport, CT: Greenwood Press, 1997).
Docherty, Thomas, *Alterities. Criticism, History, Representation* (Oxford: Clarendon, 1996).
Doyle, Paul A., *Liam O'Flaherty* (New York: Twayne Publishers, 1971).
Duytschaever, Joris, and Geert Lernout (eds), *History and Violence in Anglo-Irish Literature* (Amsterdam: Rodopi, 1988).
Eagleton, Terry, *Heathcliff and the Great Hunger: Studies in Irish Culture* (London and New York: Verso, 1995).
Edwards, R. Dudley, and T. Desmond Williams (eds), *The Great Irish Famine. Studies in Irish History, 1845–52* [1956] (Dublin: Lilliput Press, 1994).
Etherton, Michael, *Contemporary Irish Dramatists* (London: Macmillan, 1989).
Fegan, Melissa, *Literature and the Irish Famine, 1845–1919* (Oxford: Oxford University Press, 2002).
Foster, John Wilson, *The Achievement of Seamus Heaney* (Dublin: Lilliput Press, 1995).

Foster, R. F., *Modern Ireland, 1600–1972* (Harmondsworth: Penguin, 1989).
Foster, T. C., *Seamus Heaney* (Dublin: O'Brien Press, 1989).
Fussell, Paul, *The Great War and Modern Memory* (New York and London: Oxford University Press, 1975).
Garrat, Robert F., *Modern Irish Poetry: Tradition and Continuity from Yeats to Heaney* (Berkeley, CA: University of California Press, 1986).
Garrat, Robert F. (ed.), *Critical Essays on Seamus Heaney* (New York: G. K. Hall, 1995).
Genet, Jacqueline, and Elisabeth Hellegouarc'h (eds), *Studies on the Contemporary Irish Theatre* (Caen: Presse Universitaire de Caen, 1991).
Gibbons, Luke, *Transformations in Irish Culture*, Field Day Essays 2 (Cork: Cork University Press, 1996).
Goethe, Johann Wolfgang, *West-östlicher Divan* [1829], *Gedenkausgabe der Werke, Briefe und Gespräche*, ed. Ernst Beutler (Zurich: Artemis, 1948).
Gonzalez, Alexander G. (ed.), *Contemporary Irish Women Poets: Some Male Perspectives* (Westport, CT: Greenwood Press, 1999).
Goodby, John, *Irish Poetry since 1950: From Stillness into History* (Manchester: Manchester University Press, 2000).
Grant, Patrick, *Personalism and the Politics of Culture: Readings in Literature and Religion from the New Testament to the Poetry of Northern Ireland* (Basingstoke: Macmillan, 1996).
Grant, Patrick, *Breaking Enmities: Religion, Literature and Culture in Northern Ireland, 1967–97* (Basingstoke: Macmillan, 1999).
Grant, Patrick, *Literature, Rhetoric and Violence in Northern Ireland, 1968–98: Hardened to Death* (Basingstoke: Palgrave, 2001).
Grene, Nicholas, *The Politics of Irish Drama: Plays in Context from Boucicault to Friel* (Cambridge: Cambridge University Press, 1999).
Hart, Henry, *Seamus Heaney: Poet of Contrary Progressions* (Syracuse, NY: Syracuse University Press, 1992).
Harte, Liam, and Michael Parker (eds), *Contemporary Irish Fiction: Themes, Tropes, Theories* (Basingstoke: Macmillan, 2000).
Hayden, Tom (ed.), *Irish Hunger. Personal Reflections on the Legacy of the Famine* (Boulder, CO: Roberts Rinehart, 1997).
Hufstader, Jonathan, *Tongue of Water, Teeth of Stones: Northern Irish Poetry and Social Violence* (Lexington, KY: University Press of Kentucky, 1999).
Huizinga, Johan, *Cultuurhistorische Verkenningen* (Haarlem: H. D. Tjeenk Willink & Zoon, 1929).
Huizinga, Johan, *Homo Ludens: A Study of the Play-Element in Culture* [1938], trans. R. F. C. Hull (London: Routledge and Kegan Paul, 1949).
Hyland, Paul, and Neil Sammells (eds), *Irish Writing: Exile and Subversion* (London: Macmillan, 1991).
Iser, Wolfgang, *Fictive and Imaginary: Charting Literary Anthropology* (Baltimore, MD: Johns Hopkins University Press, 1993).
Jeffers, Jennifer, *The Irish Novel at the End of the Twentieth Century: Gender, Bodies and Power* (New York and Basingstoke: Palgrave, 2002).
Jordan, Eamonn, *The Feast of Famine. The Plays of Frank McGuinness* (Bern: Peter Lang, 1997).
Jordan, Eamonn (ed.), *Theatre Stuff: Critical Essays on Contemporary Irish Theatre* (Dublin: Carysfort Press, 2000).

Kamm, Jürgen (ed.), *Twentieth-Century Theatre and Drama in English* (Trier: Wissenschaftlicher Verlag, 1999).

Kearney, Richard, *Transitions. Narratives in Modern Irish Culture* (Dublin: Wolfhound, 1988).

Kearney, Richard, *Postnationalist Ireland: Politics, Culture, Philosophy* (London: Routledge, 1997).

Kelleher, Margaret, *The Feminization of the Famine: Expression of the Inexpressible?* (Cork: Cork University Press, 1997).

Kenneally, Michael (ed.), *Poetry in Contemporary Irish Literature* (Gerrards Cross: Colin Smythe, 1995).

Kennedy-Andrews, Elmer (ed.), *The Poetry of Derek Mahon* (Gerrards Cross: Colin Smythe, 2002).

Kennedy-Andrews, Elmer, *Fiction and the Northern Ireland Troubles since 1969: (De-)constructing the North* (Dublin: Four Courts Press, 2003).

Kiberd, Declan, *Inventing Ireland. The Literature of the Modern Nation* (London: Vintage, 1995).

Kiely, Benedict, *Poor Scholar. A Study of the Works and Days of William Carleton (1794–1869)* (London: Sheed and Ward, 1947).

Killen, John (ed.), *The Famine Decade. Contemporary Accounts, 1841–1851* (Belfast: Blackstaff, 1995).

Kinealy, Christine, *This Great Calamity. The Irish Famine 1845–52* (Dublin: Gill & Macmillan, 1994).

Kinealy, Christine, *A Death-Dealing Famine: The Great Hunger in Ireland* (London and Chicago: Pluto Press, 1997).

Kinsella, Thomas, *The Dual Tradition: An Essay on Poetry and Politics in Ireland* (Manchester: Carcanet, 1995).

Kirby, Peadar, Luke Gibbons and Michael Cronin (eds), *Reinventing Ireland: Culture, Society and the Global Economy* (London: Pluto Press, 2002).

Kirkland, Richard, *Literature and Culture in Northern Ireland since 1965: Moments of Danger* (London: Longman, 1996).

Komesu, Okifumi, and Masaru Sekine (eds), *Irish Writers and Politics* (Gerrards Cross: Colin Smythe, 1990).

Leerssen, Joep, *Remembrance and Imagination: Patterns in the Historical and Literary Representation of Ireland in the Nineteenth Century*, Field Day Monographs 4 (Cork: Cork University Press, 1996).

Lernout, Geert (ed.), *The Crows Behind the Plough: History and Violence in Anglo-Irish Poetry and Drama* (Amsterdam: Rodopi, 1991).

Lloyd, David, *Anomalous States: Irish Writing and the Post-colonial Moment* (Dublin: Lilliput Press, 1993).

Longley, Edna, *Poetry in the Wars* (Newcastle upon Tyne: Bloodaxe, 1986).

Longley, Edna, *The Living Stream: Literature and Revisionism in Ireland* (Newcastle upon Tyne: Bloodaxe, 1994).

Longley, Edna, *Poetry and Posterity* (Highgreen, Northumberland: Bloodaxe, 2000).

McBride, Ian (ed.), *History and Memory in Modern Ireland* (Cambridge: Cambridge University Press, 2001).

McDonald, Peter, *Mistaken Identities: Poetry and Northern Ireland* (Oxford: Clarendon Press, 1997).

Mahoney, Christina Hunt, *Contemporary Irish Literature: Transforming Tradition* (Basingstoke: Macmillan, 1999).

Malloy, Catharine, and Phyllis Carey (eds), *Seamus Heaney: The Shaping Spirit* (Newark, DE: University of Delaware Press, 1996).

Matthews, Steven, *Irish Poetry. Politics, History, Negotiation: The Evolving Debate, 1969 to the Present* (Basingstoke: Macmillan, 1997).

Morash, Christopher (ed.), *The Hungry Voice: The Poetry of the Irish Famine* (Dublin: Irish Academic Press, 1989).

Morash, Christopher, *Writing the Irish Famine* (Oxford: Oxford University Press, 1995).

Morash, Christopher, *A History of Irish Theatre, 1601–2000* (Cambridge: Cambridge University Press, 2002).

Morash, Christopher, and Richard Hayes (eds), *'Fearful Realities': New Perspectives on the Famine* (Dublin: Irish Academic Press, 1996).

Morgan, Hiram, *Tyrone's Rebellion: The Outbreak of the Nine Years War in Ireland* (Woodbridge, Suffolk: Boydell Press, 1993).

Murphy, Andrew, *But the Irish Sea Betwixt Us: Ireland, Colonialism, and Renaissance Literature* (Lexington, KY: University Press of Kentucky, 1999).

Murphy, Andrew, *Seamus Heaney*, Writers and Their Work (Plymouth: Northcote House, in association with the British Council, rev. edn 2000).

Murray, Christopher, *Twentieth-Century Irish Drama. Mirror up to Nation* (Manchester: Manchester University Press, 1998).

O'Brien, Eugene, *Seamus Heaney: Searches for Answers* (Dublin: Pluto Press, 2003).

O'Brien, George, *Brian Friel* (Dublin: Gill and Macmillan, 1989).

O'Brien, Sean, *The Deregulated Muse* (Newcastle upon Tyne: Bloodaxe, 1998).

Ó Gráda, Cormac, *Ireland Before and After the Famine. Explorations in Economic History, 1800–1925* (Manchester and New York: Manchester University Press, sec. edn 1993).

Ó Gráda, Cormac, *Black '47 and Beyond in History, Economy, and Memory* (Princeton, NJ: Princeton University Press, 1999).

O'Sullivan, Patrick (ed.), *The Meaning of the Famine*, The Irish World Wide: History, Heritage, Identity, vol. 6 (London and Washington: Leicester University Press, 1997).

Ormsby, Frank (ed.), *A Rage for Order: Poetry of the Northern Ireland Troubles* (Belfast: Blackstaff Press, 1992).

Orr, Philip, *The Road to the Somme: Men of the Ulster Division Tell Their Story* (Belfast: Blackstaff Press, 1987).

Parker, Michael, *Seamus Heaney: The Making of the Poet* (Basingstoke: Macmillan, 1993).

Paulin, Tom, *Ireland and the English Crisis* (Newcastle upon Tyne: Bloodaxe, 1984).

Paulin, Tom, *Writing to the Moment. Selected Critical Essays, 1980–1996* (London: Faber, 1996).

Peach, Linden, *The Contemporary Irish Novel: Critical Readings* (Basingstoke: Palgrave Macmillan, 2004).

Peacock, Alan J. (ed.), *The Achievement of Brian Friel* (Gerrards Cross: Colin Smythe, 1993).

Pilkington, Lionel, *Theatre and State in Twentieth-Century Ireland. Cultivating the People* (London: Routledge, 2001).

Pine, Richard, *Brian Friel and Ireland's Drama* (London: Routledge, 1990).

Póirtéir, Cathal (ed.), *The Great Irish Famine: The Thomas Davis Lecture Series* (Dublin: Mercier Press, in association with RTE, 1995).

Select bibliography

Pollak, Andy (ed.), *A Citizens' Inquiry: The Opsahl Report on Northern Ireland* (Dublin: Lilliput Press for Initiative '92, 1993).

Richards, Shaun (ed.), *The Cambridge Companion to Twentieth-Century Irish Drama* (Cambridge: Cambridge University Press, 2004).

Richtarik, Marilynn, *Acting Between the Lines: The Field Day Theatre Company and Irish Cultural Politics, 1980–1984* (Oxford: Clarendon, 1994).

Ricoeur, Paul, *Time and Narrative* [1983–5], trans. Kathleen McLaughlin and David Pellauer, 3 vols (Chicago and London: Chicago University Press, 1984–8).

Robinson, Alan, *Instabilities in Contemporary British Poetry* (Basingstoke: Macmillan, 1988).

Roche, Anthony, *Contemporary Irish Drama: From Beckett to McGuinness* (Dublin: Gill and Macmillan, 1994).

Ryan, Ray (ed.), *Writing in the Irish Republic: Literature, Culture, Politics, 1949–1999* (Basingstoke: Macmillan, 2000).

St Peter, Christine, *Changing Ireland: Strategies in Contemporary Women's Fiction* (Basingstoke: Macmillan, 2000)

Smith, Stan, *Inviolable Voices: History and Twentieth-Century Poetry* (Dublin: Gill and Macmillan, 1982).

Spargo, Tamsin (ed.), *Reading the Past* (Basingstoke: Palgrave, 2000).

Steiner, George, *After Babel: Aspects of Language and Translation* (London: Oxford University Press, 1975).

Tóibín, Colm, *The Irish Famine* (London: Profile Books, 1999).

Walcott, Derek, *What the Twilight Says. Essays* (London: Faber, 1998).

Wills, Clair, *Improprieties: Politics and Sexuality in Northern Irish Poetry* (Oxford: Clarendon Press, 1993).

Woodham-Smith, Cecil, *The Great Hunger: Ireland 1845–1849* [1962] (London: New English Library, 1977).

INDEX

n. after a page reference indicates the number of a note on that page.

Adorno, Theodor W. 51
Andrews, Elmer 98, 99, 120n.80, 147
Andrews, J. H. 116n.27
Aristotle 3, 55
Arnold, Matthew 17
Assmann, Jan 6, 52
Aubrey, John 32
Auden, W. H. 138

Bakhtin, M. M. 3, 75, 164, 166
Banville, John 61, 75
   Birchwood 61–2, 75
Barker, Francis 112
Barry, Kevin 92
Barry, Sebastian 84
   The Steward of Christendom 84
Benjamin, Walter 16, 88, 99–100, 101, 111, 112, 119n.67, 149
Bloom, Leopold 33–4
bog people 136–7
Boland, Eavan 75
Boyne, Battle of 12, 102, 104, 111, 151
Bradshaw, Brendan 82n.119
Brew, Margaret 8, 49–50
   The Chronicles of Castle Cloyne 49–50
Brown, Terence 97–8, 101, 119n.57, 120n.80, 122n.101
Buile Suibhne 22
Burke, Peter 72
Byrd, Elizabeth 8, 62–3
   The Famished Land 62–3

Canny, Nicholas 36n.11
Carleton, William 8, 45–7, 48, 50, 52, 74
   The Black Prophet 45–7, 74
Carson, Ciaran 126, 130–1, 160n.79
   Belfast Confetti 130–1
   'Bloody Hand' 130
Carson, Edward 103, 104, 121n.94
cartography
   see maps, mapping
Cicero 99
Cleary, Joe 2
Coetzee, J. M. 86–8
   Waiting for the Barbarians 86–8
Connaught Telegraph 65
Connolly, Sean 20, 116n.28
Conyngham, David Power 50–1, 58
   Frank O'Donnell 50–1, 58
Cooke, Barrie 160n.76
Corcoran, Neil 156, 159n.60
Craig, Patricia 156–7

Darby, Mildred 55–6, 59
   The Hunger 55–6
Davies, Sir John 38n.46
Davis, Graham 58
Dawe, Gerald 98, 130
   'Little Palaces' 130
Deane, Seamus 1, 4, 127, 146
Dedalus, Stephen 1, 152, 156
Dening, Greg 119n.66

Derricke, John 26, 29, 38n.46
  The Image of Irelande 26, 29
dinseannchas 135
Donne, John 15, 22
Dovey, Teresa 115n.11
Duytschaever, Joris 161n.110

Eagleton, Terry 41, 51, 78n.48, 79n.66, 81n.95, 83n.144
early modern Ireland (as represented in fiction) 12–35
Easter Rising 104, 109
Edwards, R. Dudley 59–60, 62, 64, 80n.86
  The Great Irish Famine 59–60, 61, 62
Elizabeth I 31–2
  as fictional character 14–16

Famine, Irish 8, 16, 35, 40–1
  in historiography 56, 57–62, 64–5, 68, 72, 74–5
  in literature 8, 40–75, 81n.98
Famine diary 65–7
Famine Museum 41, 42–3
Farrell, J. G. 148
  Troubles 148
Fegan, Melissa 54, 68
Field, Louisa 8, 53–4
  Denis 53–4
Field Day Theatre Company 85–6
Foster, John Wilson 138
Foster, R. F. 119n.56
Friel, Brian 8, 12, 17–21, 25, 36n.20, 37n.22, 84, 85–6, 87, 90–5, 103, 105, 110–111, 112, 116n.24, 134
  The Freedom of the City 84
  Making History 12, 17–21, 25, 84
  Translations 8, 37n.22, 84–5, 90–5, 98, 100, 111, 112, 134

Garratt, Robert 26
genre 8–9, 34–5, 165–6
Gibbons, Luke 4
Ginzburg, Carlo 109
Gleitman, Claire 84
Glob, P. V. 136, 137
Goethe, Johann Wolfgang 8, 165
  West–East Divan 165

Goodby, John 126, 165
Grene, Nicholas 104, 117n.30, 118n.48

Hadfield, Andrew 14
Halbwachs, Maurice 6
Heaney, Seamus 8, 12, 30–4, 125–7, 128, 132–41, 144, 156
  'Act of Union' 32
  'Anahorish' 133, 134
  'Belderg' 30–1
  'Bogland' 133–4
  'Bog Oak' 31
  bog poems 132–41, 158n.32, 160n.76
  Death of a Naturalist 133
  Field Work 139
  'The Grauballe Man' 137
  The Haw Lantern 132
  'Kinship' 134, 135
  North 30, 31, 32, 125, 127, 132–41, 160n.76
  'Ocean's Love to Ireland' 31–2
  'Punishment' 137, 138
  The Spirit Level 140
  Station Island 133, 139
  'Station Island VIII' 139
  'The Strand at Lough Beg' 139–40
  'The Tollund Man' 137
  'Tollund' 140
  'Traditions' 33–4
  Wintering Out 31, 33
Hewitt, John 130, 131
Hildebidle, John 135
historical imagination 5
historical novel 14
history
  from below 88–9
  as 'burden' 2–3
  and eyewitness testimony 65–8, 110
  and forgetting 2, 93–4
  and genre 8–9, 34–5, 165–6
  and ideology 87–9
  and memory 5, 6–7, 56, 65, 67, 70–1, 74, 107–8, 134, 136–7
  see also memory
  of mentality 56
  and myth 6

Index

and narrative 3–4, 19–20, 54
as 'nightmare' 1–2, 152
oral 55, 59, 67–8
and parallax 112
and representation 2–3, 48–9, 51–2, 144
and the single witness 108–9
and textuality 154
and time 2–3, 20, 99–100
and translation 104, 110–13
history play 84–6, 113
Hooch, Pieter de 141–2, 143, 160n.80
Huizinga, Johan 9, 101

Illustrated London News 53
Iser, Wolfgang 5

Johnstone, Robert 132
Jordan, Eamonn 122n.101, 122n.108
Joyce, James 33, 90
   Ulysses 33–4

Kavanagh, Patrick 27, 61
   The Great Hunger 27, 61
Keegan, Gerald 66, 67
   see also Mangan, James
Kelleher, Margaret 54, 77n.24, 78n.48, 78n.53, 79n.66
Kenny, Seán 68–9, 70
   The Hungry Earth 68–9
Kiberd, Declan 94, 95, 110–11, 112, 114, 117n.36
Kilroy, Thomas 37n.20, 84
   The O'Neill 37n.20, 84
Kinealy, Christine 58
Kinsale, Battle of 17, 18
Kirkland, Richard 99

landscape
   literary constructions of 28–30, 47–8, 57, 90, 103, 132–41, 148
   and memory 26–7, 30, 92, 94–5, 133–5, 137–8, 145
   see also memory
Leerssen, Joep 90
Lombard, Peter (as fictional character) 19
Longley, Edna 92, 95, 121n.92, 149
Longley, Michael 126–7, 129–30
   'Wounds' 129–30
Lyons, F. S. L. 6

McCarthy, Thomas 131
McCracken, Henry Joy (as fictional character) 96–8, 100
McDonald, Peter 145–6, 151, 153, 158n.18
McGuinness, Frank 8, 12, 17, 21–5, 29, 84, 85, 87, 101–10, 111, 112, 113, 114, 121n.95, 133
   Gatherers 109, 123n.115
   Mutabilitie 12, 17, 21–5, 29, 84, 111, 133
   Observe the Sons of Ulster Marching Towards the Somme 8, 85, 86, 101–10, 113
Macken, Walter 8, 62, 63
   The Silent People 62, 63
MacMorris 33–4
MacNeice, Louis 131
Mahon, Denis 43
Mahon, Derek 8, 125–7, 128, 141–50, 153, 156, 160n.81
   'Afterlives' 146–7
   'Courtyards in Delft' 141–4, 145, 147, 150
   'A Disused Shed in Co. Wexford' 148–50
   The Hunt by Night 160n.81
   'The Last of the Fire Kings' 146
   'Leaves' 147
   Lives 144
   'Lives' 144–5, 147
   'Rathlin' 146
   The Snow Party 125, 146–50
Malthus, Thomas 47
Mangan, James 66–7
   Famine Diary 66
   Robert Whyte's 1847 Famine Ship Diary 66–7
maps, mapping 91–2, 94–5, 103, 117n.33, 121n.95, 131, 143
Marcus, Steven 60
Marx, Karl 107
Medvedev, P. N. 75, 166
memory
   communicative 52–3
   cultural 5, 6–7, 11n.27, 28, 52, 90,

92, 107–8, 113, 138, 166
and forgetting 93–4
historical 43–4, 107–8, 134, 136–7, 145, 164
and landscape 26–7, 30, 92, 94–5, 133–5, 137–8, 145
see also landscape
living 57–8
personal 26, 56, 93, 107, 109
Merry, Andrew
see Darby, Mildred
Mitchel, John 50, 58, 59, 60, 80n.80
Jail Journal 59
Montague, John 8, 12, 26–30
'Like dolmens round my childhood, the old people' 29–30
The Rough Field 12, 26–30, 31, 32
'A Severed Head' 28–9
Moody, T. W. 6
Morash, Christopher 53, 66, 79n.58, 80n.80
Morgan, Hiram 36n.18
Muldoon, Paul 132
'7, Middagh Street' 132
Mullen, Michael 62, 63–4, 65
The Darkest Years 65
The Hungry Land 62, 63–4
Murphy, Tom 61, 81n.98, 84
Famine 61, 84
Murray, Christopher 90, 99, 104

Nashe, Thomas 113
Nietzsche, Friedrich 2, 40, 93–4, 95, 114, 164
Untimely Meditations 93
Nora, Pierre 6, 7
Northern Ireland, political conflict in
see Troubles (in Northern Ireland)

O'Brien, George 117n.33
O'Brien, Sean 155
O'Casey, Sean 86
Ó Cathaoir, Brendan 65–6
O'Connell, Daniel (as fictional character) 63
O'Connor, Joseph 8, 68, 71–3
Star of the Sea 68, 71–3
O'Connor, Sinéad 41–2, 43, 69
O'Faolain, Nuala 8, 68, 69–71

My Dream of You 68, 69–71
O'Faolain, Sean 37n.20, 79n.66
The Great O'Neill 37n.20
O'Flaherty, Liam 8, 55, 56–7, 59
Famine 55, 56–7
Ó Grada, Cormac 43, 81n.95
O'Neill, Hugh 14, 17, 36n.18
as fictional character 17–21, 28
Opsahl Report 128
Ordnance Survey 8, 86, 90, 91, 92, 117n.33, 134
Ormsby, Frank 128–32
A Rage for Order 128–32
O'Rourke, John 57–9
Orr, Philip 121n.93
O'Toole, Fintan 20, 116n.22

Paisley, Ian 154–5
Parker, Stewart 8, 85, 87, 88, 95–101, 105, 111, 112–13, 120n.80, 154
Northern Star 8, 85, 88, 95–101, 154
Paulin, Tom 8, 84, 125–7, 150–6, 162n.131
'After the Summit' 152
'Before History' 151
'Desertmartin' 155
The Faber Book of Political Verse 162n.131
The Hillsborough Script 84
'The Idea in History' 152
Liberty Tree 125, 151, 152–6
'Paisley's progress' 154, 156
'A Partial State' 151
'Presbyterian Study' 154
'Settlers' 151
A State of Justice 151
The Strange Museum 151
Peach, Linden 164
Pearse, Patrick 12–13, 166
Proust, Marcel 123n.126

Ralegh, Sir Walter (as fictional character) 14–15, 31–2
Rea, Stephen 85–6
revisionism (in Irish historical studies) 3–4, 5–6, 10n.16, 60, 61, 67
Ricoeur, Paul 4, 5, 44, 60, 75
Roche, Anthony 98, 122n.104
Russell, Lord John 47, 60

Index

Scott, Walter 14
Sellar, Robert 66
  'Summer of Sorrow' 66
Shakespeare, William 33, 86, 113, 136
  Comedy of Errors 136
  as fictional character 21–5
  Henry V 33–4
  1 Henry VI 113
Sidney, Henry 26
Simmons, James 127, 130
  'Ulster Says Yes' 130
Somme, Battle of 8, 86, 102, 106, 111, 130
Spenser, Edmund 13, 24, 33, 136
  The Faerie Queene 13, 15, 17, 21, 23, 31, 33
  as fictional character 12, 14–17, 21–5, 31
  'Two Cantos of Mutabilitie' 21, 22–3
  A View of the Present State of Ireland 24, 31, 32, 33, 37n.34, 39n.62
Steiner, George 93
  After Babel 93

Táin Bó Cuailgne 22
Tóibín, Colm 51, 81n.92
topography
  see landscape
translation
  see history and translation
Trevelyan, Charles 60, 77n.25, 80n.83
Trollope, Anthony 8, 47–9, 57, 77n.30
  Castle Richmond 47–9, 57

Six Letters to the Examiner 48
Troubles (in Northern Ireland) 8, 114, 125–8
  in literature 126, 128–57

United Irishmen 8, 86, 95, 97, 101, 151

Veneday, J. 40
Vere, Aubrey de 51

Walcott, Derek 88–9, 118n.40, 139
  'The muse of history' 89
  'The Sea Is History' 139
Walsh, Louis 79n.61
  The Next Time 79n.61
Welch, Robert 8, 12, 14–17
  The Kilcolman Notebook 12, 14–17
White, Hayden 3, 123n.117
Whyte, Robert
  see Mangan, James
Wilkins, Paul 132
  'A Graveyard in Ulster' 132
Williams, T. Desmond 59–60, 62, 64
  The Great Irish Famine 59–60, 61, 62
Wills, Claire 153
Woodham-Smith, Cecil 59, 60–1, 62, 64
  The Great Hunger 59, 60–1

Yeats, William Butler 136, 138, 140–1, 165
  'Nationality and literature' 165